of questions of ourselves as individuals and a society. I've changed my mind about this guy, and am glad to call him my friend.'

Doug Rushkoff, writer, documentarian and lecturer

'This provocative and honest book pushes the climate change conversation well beyond its usual edges. It conveys the enormity of the changes before us – in politics, the economy, and technology of course, but also in our psychology and even our metaphysics. I recommend it to anyone who is trying to make sense of climate change within a bigger picture that includes the evolution of civilization and consciousness.'

Charles Eisenstein, speaker and author of *Sacred Economics*

'Provides deep insight into the essential issues of our time . . . could spark the revolution of consciousness that is the revolution not just of thinking, but of acting.'

Ervin Laszlo, author and founder of The Club of Budapest

Also by Daniel Pinchbeck

Breaking Open the Head: A Psychedelic Journey into the Heart of Contemporary Shamanism

2012: The Return of Quetzalcoatl
  (published in the UK as *2012: The Year of the Mayan Prophecy*)

Notes from the Edge Times

'Daniel Pinchbeck's life is the hero's journey. Like Homer's *Odyssey*, *How Soon Is Now?* is a song of redemption for a world torn apart by the monsters of our own creation. We've dreamed up a world that is consuming itself into extinction. Pinchbeck offers us a new dream, and in doing so takes us on a powerful, magical voyage into balance and sanity.'

John Perkins author of *Confessions of an Economic Hit Man*

'Daniel Pinchbeck has emerged as a rational and clear voice of hope for a new post-capitalist future, offering alternatives to hack democracy for a better society. His expert knowledge of shamanism and ancient cultures has given him a quantum perspective from which to approach our contemporary crisis. A powerful voice providing a new narrative for alternative social movements. Pinchbeck is a prophetic change-agent with a serious message of hope.'

Jefferson Hack, CEO & Founder, Dazed and Confused

'Not only is it "sooner than you think", it's also later than you think. Here we are, humanity, caught in the moment between devolution and conscious evolution by choice not chance. Daniel Pinchbeck's new book takes us to this exact inflection point and reveals with remarkable clarity and brilliance that We Do Know What To Do in almost every field from spiritual to social to environmental, with innovations arising everywhere. He asks the Great Question: Then why are we not doing it? Let's all read it and say Yes to what we do know How to do. Let's form humanity's Burning Man team and light the fire of love in action together NOW!'

Barbara Marx Hubbard, visionary, social innovator and chair of the Foundation for Conscious Evolution

'*How Soon Is Now?* offers a spiritually driven approach to global economic and ecological crisis. This is the process through which humanity can bring itself back from the brink. With dangerous and admirable honesty, Pinchbeck tests his deepest-held assumptions and judges his life choices in a crucible of self-doubt. It's at once an initiation for himself, and an invitation for us to ask these same sorts

HOW SOON IS NOW?

From Personal Initiation to Global Transformation

Daniel Pinchbeck

Preface by STING

Introduction by RUSSELL BRAND

WATKINS

Sharing Wisdom Since
1893

This edition first published in the UK and USA 2017 by
Watkins, an imprint of Watkins Media Limited
19 Cecil Court
London WC2N 4EZ

enquiries@watkinspublishing.com

Design and typography copyright © Watkins Media Limited 2017

Text copyright © Daniel Pinchbeck 2017

1 3 5 7 9 10 8 6 4 2

Designed and typeset by Donald Sommerville

Printed and bound in Croatia.

A CIP record for this book is available from the British Library

ISBN: 978-1-78028-972-4

www.watkinspublishing.com

Contents

Acknowledgements

I want to thank a number of people who contributed to this book in different ways. First of all, I owe my mother, Joyce Johnson, a profound debt of gratitude for her editorial help. I'm amazed that I continue to learn so much from her at this late stage. I am grateful to Phil Jourdan, my editor at Watkins, whose contribution was invaluable. I also want to thank Jo Lal, the publisher of Watkins, for her care and attention. I owe a debt of gratitude to many people who worked with me at the Center for Planetary Culture, a think-tank I started. Together, we developed a Regenerative Society Wiki that provided some of the technical ideas for this book. People who contributed include Paula Santa Rosa, Ashley Taylor, David Morgan, Rachel Shearer, Mark Chasan, Ester Kim, Ryan Patrick, Harper Cowen, Rachel Wong and Jessie Brinton. I would also like to thank my managers, Jonny and Alison Podell, for their help, and my agent Bill Gladstone. I deeply appreciate the input and encouragement from friends who read various drafts of this and offered comments and suggestions, including David Sauvage, Alnoor Ladha, Ryan Wartena, Schuyler Brown and Mitch Mignano. I also appreciate other forms of help and support I received from Bob Eisenberg, Laura Hoffmann and Luke Weil. I also want to thank my supporters on Patreon.

Preface

by Sting

Our distant ancestors would never have the left the sea if there hadn't been some sort of ecological crisis that forced them over generations onto dry land. In fact, when we review the history of our species, it seems apparent that we only evolve through crisis. Individually as well as collectively, we only make progress when we find ourselves out of our comfort zone. The evolutionary record is full of short-lived species that could not adapt to change.

Because of our impact upon the planet, humanity is in imminent danger of joining this list. Earth may need a rest from its pathological guests. Daniel Pinchbeck's *How Soon Is Now?* seeks to address the enormous disconnect between our current activities as a species and the Earth's ecology. Deep down, we all know that the current status quo can't continue much longer, since there are many signs that it is already starting to crumble.

As I write this, Britain reels in shock from Brexit at the very time that global unity is needed; a fear-mongering, climate change-denying billionaire may become the next US president; and summer has come to northern Alaska earlier than it ever has before. Whatever the eventual consequences of such events, they suggest that we can no longer operate on the principle of 'business as usual', or believe that 'normality' will persist, or rely on our unravelling institutions.

How Soon Is Now? gives us the context we need to understand the chaos and turbulence of our times. For me, the take-home idea is that the biospheric emergency facing us is somehow wired into our DNA, forcing us to make an evolutionary leap as a species. I find this a compelling way of looking at our perilous situation, one that takes us beyond the stale rhetoric of political parties. It may be that many, if not most, of our problems are due to a poor level of understanding about the realities we face.

According to many scientists who study global warming, we are quickly approaching the point of no return. Although most of us don't want to face the evidence, we need to find the courage to confront it now – not just for our own sake, but because climate change will impact the lives of our children and their children. One thing I appreciate about this book is Daniel's no-blame stance, which could be more strategically effective for bringing about change than calling out the usual scapegoats. While we can't let our more egregious corporate offenders off the hook, the more important point is that we and they are all part of the same system – a system that itself needs a redesign. Likewise, Daniel's even-handed overview of revolution and its often disastrous results points to a new wisdom.

As Daniel points out in *How Soon Is Now?*, despite the very real dangers we face, the potential during this time is enormous. But we can only realize it by finding the courage to face the threats to our existence on this planet and come together to act as one.

Introduction

by Russell Brand

I first encountered Daniel through his 2010 documentary, *2012: Time for Change*. I was interested in the ideas swirling around back then that saw the year 2012 – the end of the 5,125-year-long Mayan calendar – as some sort of apocalyptic threshold. Daniel instead envisioned the prophetic due-date as an opportunity offered to humanity for a great awakening of consciousness and a global reboot – one that would depend on our actions.

In Daniel's film, I found all sorts of mind-changing information about alternative social systems, economic models and ways of thinking. I encountered the prophetic ideas of the freethinking social architect Buckminster Fuller, who in 1969 said humanity now faces a choice: oblivion or utopia. The film resonated with me on many levels. I reached out to Daniel after I saw it.

Like Daniel, I have come to understand that we first of all need something like a revolution of consciousness and a profound transformation of our social systems if we want to avert short-term regression into the primitive authoritarianism with which we are now threatened, as well as long-term ecological meltdown. I agree with him that this revolution is not simply a matter of changing our political or economic system; the solution has to be primarily spiritual and secondarily political.

This is something that the traditional left still doesn't get. The natural tribal leaders of the left are atheists, and they see the socialist or post-capitalist future as inescapably godless. Since the last century there has been a belief that religion, devotion and any idea of God must be discarded. However, once we have abandoned any sense of a sacred relation to the earth or the cosmos, we are left with nothing but a flat, depressing reality. The nihilism inherent in this worldview inexorably leads to addictions, egotism and other manias.

Through a new embrace of spirituality we must prioritize our connection to one another and the planet over other, lesser goals. Buckminster Fuller succinctly outlined what ought be our collective objectives: 'to make the world work for 100 per cent of humanity in the shortest possible time through spontaneous co-operation without ecological offense or the disadvantage of anyone'. Isn't that simply sensible, considering the ever-increasing power of our technologies, and the new communications networks that link humanity together instantly?

As Daniel explores in *How Soon Is Now?*, most of us in the post-industrial West have become prisoners of comfort in the absence of meaning. As a people, we live without a unifying myth. As the comparative mythologist Joseph Campbell has pointed out, our global problems are all due to the lack of relevant myths. This is a powerful insight. One thing that Daniel seeks to do in this book is to offer some elements of a possible new mythic structure, along with a blueprint for the future. His ideas have been drawn from tribal shamanism and quantum physics, as well as evolutionary biology and the cutting-edge of developments in fields like energy, sustainability and industrial design. He envisions a system based on cooperation rather than competition that will allow our children and their children to live in relative peace and harmony, without further annihilating the earth's fragile ecosystems, as we are now doing at a rapid clip.

Through my own explorations of yoga and meditation I have become increasingly comfortable with a mystical view on the nature of reality. I believe that as we wake up we have an opportunity, and even a responsibility, to deal with people as if they are divine – knowing that within them, ultimately, there is a divinity. The Christian mystic Emmet Fox wrote, 'Regardless of another person's behavior, the Christ within them is calling out to you.' Christ represents the archetype of the higher Self, which we all have individually, and which our species as a whole also possesses.

Daniel has a great ability to précis information and make ideas that are difficult to understand quite accessible. He also proposes ideas that may seem, at first, objectionable – like having compassion for corporations and understanding that, even though multinationals have been incredibly destructive, they are also part of our evolution and could be repurposed for the good. This may rankle many of us. I think this is a good thing. When you have reached an impasse, it is ideas that seem objectionable or absurd at first that may provide the solution. Quite obviously, the old ways of looking at things are no longer helping us. We need new ideas and insights.

The spiritual counterculture and New Age movement of the last decades focused on the power of presence, the awareness of awareness. This was good, as far as it went, but now we need to go one step further. As a new myth for this time, Daniel proposes we approach the multi-level crisis of civilization now confronting us as a great opportunity for awakening and initiation. We can focus on the great task that Fuller set for us: to make the world comprehensively successful for all.

Although we don't realize it, we already live within successive cycles of revolution that are occurring faster and faster. The Agricultural Revolution took thousands of years; the Industrial Revolution took hundreds; the Technological Revolution took tens. The Spiritual Revolution is coming – as soon as now – and we have only an instant to act.

Part One

Planetary Initiation

1

Burning Down the House

O nce, a decade ago – on 1 September 2005, just around sundown, to be exact, I tried to incite a global revolution. The incident remains one of the proudest and, at the same time, one of the most humiliating events of my life. It was inspired by a potent psychedelic catalyst, and Hurricane Katrina.

I was at the Burning Man festival at the time. As almost everyone knows by now, Burning Man, a massive annual anarcho-libertarian pseudo-utopian art event, takes place in the Black Rock Desert of Nevada every summer. The festival has grown rapidly over the last years. It has captured the attention of the global media as celebrities and Silicon Valley billionaires flock to it.

I remember, after my plane landed at Reno airport, passing TV monitors showing satellite images of Hurricane Katrina's ominous octopus arms, its vast spiralling dimensions. On the news, weathermen were plotting its likely course towards Louisiana. The emergency seemed surreal to me, an event that had nothing to do with my life.

By the time Katrina hit New Orleans, Burning Man was going strong. Thousands of costumed revellers danced each night, roaming the city during the day. Back in those days, nobody checked the Internet while at the festival. There was no cell phone service either. I found out about Katrina from friends who arrived on the playa late in the week. They described its devastating impact. I learned that the government had corralled 15,000 poor people, mostly African-American, in the Louisiana Superdome, in unsanitary conditions without water or power. Riots were spreading across the South, according to the news they brought with them from the 'default world', and National Guard reserves were being called up. It seemed that America – long a simmering cauldron of racial tension and class conflict – was on the verge of boiling over. Nobody at Burning Man knew – or cared.

Riding across the desert that day in a dusky purple haze, I entered a state of messianic megalomania, outside of the normal constraints of time or personal narrative. No longer held back by any sense of linear progress, or any concern for future consequences, I believed that the fractally rhizomatic Now was the only moment that mattered – the only moment that ever was. I felt fury at our failure, as a species, to overcome the 'system' – the military-industrial complex, Wall Street, the corporate mega-machine. This system was not only corrupt, creepy and hypocritical. It was also destroying the biosphere, and with it, our shared human future.

Revolution for the Hell of It

I first visited Burning Man in 2000. I went there as a journalist, to write a feature on it for *Rolling Stone*. I didn't have great hopes for what I would find there. It seemed a self-congratulatory, hippie-ish thing. But when I visited Black Rock City, I realized the festival far exceeded what I had anticipated or imagined. Within a few days, it permanently expanded my sense of what humanity could become.

I discovered a huge, supportive, loving community focused on self-expression, direct experience and personal freedom. Burners didn't consider the exploration of consciousness to be marginal or worthless. Most understood it as a crucial expression of human freedom. As a New Yorker, I had no idea that the psychedelic counterculture on the West Coast had evolved in such spectacular style since the Acid Test days. The festival was an initiation, in itself. It was challenging to survive in that high desert, scorching hot during the days, frigid at night. The fact that everyone had to endure the elements was part of the journey. We had all chosen, intentionally, to experience this near-emergency. This brought us together and bonded us.

Perhaps I should be embarrassed to admit this, but in the development of my personal political philosophy, Black Rock City holds a place that for me is as crucial as the Paris Commune of 1870 was for Karl Marx and Friedrich Engels. 'Working men's Paris, with its Commune', Marx enthused, 'will be forever celebrated as the glorious harbinger of a new society.' Although the French government stamped out the revolution, executing thousands, Marx went on to write many books – proving it is safer to be an armchair revolutionary than the fighting-in-the-streets kind.

The essential political insight I took from Burning Man was our capacity to reorganize society around principles quite different from the ones we have now. We can create a post-postmodern civilization where the pursuit of art, ecstasy, play and spiritual communion are central to its purpose. I believed a rapid global awakening was possible – and Burning Man pointed the way. Reinventing our fragile world as a collective art project, we would apply our technical genius and media savvy to liberate our human family, as a whole, from pointless suffering, destructive habits and outmoded belief systems.

Naively, I assumed that everyone at Burning Man understood that the festival was simply a prelude – a rehearsal for the main event. We were testing out the principles and ethos of a liberated society that at some point we would spread across the world rapidly. Eventually, we would engineer a metamorphosis of our civilization, re-creating it through the crucible of the imagination.

But suddenly, that night in 2005, I saw Burning Man's celebratory spectacle, for the first time, as an artificial paradise distracting us from the sombre reality we needed to confront. Those with the awareness and ability to change the world were caught in a hall of mirrors – a subtle trap. Burning Man was a temporary autonomous zone, a beautiful desert mirage. It showed us what was possible, but it diverted our energy from the hard work of changing the system – from confronting the powers that be, in the real world. What it promoted was cultural rebellion, not social transformation. Burning Man had turned into a culture of its own, which made people obedient and complacent.

Enraged, I rode my bike to the Center Cafe. Inside, a large band of San Francisco hipsters was playing – drumming, banjo-ing, tooting horns – to a fervent, gyrating crowd. I jumped on the stage and took the microphone from the MC – a stylish impresario known for his Steampunk couture, white top hat and improbably long beard. Everyone was startled. The band stopped. I was already a well-known figure at the festival. A day before, I had given a talk to several hundred people in the large geodesic dome of the Palenque Norte camp, as part of their speaker series. Some of my audience was in the crowd.

I began to rant, semi-coherently, about Katrina, as well as the larger ecological, geopolitical emergency confronting our species. I noted that many of us had been coming to Burning Man for many years to celebrate, to party – I said we had partied enough. Now we can do something else together that might be equally fun: establish a sound foundation for a new socio-political order. Some of the crowd listened attentively. Some booed. Various attempts were made to get me off the stage so the band could resume. I ignored them.

Finally, Paradox – a well-known circus performer in the Bay Area – convinced me to give up the mic. We went to sit outside together, in the dust. I was still enraged. I grabbed him repeatedly, pulling his hair. This was the unlikely beginning of a great friendship. As I spoke with him, still high as a kite, I hatched an ambitious plan.

I proposed that we stop the festival's annual crescendo – the burning of the Man on Saturday, followed by the immolation of the Temple on Sunday. Instead, we would invite the Burning Man community to stay in the desert for a few extra weeks while we drafted a planetary constitution together and built a social network and media platform to support the rapid transition to a regenerative, post-capitalist society. There were, I knew, so many brilliant people attending the event, leaders in many fields, from software to pop music to finance to law. Katrina was our opportunity to seize. Katrina had revealed the planetary emergency in microcosm. We would use the disaster to tap the community's genius in a focused and organized way.

I saw it all in a flash. One group of Burners – legal experts, software engineers, social scientists, anthropologists, financial analysts, workers at NGOs and more – would gather at the Center Cafe each day, to design and build the prototype for a new social infrastructure through a cooperative, consensus process. This networking platform would include tools for democratic decision-making, sharing resources and alternative instruments for exchanging value, designed to first complement and then supersede the current money system. Another group of Burners – filmmakers, journalists, poets and artists – would document the unfolding process as we wrote the planetary constitution, demanding a world based on ecological and social justice, equality, peace and righteousness. Rather than making incremental and fitful progress, humanity as a whole would make a sudden forward leap.

Around the Temple, the spiritual community of Burning Man – meditators, yogis, alchemists, Sufis, kabbalists, Wiccans – would gather in a circle for a 24-hours-a-day ceremony in which they would visualize, meditate and bring down the imprint for the new planetary culture – currently hovering above us, somewhere, in the starry night. Rock musicians, DJs, opera singers and other performers would play at the Man – a concert continuing around the clock, live-streamed to the outside world.

I assumed the wealthier Burners would happily donate tens of thousands of dollars apiece to have food and water trucked in from Reno, supporting this crucial process. Property would be collectivized, so people wouldn't have to waste any valuable time. Instead of having to look for your bicycle in a thicket of bicycles, for instance, you could grab any available ride. Rather than returning to your camp, you could catch a snooze in any nearby trailer. We would be living the revolution as we created it – we would be co-creating the New Now.

As I hatched it, I thought this plan had tremendous PR potential. We would perform revolution as a conceptual art performance piece in real time. I imagined our pitch to the world's media: the community of countercultural hedonists, hippies, druggies, geeks and Silicon Valley millionaires are making a stand, taking charge of the planet's future, at a time of ongoing war in the Middle East, corporate malfeasance, natural disasters and climate meltdown.

At first we would be mocked. But soon, the press – the global audience – would stop ridiculing us. They would grasp that this was the only way that massive social change could happen – from the dusty margins, the radical fringe. Once we built and launched our new peer-to-peer network for direct democracy and our open-source media platform promoting spiritual gnosis, equitable sharing of the world's resources for the evolution of consciousness, everybody on Earth would jump on board. I figured the whole process might take six months, give or take. By then, we would have even George Bush, Vladimir Putin, the Bilderberg elite, the Koch Brothers, the Supreme Leader of North Korea, the Sunni Imams and Shiite Ayatollahs, Bill Gates, Mark Zuckerberg and the Chinese Premier solidly on our side. We would sit down together to work things out, pausing for sessions of MDMA-assisted group therapy when necessary.

For the next two days, I didn't sleep as I sought to execute my plan. I raced from Burning Man camp to camp, trying to form alliances, building a cadre of volunteers. At one New York camp, Disorient – an established Burning Man brand, known for its bright orange costumes and digitally sequenced flashing strobe lights – I knocked a bottle of champagne out of one of the organizer's hands, pissing him off as it dribbled fizz into the dust.

'Haven't you done enough partying over the years?' I yelled at him. When they told me to leave, I lay down on the ground in protest. A few members of Disorient dragged me out of the camp by my feet. I found it ludicrous that they would drag me across the dust, from one blank spot to another – as if the campground was real real estate.

I gathered about twenty-five people together at my camp, Entheon Village, seeking to inspire them with my vision. Humouring me, friends as well as new conscripts took on the roles of lieutenants and sub-commandants in a ragged, jester army. As it became clear we didn't have the momentum we would need to stop the burning of the Man, my revolutionary project fizzled out.

A big dream for the world – however foolish or futile – leaves lingering embers in its wake. Tiny incandescent sparks. I learned so much from this embarrassing enterprise – whether blind alley or foreshadowing, I am still not sure. For a few delusional hours, I felt something similar to what a member of the Jacobin Club must have felt in 1789. I was convinced it was really happening. 'Action is the only reality,' the Yippie activist Abbie Hoffman once realized while on LSD: like a whiteboard swiped clean, our social reality can be entirely re-created and reinvented, given the proper circumstances and poetic serendipity.

System Change

But why, you may ask, do we need system change? For many of us, the reasons are blindingly obvious. The Bernie Sanders presidential campaign presented the economic case clearly. The ever-widening gap between rich and poor has reached Dada-ist proportions. Less than eighty-five individuals control more wealth than half the Earth's population – 3.6 billion people. In the US, one-tenth of 1 per cent of the population is worth more than the bottom 90 per cent. While a tiny elite has more power than ever before, vast multitudes look ahead fearfully. They see a future of shrinking hopes and increasing instability. As debt increases faster than GDP around the world, the financial system tightens its grip, like a giant anaconda suffocating the poor and the middle class. Waves of protests and rebellions – the Arab Spring, Black Lives Matter, Occupy, Brexit – reveal the ire of the masses.

We live in a post-colonial empire which uses violence – drone strikes, bombing raids, assassination, military invasion, extraordinary rendition – to impose its will on the world, as well as employing sneakier techniques, like the ballooning debts that countries across Africa, South America and Asia must pay their European and American overlords, while their resources are strip-mined away. This is already terrible. The even worse problem is that our industrial civilization has unleashed an ecological mega-crisis. We are threatened with an imminent planetary cataclysm that could drive us to extinction.

'Across the world today, our actions testify to our belief that we can go on like this forever, burning oil, poisoning the seas, killing off other species, pumping carbon into the air, ignoring the ominous silence of our coal mine canaries in favour of the unending robotic tweets of our new digital imaginarium,' Roy Scranton writes in *Learning to Die in the Anthropocene.* 'Yet the reality of global climate change is going to keep intruding on our fantasies of perpetual growth, permanent innovation and endless energy, just as the reality of mortality shocks our casual faith in permanence.'

For reasons we will explore, there is a link between our unjust economic system – which forces constant growth while it disempowers the multitudes – and the ecological catastrophe that will soon engulf us. We can't solve one without solving the other. As things go increasingly haywire, our species could easily join all the other species we are currently driving into oblivion. This could happen within this century – within the next decades. Right now, all bets are off.

Meanwhile, the corporate elite and the technocrats continue to promote the promise of new technologies to solve humanity's problems. This sounds great in theory. Unfortunately, however, our engineers have no legitimate response to many of the ecological problems we have created. Many of the 'quick fixes' they promote – like geo-engineering – could make things far worse. As a whole, humanity is sleepwalking towards catastrophe, waiting for something or someone else – Elon Musk, Bill Gates, Donald Trump, Richard Branson, Indigo Children, the Pope – to take care of it for us.

As I've focused on the ecological crisis over the last years, I have sometimes felt like Chicken Little, freaking out as I pointed to a seemingly blue, changeless sky. But as a quorum of scientists metaphorically agree, *the sky is falling.* We can feel the changes taking place all around us. Many of the solutions are blindingly obvious. But we are not applying them.

Climate Chaos

In December 2015, world leaders met in Paris to hammer out an agreement aimed at restricting the rise of global temperatures to less than 2 degrees Celsius above pre-industrial levels. Although this was celebrated as progress, it may have set back the climate movement significantly. According to a group of leading climate scientists, the pact failed to mandate the rapid, severe cuts to global emissions that we actually need.

'What people wanted to hear was that an agreement had been reached on climate change that would save the world while leaving lifestyles and aspirations unchanged', the scientists wrote. 'The solution it proposes is not to agree on an urgent mechanism to ensure immediate cuts in emissions, but to kick the can down the road.'

The Paris climate talks revealed, once again, the vast gap between what is politically feasible and what is ecologically necessary. Drastically to reduce CO_2 pollution we would have to eliminate wasteful industries, severely limit consumption, reduce air and car travel to the minimum and restrict meat-eating globally. If we want to save the Earth, in other words, billions of us have to change our lifestyles. Nobody wants to think about this – and it is political suicide to propose it because it goes against the logic of a global economy based on incessant growth. But our survival requires system change, not reform.

The fastest way for a change to occur would be for the wealthy elite – or at least a subset of them – to take responsibility for humanity's current predicament, overcome the hypnotism of privilege and use their capital to engineer a rapid turnaround. I know that sounds unlikely. Another option would be some form of revolution or global overturning of the current system, substituting new institutions for the dysfunctional ones we have now. I realize that sounds pretty difficult also.

It is much easier to build a lifeboat while you are still on dry land than to try to do it when you are caught in the middle of a never-ending super-storm. We are getting many foreshadowings of what is to come. But we keep ignoring them.

Sandy

On the evening of 29 October 2012, I was home in the East Village when Hurricane Sandy hit. An hour into it, I walked down to my corner, out of curiosity. I assumed the media had exaggerated the dangers of the storm, to boost ratings. I wanted to see for myself. To my shock, I saw brackish floodwaters rising, coming up Avenue C, engulfing cars. People were coming out of restaurants to snap pictures and selfies of this biblical menace. The police cars in front of the local precinct seemed to be floating, with water up to their windows. The flood tide was moving at a steady pace towards my street – towards my building.

I went home, threw some clothes and my laptop into a backpack, and headed off towards a friend's house in SoHo, on higher ground, as wind lashed the trees back and forth. As I hurried away, a flash of light illuminated the ominous cloud cover. I heard a gigantic explosion behind me. It sounded like a bomb. Later on, I learned that the Con Edison power plant on 14th Street and Avenue C had just blown up. An hour later, the entirety of downtown New York was plunged into darkness. For the next few days, a large area of Manhattan was without power.

The morning after the storm, I walked back to my house. Everything was closed except for a few delis and restaurants serving hastily made sandwiches and coffee out of thermoses. Deli workers were trying to get rid of everything perishable from their refrigerators and freezers. In the East Village, people stood around on street corners, dazed expressions on their faces, inspecting the damage from the flood. I biked uptown, to stay with my mother on the Upper West Side, an area that was comparatively untouched.

I was supposed to fly to Mexico the next day to give a TEDx talk at a festival, commemorating the Day of the Dead, in an old colonial town popular with expatriates from the US and Europe. My talk was going to cover, in condensed form, the theme of this book: the ecological crisis as initiation – as an opportunity for us to engineer a self-willed, rapid mutation in human consciousness. But the airports were closed and my flight was cancelled. I assumed I wouldn't be able to go.

Then I received a call with an invite to fly on a private jet to Mexico. The jet belonged to a media mogul, the CEO of a major conglomerate. The CEO and his wife were dedicated Burners – they were power players in the scene. They had started the festival in Mexico to bring some of the Burning Man vibe to their second home. They owned a beautiful villa overlooking the town as well as a company making the world's most expensive tequila.

Riding High

As an aside, I should note that I have been on quite a ride since I attained a moderate level of fame as a psychedelic author and visionary. In 2007, when Steven Colbert called me a 'psychedelic drug advocate' during our TV interview, he solidified my position as a public spokesman for the altered states and shamanic practices I had written about in my books.

'Timothy Leary died recently. We just got rid of him. Why do we need another one?' he asked me on air.

While I have taken pains to differentiate myself from Leary – the Harvard psychology professor turned psychedelic psychopomp, called 'the most dangerous man in America' by Nixon, who told the 1960s generation to 'tune in, turn on, and drop out', with unfortunate consequences – I have inherited a bit of his social cachet as rebel and outsider.

Over the last decade, I have had a unique opportunity to pass through many different worlds, learning and carrying ideas from one to the next. For a German TV show, I wandered the streets of Paris with Alejandro Jodorowsky, legendary director of *Holy Mountain*, and psycho-magician. I flew in a chartered helicopter with Sting and his family over crop circles in England, looking for extra-terrestrials. I hung out in the trenches of Occupy Wall Street with tousled anarchists. I visited the mountains of Colombia to study the rituals and philosophy of the Kogi and Arawak people. I debated with the comedian Russell Brand in a geodesic dome in Utah. I visited a 'free love' community, started by German radicals, in rural Portugal. I helped organize a summit on climate change at Facebook headquarters in Palo Alto, with slick marketing geniuses and non-profits like Greenpeace and 350.org. We failed to convince Zuckerberg's minions to support the ecological movement with more than tokenism.

As much as I could, I sought to influence the influencers. Particularly, I thought drinking ayahuasca, the visionary medicine from the Amazon basin, would be extremely beneficial for many of them. In Big Sur, I attended one of the most lavish weddings of our transhuman times, as the guest of Sean Parker, co-founder of Napster and the ex-president of Facebook. The roster of invitees included numerous rock stars and dot-com tycoons, founders and funders of Internet leviathans. Like almost all of them, I wore an outfit custom-made for the occasion, a long tailored jacket and silk-embroidered vest. We partied all night in a grove of majestic redwoods, transformed into a Hollywood phantasmagoria of Renaissance ruins and flower gardens for one multi-million-dollar night. The ceremony set world records for excess, triggering incensed editorials and local outcries. The wedding was easy to criticize. On the one hand, I found it a beautiful expression of love. On the other, it was a painful reminder that a tiny elite gets to enjoy the most fabulous Gatsby-like extravagance, while billions around the world remain stuck in poverty and desperation.

For Summit Outside, a weekend retreat, I visited a mountaintop in Utah. A group of young entrepreneurs had bought the entire mountain – a sky resort – to build a utopian community for the privileged, taking a page from the libertarian fantasies of Ayn Rand. We dined on one long table crossing an entire valley. A battalion of waiters served over a thousand of our society's best and brightest, a well-meaning, khaki-tinged mob that included heads of charities, venture capitalists, documentary filmmakers and CEOs of tech start-ups.

On a private beach in Mexico, for the end of the Mayan calendar's 5,125-year-long count, costumed dancers in Aztec headdresses gyrated to electronic beats among life-size reconstructions of Stonehenge, Easter Island's massive heads and monumental sculptures of Greek deities. I spent the night tripping with one of the world's wealthiest art dealers, a Brit. He offered me free career advice, telling me I should 'be the messiah, play the pariah'. Back home, following his lead, I wrote him a long, histrionically irate email linking the planetary mega-crisis to the decadence of the art world. He never replied.

I write this having just returned from New Zealand where I attended a futurist conference organized by two tech geniuses in their early thirties, who dropped out of Harvard ten years ago to build a massive data-processing company, which they sold for a fortune. With the proceeds, they acquired 2,000 acres of Kiwi forests and dairy farms. They are integrating the most up-to-date methods of organic agriculture, food forestry and solar-powered villages, assembling a dream team of yogis, reiki healers, permaculture designers and software engineers. They chose New Zealand, after surveying the options, as the most likely place in the world to survive runaway climate change, global social breakdown and everything else that's coming. They may be the smartest people I know.

The Day of the Dead

Let's get back to Sandy: the day after New York was humbled by the super-storm, I biked back to my apartment. Below 28th Street, the city was plunged into a velvety darkness, unlike anything I had experienced. A few bars had stayed open, illuminated by candlelight. Some blocks were so dark that when people passed me, all I could see of them was the reflective strip on their sneakers, caught in bike light for a flickering instant. It was like the darkness of the void – before the beginning, after the end. There was a thrilling ambience of lawlessness – no thief would ever be caught in the depths of that blackness.

My building had a dank, foetid smell. The flood had engulfed the already mouldy basement. My apartment was without heat or cell phone service. I threw every blanket over me and shivered through the cold night. Early the next morning, I was picked up by a chauffeur-driven SUV. The car gathered up a small group of fashionable Burners – photographers, event planners, stylists. We headed out of town to a small nearby airport.

I had never flown on a private jet before. To my surprise, there were no security checks before boarding. We didn't need to remove our shoes, get bombed by malevolent millimetre waves, or throw away forbidden tubes of lotion and canisters of hairspray. Any one of us could have been carrying an assault rifle strapped across our chest and a suitcase nuke. Nobody would have checked. This was a gentle reminder that our world works a bit differently for the super-wealthy compared to everyone else. According to the net, the owner of the plane was worth close to a billion. He owned boats, private islands, as well as tequila companies and jets. Of course, he also contributed to many charities. They all do.

In a world plagued by so much unnecessary suffering, we might consider extreme wealth – and the entitlement and insulation it brings – a spiritual disease. Most of us are prey to outbreaks of it, on much smaller scales. I admit – in this regard and many others – I am no better than most.

When I was in my twenties, I got my first good-paying job as an editor at a magazine – a crass competitor to *Vanity Fair*, called *Fame*. Suddenly, with money in the bank, I felt far less sympathetic and compassionate than I had when I was poor. Where previously I would give money to homeless people, now I would scoff when, wearing my new double-breasted Armani suit, I walked past them sprawled out on the sidewalk. I wondered why they couldn't pick themselves up off the ground and find a career.

Now for a far more embarrassing admission. Just a few years ago, I received a sizable grant from a foundation. When I had an influx of funding, after years of feeling grumpy and cash-starved, I sought to redress what I saw as old wrongs. I felt I 'deserved' a taste of the luxury lifestyle enjoyed by my many wealthy friends with their endless skiing vacations, boating trips and spa treatments. Instead of using every penny to fuel the social and cultural revolution I believe is necessary, I upped my lifestyle in various ways – fancier suits, better restaurants, a trip or two. I felt it was my due.

In some ways, it is easier to be poor. One has less choice and less responsibility. I am sure, at the mogul's level of wealth, there is powerful peer pressure, among CEOs, to throw the best party, buy the coolest island or vintage car collection or whatever. Sitting on the private plane to Mexico in 2012, I wished I could find a way to speak to my host, to convey to him the pressing needs of our moment – what might happen if his genius for building companies could be channelled, used to liberate the masses from the mental prison the media has built around the human mind. But I could tell my views would mean nothing to him.

We landed. I dropped my bag in my hotel, then wandered through the mustard-coloured streets of the colonial town, appreciating its baroque facades and vibrant street life. A massive stone cathedral presided over the elegant central square. Locals, as well as expats, were costumed as skeletal phantasms. They wore tuxedos, evening gowns, white gloves. Delicate traceries of black ink decorated their bleached faces. Altars made of flowers, papier-mâché tombstones and giant sculpted skulls were set up all around town.

This extreme journey – from Hurricane Sandy's urban wipe-out to the private jet to the elegant ghost world of the Day of the Dead – seemed a garish presentiment of what humanity may be rapidly approaching: an abrupt passage between worlds. It was just one year after the end of the 13th Baktun, completing the Mayan calendar's long count, the focus of my second book.

It could be the case that the 'dimensional shift' that many mystics speak about, which the visionary philosopher Rudolf Steiner described as different incarnations of the Earth, and which indigenous cultures like the Hopi call a transition from one 'world' to the next, requires our total annihilation. After all, even for those of us who believe in great mysteries and subtle realms, we really know nothing about the workings of the invisible, occult dimensions. Death remains the biggest question mark. Maybe we all need to croak together, in one massive methane eruption, biospheric cataclysm or Dr Strangelovian plunge into nuclear winter, to work our stuff out on the astral plane.

Hurricane Sandy had revealed vividly to me the fragility of our instruments and our dependence on the grid. If the blackout had gone on past a few days, the bow and arrow would have seemed futuristic.

After Sandy, city agencies and volunteers from the Occupy movement banded together to rebuild those sections of the city that the storm had decimated, like Rockaway Beach and Red Hook. This was a noble effort. But it also seemed a doomed one. All of the evidence tells us climate change is intensifying. Why restore beachfronts and barrier islands if they will soon be abandoned in any case?

What Happens Next?

When it comes to the future, we appear to suffer from a severe lack of direction. Collectively, we are lost, fumbling in the dark. How can it be that we have so little idea of where we are going – or want to go – as a species? Perhaps people believe there are experts taking care of the problem – but what if the experts turn out to be self-deluded in various intricate ways? What if there are no experts, as of now, in what the future can bring?

And yet, we can say a few things about the future with a fair degree of certainty. By 2050, without some drastic, as of yet unimaginable intervention – without a radical, globally orchestrated programme to reduce CO_2 levels through conservation and sequestration – the Earth will be considerably hotter than it is today. With climate change quickening now, by then the planet could be two, three or more degrees warmer. Accelerated warming might cause three metres, at least, of sea-level rise, according to climate scientists. This would have disastrous impacts.

Let's admit what we all know. We are already experiencing crazy, rapidly fluctuating weather. As I write this, New York is colder in May than it was in January. In a few decades, the situation could be far more chaotic than we can even predict. We depend on plants to provide us with sustenance. In order to blossom and grow – to feed us, in other words – they need climate stability.

The Arctic is melting rapidly now; month by month, gigatons of ice are released into the seas. Many of the world's low-lying coastal cities – including New York City, my home – could be deluged, made uninhabitable within a handful of decades. If that happens, hundreds of millions, if not billions, of people will start migrating inland in either a somewhat controlled or chaotic fashion.

Let's assume the current political system finds a way to stay in place despite panics and paroxysms. In that case, a tiny elite will still maintain control over the vast preponderance of the world's wealth and property. They will employ private armies, killer drones and government surveillance to guard and protect their privileged status in a disintegrating world – if they haven't found a more insidious method, like hacking the brainstems of their serfs or developing the next tier of mood- and mind-altering drugs to control the nervous systems of the sheeple directly.

It is inevitable that the melting of the mountaintop glaciers that provide fresh water to several billion people, and other drastic changes in climate and weather patterns, will induce unending droughts. Famines could be endemic across much of the world. With these cataclysms, along with spreading diseases, we might undergo significant, if not severe, population die-offs. These conditions, in all likelihood, will lead to regional wars over resources, the scapegoating and persecuting of minorities, as well as the collapse of many nation-states.

Industrial disasters like Fukushima and the Gulf of Mexico oil spill will become regular occurrences in the wake of tsunamis and super-storms. All the big cats and great apes will go extinct, and mosquitoes and insect pests will migrate north. Seeking escape from physical hell, the masses may zone out on immersive games and virtual reality spectacles. As the world turns into a giant refugee camp, engineers will experiment with massive geo-engineering schemes. They will pour sulphur particles into the atmosphere and iron filings into the oceans with unpredictable, perhaps even more disastrous consequences.

This scenario is, of course, only an outline, with many X factors. Perhaps advances in medicine and nanotechnology will bring life extension and superhuman capacities to the privileged few, creating a deeper biological divide between the Haves and Have Nots. Populist fury may erupt against the First World – the primary source of economic injustice and ecological decimation – as the Earth becomes hotter, more crowded and more barren of life. This could lead to the detonation of 'suitcase nukes' in major cities and bioterrorism or false flag events involving weaponized or genetically engineered viruses.

Mass panic would force a descent into martial law. People may be electronically tagged, their every move under the surveillance of sophisticated artificial intelligence agents. This would be a hotter, drearier, more despicable world – but one that seems quite likely, from where we are now.

Another scenario is plausible and far more extreme. Soon – any time now – we may face runaway climate change – rapid warming, beyond the worst predictions. Over the last decade, scientists found that positive feedback loops accelerate warming. For instance, the disappearance of Arctic ice means that more sunlight is absorbed and less is reflected, turning up the thermostat.

One way this can happen is through an eruption of methane. Methane is roughly 30 times more potent as a heat-trapping gas than CO_2. While methane only stays in the atmosphere for ten years, whereas CO_2 circulates for over a century, there are huge quantities of it frozen in the oceans and the Siberian peat bogs. Scientists believe a sudden eruption of methane caused the Permian Mass Extinction 250 million years ago, when 95 per cent of all life on Earth went extinct within a few decades.

From the study of past geological epochs, we know that once warming passes an unknown tipping point, the Earth can heat rapidly, becoming a biological desert in a half-century. Through studying the climate record, preserved in ice-core samples, geologists have learned that the climate generally doesn't make a slow, incremental transition from one steady state to another. Instead, it tends to make a drastic lurch in a short timeframe.

When you take the time to study the ecological data, you can feel as though you are on a bad acid trip, in danger of losing your moorings as well as your mind. The situation can seem irrevocably, almost absurdly grim. Even so, I believe there are many good reasons to hope. The human species is creative, innovative, highly adaptive. We can change quickly. We might be on the cusp of a rapid transmutation now. Because we are meshed together into one global brain via the Internet, new ideas, new ecological techniques – even new currencies or ways to practise democracy – can spread across the world in a micro-millisecond.

Although a tremendous amount of damage has already occurred, and more is unavoidable, it is still possible that we can rally ourselves. We can redirect our civilization along a different path and we can do it quickly. As *Peak Everything* author Richard Heinberg notes, 'In order to save ourselves, we do not need to evolve new organs; we just need to change our culture. And language-based culture can change very swiftly, as the industrial revolution has shown.'

Similarly, Alexis Zeigler writes in *Culture Change*, 'The solution to changing the Western lifestyle is the simple impossible act of creating social networks that build social support outside of the mainstream in the context of a truly sustainable society.' If we haven't accomplished this yet, it may be because we haven't really tried.

Psi

Materially, we can shift global practices in farming, industry and energy production within a few decades. We can reforest the planet. This would put a massive amount of excess carbon back in the Earth. But along with the material, industrial aspects of this transition, we will need to undergo a shift in our values, beliefs and habits. In other words, we need to change our technical and industrial base, our political and economic system, as well as our consciousness and our culture – our way of relating to the world. I know this is no small feat, but it is possible. It could occur through a tipping point, where a small group discovers a new way of being that quickly spreads out to encompass the whole. And it could happen fast.

Also, from my perspective – as we will explore – there are reasons to hope that fall far outside what mainstream thinkers, scientists or our academies imagine possible. There are aspects of reality that remain unknown, inaccessible, to most people. For instance, there is a great deal of evidence that we possess latent psychic abilities, which some researchers call Psi.

Psi could be exponentially more powerful as a transformative force than electricity, if we can figure out how to use it. 'Psi is a terribly important adventure. It is the wild card in our seemingly hopeless attempt to get the human race off the endangered species list,' writes Lawrence LeShan in *A New Science of the Paranormal*. 'We must be open to facing the possibility that we will find things so new and startling that they change our preconceptions about ourselves and about the universe we live in,' he writes. 'So far, we have not had that courage. Perhaps now with species extinction looming before us, we will find that courage.' I consider it possible that the ecological crisis could be a 'cosmic trigger', forcing not only rapid technological and social innovation, but also a psychic evolution.

Prophecy

In *2012: The Return of Quetzalcoatl*, my last book, I explored the thesis that humanity is undergoing an evolutionary leap from one level of consciousness – one state of being – to the next. Although I dealt with the 5,125-year-long count cycle of the Mayan calendar, which ended on 21 December 2012, I never anticipated either the Apocalypse or Rapture at or around that date.

I proposed instead that the purpose of the calendar was to mark the transition – to help us make the jump. I saw the end of the long count as an invitation for humanity to undergo a global awakening and take a different path. This would mean adopting aspects of the worldview and some of the practices of indigenous and aboriginal cultures.

These small-scale, traditional societies developed methods of long-term continuity based on their spiritual ethos of interdependence and connection to nature. As Native American sociologist Jack Forbes puts it, 'The life of Native American peoples revolves around the concept of the sacredness, beauty, power and relatedness of all forms of existence. In short, the ethics or moral values of native people are part and parcel of their cosmology or total worldview.' We can, I think, merge crucial aspects of the indigenous worldview – as well as the ecological and social practices that stem from it – with our advanced technical capacities. If we manage this, we can learn to respect the limits of the Earth and bring our global civilization back into balance.

In the modern world, time is linear and spatial – you can waste it, run out of it or equate it with money. We are supposed to be making 'progress' towards some ineffable, technological goal. But this is just one way of conceiving time, of exploring its many dimensions. There is also the dreamtime, the ever-present origin, known to aboriginals.

Aboriginals don't conceive of history, of progress and redemption, or decline and fall. For them, the universe is a sacred continuum, an ongoing ceremony. There is only one holy moment, infinitely extended. This way of understanding time is at least as sensible as ours.

In the modern world, people tend to think of humanity as separate from nature – somehow above or outside of it. We forget that all of our abilities are extensions of what we have received from the natural world. I think this gives us reason to hope. The development of modern industrial civilization may also be part of a natural cycle. Most probably, the evolution of society – the development of consciousness – is as exquisitely timed and purposeful as other processes we observe in evolutionary biology. We may be following a programme or sequence – much like foetal development, where the mother transmits chemical signals to her infant, at precise intervals, up to the moment of birth. How we understand and articulate it is part of the programme, executed by the code as it writes itself.

Right now, I believe we are in transition – in the birth canal – approaching the next threshold of our awakening, the next phase of our life as a species. In quantum physics, for example, we are realizing the union of Western science with Eastern metaphysics. In the Middle Ages, modern science emerged out of magic and alchemy. Science began with observation of the physical phenomena we observed outside of us. It has slowly turned inwards. Mysticism starts from the other direction. It begins with our subjective experience – the phenomenology of perception – and opens to the world in its totality. As we approach the end of history, the edge of the abyss, these forms of knowledge are fusing together, merging and unifying. I consider this to be part of the prophetic shift we are undergoing.

The world – according to Hinduism and Buddhism, is '*maya*', illusion. Similarly, Carl Jung saw the world as a projection of the psyche, a parable of the imagination. I take this to be true, to the deepest level. The imagination is not just a faculty. William Blake considered it to be human existence itself. We are living a fable devised by one underlying source, pure consciousness – the 'I Am That', which we are. When we deepen our consciousness – when we ratchet up our awareness of unity within multiplicity – the world shifts correspondingly.

We can no longer allow ourselves to be carried along by the forces of history. Humanity has reached a juncture where, in order to survive, we must become co-creative with the evolutionary process, inflecting and shaping it. We can take responsibility for the plot, its twists and dizzying turns. This requires a new vision and shaping intention.

I don't think everyone needs to drink ayahuasca, go to Burning Man, or explore the prophetic or esoteric aspects of reality. There are many different pathways to self-knowledge and happiness. I also believe that it makes no sense to separate out the 'spiritual' and the 'material' – or the spiritual and the political – as if they are opposites. That is a flaw in our thinking that we inherited from outmoded religions. The separation between spirituality and matter was absorbed into New Age spirituality, which has often been self-centred. Now we must grow beyond it to make a spiritual commitment to our human family, as a whole, as well as to the greater community of life on Earth.

It is hard to imagine how we can make a rapid systemic transition without a mass awakening or a consciousness revolution. As unlikely and implausible as it seems, we need to transform the basis of our post-industrial, ecologically suicidal, hyper-individualist, deeply unjust society. We can establish, in its place, a system that supports the collective health of humanity as it restores and replenishes the biosphere. Considering the severity of our biospheric emergency, we must find technical as well as social solutions that can replicate quickly and scale exponentially. If it helps to focus our minds on the alternative, we can call it a regenerative society.

Sustainability, the ability to maintain life in its current form over a long duration, needs to be eclipsed by a new paradigm. As a call to action, what sustainability seeks to sustain, above all, is some version of our current way of life, even though the evidence is quite overwhelming that it cannot continue. Living processes, generally, don't just endure or persevere. Life either flourishes and blooms, evolves and transforms, or it stagnates and dies. The rhetoric of sustainability tends to support the belief that our current form of post-industrial capitalism can be reformed – that it can persist, in something close to its present order.

The emergent paradigm defines its ideal as a *regenerative culture*. We can look at our current institutions and ideologies as a substrate, a foundation, providing the conditions for another level of trans-formation, just as modern bourgeois society, based on market relations and competition, emerged from monarchy, based on feudalism and obligation. According to chaos theory, the nonlinear dynamics of living organisms allow for the emergence of new orders of complexity, when a system reaches a high level of instability. As the mono-cultural, technocratic approach of post-industrial capitalism crumbles, a new worldview – a new way of being – is crystallizing.

To understand what I mean by a regenerative society, we can contrast it with the consumerist society we have now. In a consumer society, the main focus of cultural and industrial production is making and selling consumer goods to those who can afford them. Industry creates profit for corporations and shareholders. A regenerative society, in contrast, would apply technology and industry to restore and replenish the ecosystems of the planet, while also seeking to enhance the quality of people's lives. The focus would not be on accumulating wealth for the few, but on distributing goods and resources fairly. The goal of such a system is a world where humanity thrives, living in harmony and symbiosis with the planet. This requires a greater emphasis on resilient local communities and bioregions, rather than global corporations and nation-states.

Rebellion and the Sacred

Albert Camus – chic existentialist, renowned hipster intellectual of his time – saw rebellion as a metaphysical principle. When men rebel, they overcome their individuality and alienation. They identify themselves with all those who suffer under oppression. In *The Rebel*, he wrote, 'only two possible worlds can exist for the human mind: the sacred (or to speak in Christian terms, the world of grace) and the world of rebellion. The disappearance of one is equivalent to the appearance of the other, despite the fact that this appearance can take place in disconcerting forms.'

Modern civilization represents rebellion from the past. We rebelled against any idea of God or the sacred, declaring, with Nietzsche, 'the death of God'. Is it possible we are leaving the time of rebellion behind us? Has nihilism, hyper-individualism, domination, patriarchy, run its course? Are we finally losing interest in our own extended tantrum? Is the pendulum swinging back from the world of rebellion to the world of the sacred? Personally, I believe this is our evolutionary destiny.

Since the 1960s, consumer society has diluted the pursuit of enlightenment into a lifestyle option, as meaningless as all the rest. People seek enlightenment at weekend workshops, or by mantra chanting twice a day, while they pursue careers in corporate finance or advertising. Mindfulness is taught to project managers at Google to boost their efficiency.

Spirituality has become trendy; shamanism is a fad. For the post-Marxist critic Slavoj Žižek, Westernized Buddhism, as well as yoga and urban shamanism, 'enables you to fully participate in the frantic pace of the capitalist game, while sustaining the perception that you are not really in it, that you are well aware how worthless this spectacle really is – what really matters to you is the peace of the inner self to which you know you can always withdraw . . .' Žižek proposes that 'New Age "Asiatic" thought' – reflected in bestsellers like *The Power of Now*, *The Seven Spiritual Laws of Success* and *The Secret* – has become 'the hegemonic ideology of global capitalism'. I find this a helpful insight.

The elite of our society – mainly Baby Boomers now – tend to indulge in a feel-good, Diet Coke version of spirituality, without sacrifice or commitment. They nibble at the edges of mysticism, toying with The Four Agreements, mastering The Seven Laws of Spiritual Success, flying to Hawaii for weekend Tantra workshops designed to enhance their orgasms. They scrupulously avoid the surrendering of ego meant to accompany enlightenment, as well as its political, social and ecological dimensions.

But right now we need to wake up for real. We must wake up – not because spirituality makes us feel good, or chanting a mantra gets us a new car, or because avowing Advaita Vedanta non-duality assuages our guilt at not doing enough for the world. We need to wake up because the Arctic was 30 degrees Celsius warmer than usual in the winter of 2015. We are polluting every ecosystem on the planet. Somehow, we have to overcome distractions to confront the destruction we have unleashed on the world – and hopefully reverse it. At this point, our planet's future – the lives of our children and all children – depends on us, on our passion, commitment and critical discernment; on how we make use of our limited time and resources.

We must overcome self-interest to see ourselves in a new way. Our species can evolve to play a supportive role in the Earth's ecology: that's our opportunity. As individuals, we can see ourselves as secret agents or midwives, helping to birth a new human society. We can be catalysts who create change with our words and our deeds. As part of this initiation the cosmos has delivered to us, I am afraid we must be willing to make serious short-term sacrifices.

I meet many well-off people who are constantly trying to heal themselves. While healing ourselves is important, it can also become a trap. Instead of waiting for some magical healing to occur, the most advanced and aware among us need to lead by example – to take courageous risks, pointing the way forward for everyone else. Perhaps we can only truly be healed when we overcome our sense of entitlement by embracing a new collective mission, acting together as one.

Multitudes of people are getting angry and desperate. As the old world collapses around them, they will turn to Trump-like demagogues, choose hatred and pursue short-sighted goals that will further damage the Earth. These people need to be shown another path, but we can only do so once we have found it ourselves. At this point, we need more than a vague idea of the alternative – we can't just hold hands together and sing 'Imagine', waiting for a more beautiful world spontaneously to emerge. We have to understand what's wrong with our system while we work on building the tangible alternatives. We should demand a world that works for everyone – including the most desperate, marginalized and deprived people.

We all know, in our hearts, that liberation – authentic illumination – requires a Christ-like dedication to service. Buddhists take the Bodhisattva vow – they commit to awaken all sentient beings, out of compassion, through innumerable cycles of death and rebirth. What does this mean for us? We must find a way to embody, to express, our solidarity with the sorrowing Earth.

If we are aspects of that one being – the eternal principle, the Absolute, the Void, the Creator Spirit, the Artist formerly known as God – then the original revelations of Christianity shine in a new light: *I and the Father are one. Love your neighbour as yourself.* If there is only one non-local source – one consciousness, infinitely variable and indivisibly the same – then all separation is illusion: we are one.

Gandhi and Martin Luther King remain intimidating figures because of the way they lived their values and ideals. For Martin Luther King, 'The Kingdom of God' existed now, not in some imaginary future. The Kingdom comes into being whenever we unite our ideals with our actions. Gandhi built a mass movement of nonviolent activism based on principles of *satyagraha*, or 'truth force'. He overthrew British colonial rule in India based on this principle: 'The followers of truth and nonviolence will offer *satyagraha* against tyranny and win over the tyrant by love, he will not carry out the tyrant's will but he will suffer punishment even unto death for disobeying his will until the tyrant himself is won over.' Gandhi's thought is so unadorned, so pure, it is still shocking to encounter it.

We have unleashed planetary catastrophe through our actions as a species. We have induced an initiatory crisis for humanity as a whole. I think that on a subconscious level we have willed this into being. We are forcing ourselves to evolve – to change or die – by creating this universal threat to our existence. We will either squander our chance and fail as a species, or we will seize it, making a voluntary, self-willed mutation in how we think and act. This is the choice that faces us now.

2

Ecstatic Contact with the Cosmos

When I was a child, I remember feeling certain that a great secret was waiting to be revealed to me. I felt the whole world trembling with this mystery that lurked behind the surface of ordinary reality. It was hidden under the sidewalks of New York City, within the windows of the apartment buildings that stared out at me like ten thousand unblinking eyes. It was whispered by the wind that blew teasingly through the leaves of the trees, causing ripples across the Hudson.

I was sure this mystery waiting to unveil itself to me was the core of existence. When I found it, I would know my purpose and mission and become a whole being. I assumed all adults had passed through the portal of this unfathomable event. I believed this must be the secret subtext of their conversations, which otherwise seemed nonsensically dull and boring.

In high school, I began to grasp, then to accept morosely, that no hidden revelation awaited me or anybody else. It slowly dawned on me that the adults I knew did not have access to anything beyond the ordinary and day-to-day. I felt baffled, betrayed, by this realization.

I think many of us can recall the anticipation, the expectancy, that the world was designed to reveal a great secret. We can also recall the sense of despair we felt when our hope was extinguished.

The yearning we feel as adolescents, when all of our senses strain for some deeper intensity of being, is the desire for initiation and transcendence. We seek access to something sacred – something greater than ourselves. Because our culture denies us the fulfilment of this yearning, we become alienated and jaded. Over time, we learn to accept our disappointment, to forget our hopes. We are forced to accept degraded substitutes – to find a limited form of transcendence in media spectacles, sporting contests and artworks.

I believe modern civilization is founded on this original betrayal. All traditional societies around the world – all premodern cultures – had some form of rites of passage, of initiations, which marked the transition from childhood to maturity. At some long-ago point in our history, Judaeo-Christian civilization abandoned the techniques of initiation, which allowed each person to reach self-knowledge or gnosis, in favour of indoctrination. Spiritual knowledge was no longer available to everyone. It was controlled, held in secrecy, by the priests and the rulers.

This history can be traced back to the closing of the Mystery Schools that were crucial institutions up until the rise of Christianity. All of the great figures of antiquity congregated annually at Eleusis in Ancient Greece, where they imbibed a potion together, the *kykeon*, which most probably contained psychedelic plants. In the Middle Ages, the Church stamped out the European remnants of plant shamanism with the Inquisition, where those who possessed second sight, who used substances like belladonna and henbane to undertake visionary flights, were burnt at the stake as witches.

A civilization developed that promoted only one kind of consciousness – a rational, day-lit form of awareness, denigrating the intuitive, the visionary and the mystical. These forms of holistic right-brain awareness can also be considered feminine. Modern civilization not only repressed women and demonized female sexuality; it also suppressed the feminine, intuitive aspects of consciousness. It only considered the left-brain or masculine aspect to be valuable. As this patriarchal civilization developed science, logic and military discipline, it was able to extend its reach across the world, constructing a global empire.

Because it is innate to us, the yearning for transcendence and initiation always reappears in some form. If it is not integrated into the culture in a healthy and useful way, it expresses itself through nightmarish deviations. Writing between the First and Second World Wars, the German Jewish critic Walter Benjamin thought that humanity could not avoid collective experiences where we enter into 'ecstatic contact with the cosmos'. Either we create such ceremonies consciously, or they will be inflicted upon us through catastrophes. Benjamin saw the First World War as an example of this. It was an 'attempt at a new and unprecedented mingling with the cosmic powers', unleashing gargantuan powers of death and destruction.

Today, we see our innate human yearning for transcendence displaced onto technology. In Silicon Valley, the Singularity has become a quasi-religious faith supporting the ideology of corporate progress. The idea of the Singularity is that humanity's destiny is to merge with our machines or be replaced by them entirely. As I will discuss in more depth later, I think this is a wrong direction. I don't believe we should reject technology. I believe our evolution of technology is part of the evolution of consciousness. But we should seek to master our mechanical and virtual tools for humane, regenerative purposes.

The world wars that defined the twentieth century could be seen as expressions of the suppressed, primitive parts of our collective psychology – what Carl Jung called the shadow – projected on a massive scale. They reflected the level of unconsciousness existing at that time. In the same way, I believe we have unconsciously unleashed the ecological mega-crisis in order to force a collective awakening and to bring about the next level of our unfolding as a species.

Our governing elites and educated classes have known for over a half-century that we are charging towards ecological collapse. Abundant data, the Club of Rome reports, books like Rachel Carson's *Silent Spring* made this clear decades ago. But we have been unable to change our direction and, in fact, we have continued to accelerate towards disaster. Underlying the momentum of post-industrial civilization is a deep well of suppressed grief over our assault on the biosphere. This also must be brought into our awareness, and acknowledged.

We see the same pattern occurring in ourselves and in the lives of the people around us. People will persist in addictive and self-destructive patterns until they find themselves forced to choose between a path of self-knowledge or disintegration and death. On a neurological level, they seek to push themselves to the limit, pursuing different states of consciousness – seeking some intensity of communion that the normal world has denied them.

Collectively, the human species is revealing the same pattern of self-destructive impulsion – suppressed yearning leading to heedless abandon – that we see on the individual level. We are pushing against the boundaries of ego-based individualism, seeking to reach the next expression of our human being-ness. In order to evolve, we have to recognize the pattern.

A Collective Rite of Passage

We can conceive of the biospheric meltdown humanity has caused as a rite of passage for our species as a whole. Anthropologists have noted that rites of passage invariably pass through a series of stages. In the first stage, the candidates are taken away from their homes. They are forced to undergo a process that is shrouded in mystery, considered life-threatening as well as sacred. During this stage of separation, they undergo certain ordeals that force them into an altered state of consciousness, where they receive visions. The elders help them to understand and interpret what the spiritual world has revealed to them. In the final stage of reunion, they are welcomed back into the community, which celebrates their return.

Initiations can take many forms. They can involve long fasts, vision quests, solitary walkabouts in the wilderness. Initiation can mean taking psychedelic plants like peyote, iboga, mushrooms or ayahuasca. They vary widely in intensity and duration. One form of initiation, for Australian aboriginals, involves being buried up to your neck in the earth for one excruciating, interminable night. In the tradition of the Kogi people who live in the mountains of Colombia, the young boys who are destined to be the Mamas, the teachers of their community and those who perform divinations, must spend many years in darkness, to develop their visionary capacities. For an initiation ritual of the Hopi snake clan, poisonous snakes are collected from the wilderness. The members of the clan sit in a circle, with their knees touching. The snakes are dumped out of a sack into the centre of the circle. The men must remain in absolute stillness until all the snakes have slithered away, passing over them.

Modern civilization maintains faint vestiges of initiation rites in ceremonies like baptisms and Bar Mitzvahs, or hazing rituals at college fraternities. For the most part, these ceremonies are comparatively sedate. They do not force people to risk their lives, undergo personal transformation, face their fear of death and the unknown, or access a visionary trance. A diploma rather than any threshold of inner realization tells us we have reached adulthood.

We seem to be subconsciously impelling ourselves towards planetary catastrophe to break our alienation and ego-centrism, to reach a new intensity of communion. We are making this happen through collective catastrophe because we no longer have rites of passage which create the same effect through intentionally guided ritual. But the chaos and catastrophe we are unleashing may have an unforeseen result. Collectively, humanity can realize love – universal, unconditional love – as the root of our solidarity, the basis for healing our world. Through a shared experience of catastrophe as well as the witnessing of mass suffering, we may be forcing ourselves to open our hearts individually and collectively.

In *A Paradise Built in Hell*, Rebecca Solnit visited communities in the wake of major disasters, such as New Orleans after Katrina. We are conditioned by the mass media to believe that people will behave like monsters or criminals when society breaks down, but Solnit found the opposite. For the most part, people go out of their way to help each other when catastrophe strikes. 'In the wake of an earthquake, a bombing, or a major storm, most people are altruistic, urgently engaged in caring for themselves and those around them, strangers and neighbours as well as friends and loved ones,' she writes. Years after a disaster, many people recall their experiences as the best time of their lives, when they briefly felt a sense of belonging and togetherness. Ironically, before modern civilization, this was our natural state, going back tens of thousands of years.

'Disasters, in returning their sufferers to public and collaborative life, undo some of this privatization, which is a slower, subtler disaster all its own,' Solnit writes. 'In a society in which participation, agency, purposefulness and freedom are all adequately present, a disaster would be only a disaster.'

Our current civilization artificially keeps us alienated and isolated, in competition with each other. The system functions mechanically to benefit those at the top of the financial pyramid, who control humanity through mass media and government, instilling fear and insecurity. We subconsciously strain against this condition of slavery and serfdom. We require a breakthrough to a new system to express the full range of our humanity – our innate altruism, our empathy for one another. The oncoming emergency will force us to access the deep reserves of intelligence, compassion and creativity that we need to bring about this metamorphosis.

As individuals, we don't need to wait for catastrophic rupture of our planet's support systems before we shift into an actualized, empathic state. We can make it our conscious choice; we can live that way now. But tragically, it seems that humanity, as a collective, requires a universal crisis to bring about our mass awakening.

The Prefrontal Cortex

Initiations are more than cultural or social processes. They may have a crucial impact on how our brain functions. They may be neurological events that have a permanent impact on how we relate to the world.

The newest structure in the brain separates us from our primate ancestors. This structure is called the prefrontal cortex and is part of the neocortex. It has only reached its current level of complexity over the last 100,000 years – barely a blink of evolutionary time. The prefrontal cortex is an evolutionary mutation that allows for higher-order thought, language and abstract symbol processing. As Joseph Chilton Pierce writes in *The Biology of Transcendence*, this region of the brain governs 'all higher intellectual capacities such as our abilities to compute and reason, analyse, think creatively, and so on'. Our sense of self-identity and awareness develops through adolescence, but we may require a culturally induced ordeal – an initiatory shock – to reach our full potential.

Through extreme events or initiation rituals, the individual can attain visionary states, overcoming the limits of the ego. This often happens, for instance, in Near Death Experiences, which can permanently change how the survivor sees the world. The visionary or non-ordinary state that brings a sense of unity with the cosmos, or awareness of the multi-dimensions of the psyche, may be very fleeting. Even so, such non-ordinary states of consciousness can provide a stable reference point, like an anchor, particularly when the society recognizes their importance and value.

One function of initiation, according to Pierce, is to connect mind and heart. The heart is also a thinking organ, possessing neurons. It emanates a measurable field of electromagnetism in the shape of a torus that surrounds the physical body. Almost universally, Pierce writes,

> A poignant and passionate idealism arises in early puberty, followed by an equally passionate expectation in the mid-teens that 'something tremendous is supposed to happen' and finally by the teenager's boundless, exuberant belief in 'the hidden greatness within me'. A teenager often gestures toward his or her heart when speaking of these three sensibilities, for the heart is involved in what should take place.

When society thwarts our innate drive to find meaning and transcendence through inner experience, the deepest, most sensitive parts of ourselves go numb.

With no access to transcendent states, people are trapped by constant cravings, seeking empty gratifications. They try to solidify their sense of personal identity through material possessions or by seeking power over others. They cannot reach maturity, which, for a member of a tribe, means taking responsibility for your community, revering and caring for the natural world, and accepting also the place assigned to you in the cosmic order.

My Journey

When I was in my late twenties, that suppressed yearning I had felt as an adolescent reappeared in a deeper form. I don't know why I was afflicted with it to such a degree. All I know is that my life seemed increasingly empty and meaningless without some way of reaching transcendence. I'd grown up without any religious or spiritual beliefs. My parents were artists who had rejected the religion of their ancestors.

My Irish Catholic father, Peter Pinchbeck, painted in the tradition of the Abstract Expressionists. He brooded over huge canvases in his bare SoHo loft. My Jewish mother, Joyce Johnson, belonged to the Beat Generation as a young woman in the 1950s. She wrote about her relationship with the novelist Jack Kerouac and her adolescence in her memoir, *Minor Characters*.

Art was their replacement for religion. It was their life and their faith. From childhood, I wanted to be a poet and novelist. I imagined myself, eventually, writing novels in the tradition of the European avant-garde, following in the footsteps of Virginia Woolf, Kafka, Samuel Beckett, Nabokov, Georges Perec and other authors that I loved.

I was influenced by the Beat writers, particularly Kerouac, Allen Ginsberg and William Burroughs. These authors confronted their own existential crises as young men, hovering around Columbia University in the 1940s. The Beats flitted in and out of mental institutions and prisons, exploring the edges and underworlds. Fighting against the mainstream culture, its stereotypes and hypocrisies, they sought knowledge through direct experience. They explored psychedelics and other ways to reach what the poet Arthur Rimbaud called a 'systematic derangement of the senses'.

In the late 1940s, Kerouac conceived of the Beat Generation as a 'subterranean revolution' outside of politics, growing up under the shadow of the atomic bomb, seeking to build a new society based on 'apocalyptic love' and the rediscovery of joy in a liberated society, free of guilt. They rejected the mainstream construct of an adult maturity based on sexual repression, conventional careers and constricted rationality as false. The goal of the Beats was to break free of received ideas and stale conventions. They wanted to recover originality, spontaneity, mystical truth. They believed everyone could access their innate brilliance, once they liberated themselves from social conventions. Kerouac wrote, 'You are a genius all of the time.'

I suffered a long illness as a child, an infection of the spine which kept me in hospital for eight months between the ages of 11 and 12. I wore a full body cast for most of that time. In the wake of it, I developed scoliosis. My time in the hospital shaped my consciousness in many ways. I felt like an outsider, exiled from my body. I also had to learn to find comfort even in the most painful and difficult circumstances.

I suspect this long childhood illness accidentally left me with unusual abilities and tendencies. I couldn't forget the hovering nearness of death, which made me want to find some meaning or purpose to life. As a writer, I developed the ability to pursue subjects that were too difficult, abstruse or threatening for most people to explore in depth. I think I also developed some inner detachment which helped me look at the world from an impersonal, systems-level viewpoint.

In my late twenties, as I plunged ever deeper into an existential emergency, I kept thinking about my handful of psychedelic trips back in college. They were the most powerful indicators that there might be other aspects of reality – other levels of consciousness – that modern civilization had suppressed or rejected. I went back and took LSD and mushrooms again. These substances seemed to reveal so much.

On the one hand, they were deconditioning agents. They made me aware that our civilization was an artifice, a consensual hallucination, and that our world could be constructed differently. I also experienced closed-eye hallucinations, incredibly intricate geometrical patterns and images that didn't seem like anything produced by my mind alone. They seemed to demonstrate the existence of archetypal dimensions, the collective field of the psyche that Carl Jung explored in his work.

As I researched psychedelics I learned about the ritual use of ayahuasca in South America and iboga in West Africa. As a journalist, I was able to get magazine assignments to undergo these rituals in their original context. I went to Gabon, on the equator of West Africa, to eat the iboga root in a ceremony with the Bwiti tribe. During this all-night event, as I lay on the cool ground in the Bwiti temple, I was taken on a journey through my life up to that time.

As I wrote in *Breaking Open the Head*, I was shown a series of scenes from my past – they weren't just visual images. They were like holographic, sensorial recreations. I recalled myself as a child, with my parents fighting in our loft. I remembered how I made myself terrified that there was a monster hiding under the bed or in the closet. I remembered how sad I felt when my parents separated and I moved uptown with my mother.

Later, I saw myself in my twenties going to literary cocktail parties and getting hammered on alcohol. I saw how this drinking had a negative impact on my character, my work and relationships. The scenes appeared again and again, as if mocking me with my stupidity. I had the uncanny feeling there was a guiding intelligence in the iboga – a plant spirit – that wanted to communicate with me, to teach me.

I went to the Amazon jungle in Ecuador to participate in ayahuasca ceremonies with the Secoya people. The Secoya were a tribe of 30,000 at the beginning of the twentieth century. By the time I visited, there were fewer than 700 of them left, split between two small reservations.

Only a few elder shamans remained – tiny, wizened men in their eighties who wore coloured tunics and crowns woven from local branches. The elders walked us through the dense jungle, pointing out many plants with healing powers, giggling frequently. The oil companies were decimating the jungle, poisoning the rivers and building roads. The roads attracted poor *mestizos* who slashed and burnt the forest to create subsistence farms.

Of all the substances I explored, ayahuasca remains my favourite. The substance has now become popular around the world, with shamans bringing the plants to Europe, Asia, South Africa and everywhere. Ayahuasca is a bitter drink that requires two plants, the ayahuasca vine – *Banisteriopsis caapi* – and the DMT-containing *psychotria viridis*. The brew induces a huge range of visionary effects. You can find yourself immersed in the liquid medium of the aboriginal dreamtime, entering pure consciousness or the *samadhi* state, or visiting myriad spirits and deities who take you on journeys to other worlds and dimensions. Ayahuasca can also bring you profound, healing insights into the nature of your own soul.

I visited Huautla de Jiménez, a mountain town in Oaxaca, Mexico, where magic mushrooms were found in the early 1950s by the investment banker and amateur mycologist Gordon Wasson, and Valentina, his Russian wife. I explored the postmodern world of psychedelic chemistry. In Marin County, I visited grey-bearded, legendary Sasha Shulgin in his laboratory and tested a number of his experimental compounds.

I attended an ethnobotany conference in Palenque, Mexico, where I tried dimethyltryptamine, nn-DMT, for the first time. DMT is a chemical produced by the human brain, and also found in many plants. When I smoked it, my body and my surroundings vanished. I broke into a fully realized other reality – a kind of hyper-dimension – that seemed far beyond anything the wiring of my brain could concoct. I felt I was communing with a superconsciousness that was extra-terrestrial, overwhelming. I was immersed in a crystalline, fluorescent lattice made up of one being that was simultaneously many beings, all of them chattering at a high pitch. I felt they were omniscient, aware of me as part of some programme or of what the science-fiction writer Philip K Dick named a Vast Alien Living Intelligence System (VALIS).

Breaking Open the Head became a record of my transformation. By following a personal path of self-discovery, my understanding of the nature of reality changed profoundly. I started as a secular materialist, a Freudian and sceptic. I ended up converted to a mystical and shamanic worldview. This didn't happen all at once. It took a series of ceremonies, adventures, good and bad trips, as well as extensive research through the literature on visionary experience and interviews with many people who had undergone similar journeys of initiation. I experienced inexplicable psychic phenomena: synchronicities, occult apparitions, visitations, telepathic links and much more. These experiences convinced me that consciousness is not ultimately brain-based but a fundamental property of the universe.

Biocentrism

Reductive scientific materialism is unproven and therefore a kind of religious faith. The belief that consciousness is brain-based – an epiphenomenon of evolution, caused randomly by neurological wiring – remains a hypothesis. For scientists like Robert Lanza and Amit Goswami, the last decades of experiment support the opposite view: consciousness is the underlying reality. The universe – all matter – gives transitory expression to its infinite, ever-changing potential.

In *Biocentrism*, Lanza notes that space and time have no reality outside of our awareness of them. They are, finally, 'tools of our animal understanding'. He believes the universe has been fine-tuned for our emergence and that it exists in order for living beings – we ourselves – to experience and participate in it. Consciousness – the 'I Am That' of Eastern mysticism – has devised this adventure for itself, and we are its expressions.

According to quantum physics, the existence of a material world depends on an observing consciousness, which collapses the incessant quavering of energy waves into a definitive, perceivable state. We have also discovered that electrons, once connected, maintain their link no matter how far they travel away from each other. Time, it would seem, does not exist for these subatomic particles. This fact subverts our conventional understanding of time.

In *The Self-Aware Universe*, Goswami, a physicist, theorizes that principles of quantum theory allow for the existence of subtle bodies and aspects of an immortal soul. What mystics call spirits or souls could be energetic complexes bound together, as quantum waves, via Action at a Distance. Such complexes may remain connected after the death of an individual.

The individual spirit may seek to develop its patterns of thinking, feeling and willing further through reincarnation, assuming bodily form again and again. Such energy-clusters eventually fulfil their potential, Goswami suggests, when they realize their self-identity with the underlying spaceless and timeless reality. This would be what various traditions call enlightenment, illumination, attainment or realization.

Both scientists propose that consciousness is primary and precedes material manifestation. Goswami believes we must develop a 'science within consciousness', rather than conceiving an objective reality that exists outside of it. A great bulk of evidence, as well as repeated experiment, demonstrates that such an objective reality simply does not exist. Yet, for the most part, we continue to act as if it does.

Sex and Drugs

I am sure some readers will find some of my ideas to be objectionable, dismissible, even absurd. That is okay. We are at a crisis point. We need to be willing to think differently and consider alternative possibilities, even radical ones, in all areas. We need to do this simply because the system – industrial, social and ideological – we have inherited is destroying the biosphere upon which all life depends.

What I learned from my own journey is that initiation is not a single threshold experience. Even after one accepts the existence of a spiritual world, there are many levels of initiation and development to undergo. My own development has, unfortunately, been very uneven. Although I accessed some forms of occult knowledge and many new ideas through shamanic work and psychedelic exploration, I was unable to face some flaws in my character for quite a long time.

I now believe that prolonged psychedelic use amplified some of my flaws. Some people have an innate tendency to push themselves to the edge, seeking to know what lies beyond it. Those are the people who become artists, shamans, visionaries – or criminals, psychopaths or lunatics. We all have these tendencies to some degree.

I published my second book, *2012: The Return of Quetzalcoatl*, in 2006. The book became a bestseller, and I became an eccentric counter-culture celebrity in middle age. Driven by urgency about the planetary crisis, I launched companies and think-tanks before I had reckoned with my own childhood wounds – before I had sufficiently seen or integrated my shadow.

Suddenly famous, I found I had a great many more sexual opportunities than when I was young, poor and unknown. A deep well of erotic disappointment and dissatisfaction, even bitterness, had accumulated over the years. I think this is the sad, suppressed truth for many men. Given the opportunity, I wanted to make up for lost time. I took advantage of these openings; sometimes, I acted in ways that were thoughtless and self-serving, that I now regret. I didn't realize my sexual quest had become a nasty compulsion until the pattern revealed itself.

What made the situation more complex is that I honestly believed I was promoting 'free love' in a positive way. I went out of my way to be honest. I thought I was following in the footsteps of the poet Allen Ginsberg, who believed that society should support 'lifestyles of ecstasy, for whoever wants them'. In fact, I still agree with him.

Part of my problem was that I still saw myself as a wounded, sensitive person – an underdog – seeking to grow and understand himself. With the success of my work, other people, particularly younger people in the counterculture world, saw me as a leader or an authority figure. Innately dissident, I wasn't ready, at that point in my life, to be anyone's role model.

Personally, I think we need to break away from the nuclear family and the monogamous couple as our ideal. I believe that a liberation of Eros – encompassing love and compassion, as well as sexuality – is a critical aspect of the next phase of our evolution as a species. As I will discuss later, this evolution requires a new level of cooperation between the genders which will benefit everyone. It also requires deprogramming from inherited patterns of jealousy and competitiveness, and an eventual transformation of our socio-economic system.

Although I have made many mistakes in my life, I believe my perspective still has value – in fact, it probably has more value because of the errors and missteps. I took some uncharted detours through murky swamps of the psyche, seeking to integrate my personal dark matter. I believe our individual suffering can illuminate larger processes happening in the collective. By healing ourselves – by understanding the forces that work on us and making peace with them – we contribute to the healing of the whole. As Nisargadatta Maharaj says in *I Am That*: 'Don't be afraid, don't resist, don't delay. Be what you are. There is nothing to be afraid of. Trust and try. Experiment honestly. Give your real being a chance to shape your life. You will not regret.' I have experimented honestly, and I don't regret.

Global Reboot

This book is – I admit it – a continuation of my attempt to spark a revolution at Burning Man over a decade ago. As unsuccessful as that attempt was, as crazy as I am, I still feel I had, in essence, the right idea. I know it is difficult and painful to contemplate what is happening to our world. Most of us are experts at distracting ourselves from the mega-catastrophe that threatens to engulf all of us, even laughing it off. But if we are brave, I believe we can come to see it as a necessary and even positive threshold in the life of our species. It is only by embracing this crisis in all of its mind-bending complexity that we can find the will and the incentive to change ourselves and our world.

From the 1960s until today, many people have taken personal journeys of initiation, rediscovering mysticism and shamanism, and embracing an expanded awareness of psyche and cosmos. This collective voyage of initiation can't be completed, however, until those who have taken their personal vision quests are able to bring their new knowledge back into our society – to have it fully absorbed, welcomed and integrated. The best option is that we undertake a peaceful, deliberately designed and non-destructive system change.

We can think of our current civilization – its technical and socio-political infrastructure, its ideology and beliefs – as an operating system, much like the software that runs our computers. Now we need to reboot and install a new system software. A new social design could, eventually, give every human being the opportunity to flourish and thrive, to live creatively, without fear for their future. Accomplishing this is a great mission that will require a truly rational, empathic application of our technical and creative powers.

We must build this new programme – engineer this global reboot – within the next decades. If we can accomplish this, we will have passed the test that the universe has set for us. I realize that some people will worry I am proposing a nefarious form of 'social engineering'. The truth is that we have already been socially engineered. As Terence McKenna noted, culture is our operating system. We have been conditioned since birth to accept a system of global control, elite privilege and military domination. Identity is, to a great extent, a social construction.

'The only thing that one really knows about human nature is that it changes', Oscar Wilde wrote. 'Change is the one quality we can predicate of it. The systems that fail are those that rely on the permanency of human nature, and not on its growth and development.' I think this is true. It points towards the enormous task as well as the great opportunity confronting us now. The Earth will not be able to support a global civilization based on hyper-consumerism and hyper-individualism for much longer. Therefore, we must change human nature as it is currently known. We must do this – not only to survive, but also to reach our full potential as a species.

Our technocratic society uses the mass media as an instrument of mind control and threatens those who dissent or resist with violent reprisals (for example, nonviolent drug offenders seeking to explore their own consciousness face draconian prison sentences). Through incessant media bombardment and government fear-mongering, people are conditioned to believe that oppression, injustice, violence and inequality are normal and inevitable. What we require is a new social design to liberate humanity from its prison. This redesign must also reckon with our darker and more destructive impulses and find ways to channel them.

My mission with this book is unabashedly utopian. To quote Wilde again (although remembered mainly as a playwright and dandy, he was also a brilliant social critic): 'A map of the world that does not include Utopia is not worth even glancing at, for it leaves out the one country at which Humanity is always landing. And when Humanity lands there, it looks out, and, seeing a better country, sets sail. Progress is the realization of Utopias.'

Postmodern civilization is already a pseudo-utopia. Over the last few centuries, we have constructed an artificial paradise of consumer goods – the society of the spectacle – for those with the resources to enjoy it. Unfortunately, this artificial paradise is built on excessive waste and ecological destruction. It has created misery for those on the margins, the victims of famines, wars and genocides. By addressing its flaws, we can realize the next manifestation of our genius as a species – and achieve, in comparison, a true utopia.

I know it seems strange to discuss the imminent prospect of ecological meltdown on the one hand and the attainment of a practical utopia on the other. But such is the schizophrenic nature of our time. As we shall see, both outcomes seem plausible. In the near term, we may get a bizarre mix of the two.

I don't think a massive dieback of the human population is inevitable – perhaps I refuse to believe it. But the longer we wait to relaunch our social operating system, the more difficult it will be to avert planetary catastrophe. We have already waited too long.

I seek to bring together the archaic and the postmodern, the visionary and the rational, the corporate and the anarchistic, in a viable synthesis. I don't expect us to revert to old-fashioned eighteenth-century agrarianism, although I do think communities will need to grow more of their own food and become as self-sufficient as possible. I also don't think we can regress all the way back to small-scale bands of hunter-gatherers, although there is a great amount we need to learn from indigenous and aboriginal cultures that supported their local ecology for thousands of years. Out of compassion, we must seek to maintain the current human population even as we radically reduce our burden on the Earth.

I don't reject the potential of futuristic technologies – artificial intelligence, nanotechnology, biotechnology and so on – out of hand. But I think we must explore them with great caution, and with constant oversight from civil society. Right now, crucial decisions that impact on the biosphere in its entirety are left to engineers, corporations and financiers. Our current form of government was established in the late eighteenth century, when news as well as progress moved at a much slower speed than today. To deal with our rapidly changing circumstances, we need more than a reform – we need, I think, a new political-economic operating system.

In many cases, the promise of advanced technologies has been far greater than what they delivered. Each new level of technology also brings with it unforeseen negative consequences, requiring more innovation to fix. As the dark ecologist Paul Kingsnorth has noted, this has created an increasingly alarming, even world-endangering 'progress trap'. As our civilization becomes more technologically complex, it also becomes more fragile. The prospect of the Singularity, promulgated by Google engineer Ray Kurzweil and other techno-utopians, is one we must investigate carefully. It is something like a ticking time bomb we must defuse.

Competition to Cooperation

The study of biological evolution – the history of life on Earth – reveals an inveterate tendency towards greater levels of cooperation, coordination and symbiosis. This idea may seem surprising at first. As part of the paradigm we inherited – the one we are now leaving behind – many thinkers and scientists placed their focus, instead, on the competitive, aggressive and destructive aspects of nature. This view of biology as a constant struggle for life meshed perfectly with the predatory economic mode of capitalism. This idea has now been superseded by a new view of life as an intricately networked phenomenon, where organisms support each other far more than they compete.

According to biologist Lynn Margulis, the author of *Microcosmos*, who developed the Gaia hypothesis with scientist James Lovelock, 'The trip from greedy gluttony, from instant satisfaction to long-term mutualism, has been made many times in the microcosm. While destructive species may come and go, cooperation itself increases through time.'

We can find the most accessible example of cooperation and symbiosis as the pattern of evolution in our own bodies. Our bodies are made out of a hundred trillion cells and vast colonies of microorganisms that work together seamlessly. In a previous stage of the Earth's evolution, these organisms were fighting against each other for scarce resources. During a period of crisis, they figured out ways to collaborate to construct more complex structures – organs, like skin, eyes and lungs. In a way, all human technologies are just recapitulations of technological feats we already find in the microcosm. Long before the Internet, viruses exchanged information – genetic code – around the world at high speed.

When humans cooperate to build a satellite dish, it is not that dissimilar to the communities of specialized cells and microorganisms that assemble an eye or an ear. 'As tiny parts of a huge biosphere whose essence is basically bacterial, we – with other life forms – must add up to a sort of symbiotic brain which it is beyond our capacity to comprehend or truly represent,' Margulis wrote.

Individual cells in our bodies do not hoard wealth – excess energy – but store it in deposits of fat that are freely available to the cellular community as a whole. Cells contribute their efforts to the collective body without seeking more for themselves, as energy flows seamlessly, going wherever it is needed. Without any competition, cells as well as organs work with maximum efficiency for the success of the whole.

The Noosphere

We can understand the process we are undergoing as purposeful, teleological and even implicitly designed – in the same way that nature designs conception, foetal development and birth on the level of an individual organism. Humanity, as a whole, constitutes a planetary super-organism, one unified being, in an ongoing, symbiotic relation-ship with the ecology of the Earth as a whole system.

The more we can individually prepare and awaken to our situation now and choose to undergo initiation, the less collective suffering will be experienced by humanity, as a whole. I believe each of us can realize this crisis we face as a great adventure and a mission which dignifies human life and gives it meaning.

In *Non-Zero: The Logic of Human Destiny*, Robert Wright noted that humans keep developing increasingly larger and more complex forms of social organization – from the small tribe to the city-state, from national governments today, to extra-national bodies like the United Nations and the European Union. For Wright, this suggests an eventual transition to global government. I look at this transition differently, believing that we will eventually transcend national governments by establishing a harmonic planetary orchestration, where local communities will function like the cells and organs in an efficient, self-regulating body. Once we evolve, we will have governance – planetary self-regulation – without governments.

Wright gives credit to the earlier work of the Catholic mystic and palaeontologist Teilhard de Chardin, who introduced the idea of the noosphere (from the Greek word *nous*, meaning mind), which he described as a layer or envelope of thought that encompasses the Earth. Writing in the first decades of the twentieth century, de Chardin proposed that, just as the Earth has an atmosphere, a lithosphere and a hydrosphere, it also has a surrounding layer made up of thought. For de Chardin, the noosphere already exists although most are unaware of it. Humanity will reach a point where we consciously activate it by attaining a collective realization.

De Chardin believed humanity's realization of the noosphere to be a mystical process through which we will discover, and celebrate, our inherent communion with the cosmos: 'Some day, after we have mastered the winds, the waves, the tides and gravity, we shall harness for God the energies of love. Then for the second time in the history of the world, we will have discovered fire,' he wrote.

The inception of a harmonized planetary collective would light up the noospheric switchboard. Our socio-political reality would no longer be distorted by greed. Our world would be shaped by wisdom, encompassing a long-term vision for human beings to live in healthy communion with our shared sister Earth. If we were to consider love – what Sigmund Freud called Eros – as a biological drive, we might define it as the instinct that binds separate entities into greater aggregates.

For de Chardin – as well as Wright and a number of other thinkers – humanity's social and technical development, seen as an extension of the Earth's biological processes, suggest that our evolution has an underlying purpose and direction. Just as a plant flowers or a caterpillar morphs into a butterfly, we are inexorably, whether we like it or not, undergoing a metamorphosis into a harmonized collective – a super-organism. As we attain that state, we may find that our interests and capacities change profoundly, just as a butterfly, no longer crawling or devouring leaves, gains an added dimension of flight and starts to pollinate. Rather than fearing what is coming, we can welcome it and rejoice in an opportunity to create a new world.

Part Two

Hard Limits

3

Earth Changes

Many journalists have written surveys on the ecological mega-crisis and its social impacts. These chroniclers have travelled across the world, visiting the front lines in Africa, Asia, South America and the Arctic. They have been part of the action at global climate summits, watching in horror as the US and Chinese governments undermined agreements that could have helped stave off decimation. Many of these writers also explore a range of possible strategies for adapting and mitigating, as well as preventing, the worst effects. Among the works in this genre, I include Elizabeth Kolbert's *The Sixth Great Extinction*, Naomi Klein's *This Changes Everything*, Mark Hertsgaard's *Hot: Living through the Next Fifty Years on Earth*, Mark Lynas's *The God Species*, Fred Pearce's *With Speed and Violence: Why Scientists Fear Tipping Points in Climate Change*, Bill McKibben's *Eaarth* as well as his earlier *Deep Economy*, and Rebecca Solnit's *A Paradise Built in Hell*.

Although I recommend all of these books and consider them essential reading, my own contribution at this juncture is to offer something more philosophical – systemic in its critique, as well as strategic in its approach to how we make change. I have been inspired by Murray Bookchin's approach to social ecology, Hannah Arendt's political philosophy, as well as Buckminster Fuller, who applied nature's design principles to our species-wide crisis.

Let's start by looking back in time briefly. Over the last 60,000 years, since leaving Africa, the human species has developed language and culture, increasing in numbers, slowly at first, as we spread ourselves across the surface of the world. For most of that time, we lived as small tribes of hunter-gatherers. Around 10,000 years ago, we began growing crops, building cities and launching empires. Over the last few centuries, our species discovered steam power, electricity, coal, oil, mechanical technology and industry. We split the atom and beached on the moon.

As its science and technologies advanced, the modern West constructed a new social model based on conspicuous consumption and planned obsolescence. We exported this experimental way of life across the world. In a short span of time, because of our capacity to exploit energy from fossil fuels – one barrel of oil holds the equivalent of 23,200 hours of manpower – humans went from biospheric nonentity to the catalysts of a geological event. The crisis confronting us is the result of what might prove to be our very short-lived success as a species.

As modern society became increasingly severed from nature, our science-based culture propagated an ideology of materialism, dismissing any mystical or religious belief system as antiquated and false. We rejected the natural, the feminine and the intuitive, replacing them with the masculine ideals of order, logic and rationality. Faith in science and technology replaced religion for many people.

This technological worldview has revealed its own internal contradictions and is reaching the point where it is starting to self-destruct. I recently held a dialogue with the neoliberal economist Nouriel Roubini, who was on President Bill Clinton's cabinet and gained the nickname 'Doctor Doom' for accurately predicting the 2008 economic meltdown. Looking at the advance of robotics and artificial intelligence, Roubini predicts that robots will eventually replace humans in all fields of activity, and that, in fact, the future belongs to the machines. This sterile *Terminator* scenario will happen, he believes, within the next fifty years.

I see this fatalistic viewpoint as the result of a narrow, reductive rationality. Rather than forfeiting our future to robots, we must learn to master our projections of technology, applying our genius for innovation to humane and benevolent pursuits. We can then define a new trajectory for our species, where we use our technologies to emancipate humanity, establish societies of sustainable abundance and explore the creative capacities of the liberated imagination – not a zero-sum game, but an infinite one. We are at the start of a fantastic adventure – the plot we are in is just as dramatic as anything we have seen in films like *Star Wars*, *Mission Impossible*, *The Matrix* or *2001*.

But before we can get to my proposed solutions and strategic action plan, we need to be on the same page about what's happening to our Earth. We must have a shared understanding of what we are doing to ourselves and our world. What I believe to be my contribution to this debate won't make much sense if we lack a coherent picture of what the science is telling us and what we can expect in the coming century. Therefore, I am going to devote this chapter to the evidence and the facts.

For some readers this may be revelatory and fascinating. Perhaps it will be enough to spur them to action. For others, however, these sections may seem heavy going, drearily academic – the term 'fucking depressing' comes to mind – even though the subject directly relates to their future lives and the lives of their children. For the benefit of these readers, I will interrupt the flow from time to time, summing up the key points, riffing a bit along the way.

Critics might assume that because I have a 'spiritual' (the terms I prefer are occult or esoteric) perspective, I don't care about the science. The truth is the opposite. Our choices and our actions must flow from the cold, hard empirical evidence. I believe I am able to engage with it, frightening as it is, because I have explored the mystical and prophetic dimensions of what's happening.

When we fully accept and realize that this crisis is our invitation to undergo a collective metamorphosis – to establish something much better than we have now – then we can find the will and courage to handle the distressing specifics. Deepening global crisis is going to force transformation, one way or another. The best thing we can do is seize this chance to leverage a mass awakening.

Dread or Detachment?

Most people have, I find, a schizophrenic approach to the ecological threat hanging over us. On the one hand, they feel dread – a sense of impending disaster. Young adults, kids in their twenties, tell me they believe we are doomed. Therefore it doesn't make sense even to try to do anything at this point to change the situation – you might as well dedicate yourself to indie rock, Tinder hook-ups or other distractions. When we feel helpless to change something, we push it out of our minds. We treat it as a joke.

Paradoxically, many people also believe that technology is going to develop so quickly that it will save us without them needing to lift a finger. Both of these ideas – that we are doomed and can't do anything, so there is no reason to try, and that technological innovation will save the day – are popular memes, spread through the media. Although they are contradictory, many people think both of these things at the same time. One theme the two ideas share is a rejection of any sense of agency or responsibility: any possibility that we can, and must, change ourselves.

I find the ecological movement guilty of this. Many well-funded groups organize marches against pipelines, drilling and fracking – or against climate change itself. But we can protest these things all we want and it won't change anything as long as we are still using way too much energy and squandering our natural resources. We might stop a pipeline in one area, but the energy companies will simply build one someplace else. Ultimately, the system is responding to consumer demand. If we are going to avoid the most catastrophic outcome, social behaviour – as well as the beliefs propelling it – needs to change.

People make the argument that it doesn't matter if we in the West now change our path, because China – or India, or other still-developing countries – will never change theirs. This is an assumption that supports continued passivity and abdicates responsibility. The fact is that Western society has not only spread our industrialized, hyper-individual, consumerist model around the world, but has relentlessly marketed it as the best way for everyone to live. On the one hand, we've used financial pressure and biased trade agreements to force developing regions to adopt our values and conform to our agenda. On the other, we have bombarded these cultures with shallow, seductive, hypnotizing media – *Dallas, Lifestyles of the Rich and Famous, Sex and the City*, the Kardashians – which have made it seem that everyone should aspire to the same standards of material wealth and glamour.

As our postmodern society undergoes a transformation of values and practices, we will apply the same genius we use to sell innumerable gaudy, useless, breakable things to promote and distribute a different way of living and being across the world. We now know from many studies that our commercial, self-centred lifestyle does not produce real contentment. Many commentators note that people in traditional societies, living within ecological limits, seem far happier than those who have adopted the Western consumer mindset. In traditional societies, we find far less crime, a deeper connection to nature, and vital spiritual traditions. In these cultures, most people live in villages or small communities. They trust and care about each other.

I believe that the only way we can engineer a rapid turnaround is to repurpose the mass media and communications infrastructure the capitalist system has bequeathed to us. Instead of marketing consumerism and keeping people fearful, our networks of media and social tools can promote different values – responsible, Earth-honouring ones – and solution-based approaches to our current problems. We can provide people with tangible tools for changing their lifestyles in major and minor ways – sharing resources, conserving energy, building communities and so on. We can shift people away from dependence on distant authorities towards local autonomy and resilience. Because human beings are extremely adaptive, this transformation could happen surprisingly quickly. It requires, first, an imaginative leap.

Modern society traps us in alienation. People continue to act as if the increasingly obvious changes in climate and environment have no connection to their lives or our collective future. If we are going to address our critical situation, we need to develop a wide-ranging vision, a systems-level perspective. Individuals must step into leadership roles, not to amass power and wealth, but because they truly want to help.

One big problem is that our brains evolved to deal with short-term dangers, like being stalked by a lion. We are not used to responding to threats that unfold slowly, over a matter of decades. Doing so requires an act of will, intellectual apprehension and courage.

We have been told there are experts in every field, with specialized, technical knowledge far beyond what we can fathom. We count on these experts to handle those problems that seem beyond the scope of our abilities. Immersed in their daily lives, most people don't entertain the prospect that these experts and specialists may themselves be mistaken. They may be operating with such fragmentary knowledge that they lack the ability to comprehend the whole picture, or to envision, let alone institute, the level of systemic transformation that will be needed.

What if there are no experts in what the future will bring?

Humanity has been put in command of what Buckminster Fuller called Spaceship Earth. Fuller noted that although our spaceship was flawlessly designed, it lacked an instruction manual:

> In view of the infinite attention to all other details displayed by
> our ship, it must be taken as deliberate and purposeful that an
> instruction manual was omitted . . . The designed omission of
> the instruction book on how to operate and maintain Spaceship
> Earth and its complex life-supporting and regenerating systems
> has forced man to discover retrospectively just what his most
> important forward capabilities are. His intellect had to discover
> itself.

There is no doubt that our use of the planet's finite resources must change drastically while we seek to repair, as best we can, the damage we have already done. We must apply our intellect to this task.

For the sake of future generations and the greater community of life on Earth, we must find ways to overcome distractions, building a wave of collective action that will gather enough strength to overcome the resistance of those entrenched and powerful forces that stand in our way. Such a movement can only be effective if we possess a clear idea of the positive outcome we seek as well as the methods we must apply to attain it.

Because we are afraid of what's coming, because we feel it is not our responsibility, and because the mass media doesn't focus our attention properly, most people lack even the most rudimentary knowledge about what we are doing to the Earth. I have spoken to graduate students studying sustainability and design at the School of Visual Arts in New York, and even they didn't know the most basic information about species extinction, ocean acidification, climate change and so on. In America, the typical adult can name over a thousand corporate logos but fewer than ten species of native plants.

People find themselves disconnected, detached from what is taking place, watching it like a movie. Conditioned and indoctrinated by a system designed to disempower them, many feel cynical about any possibility of changing the status quo. This needs to change. We can educate ourselves about our situation and then share that information in a productive way. We can't galvanize people into action by making them scared or miserable. The only thing that will inspire people to act, I believe, is a compelling and beautiful vision of the future – a future they want to see for their children and grandchildren.

'Restoring the earth will take an enormous international effort, one far larger and more demanding than the often-cited Marshall Plan that helped rebuild war-torn Europe and Japan,' writes Lester Brown, the founder of Worldwatch Institute, in *Plan B 4.0: Mobilizing to Save Civilization*. 'And such an initiative must be undertaken at wartime speed lest environmental deterioration translate into economic decline and state failure, just as it did for earlier civilizations that violated nature's thresholds and ignored its deadlines.'

Brown notes that the US industrial economy was able entirely to restructure itself in just a few months, following the 1941 Japanese attack on Pearl Harbor. This required a three-year ban on the sale of automobiles, as factories shifted to producing planes, tanks, guns and other forms of military hardware. A similar, rapid redirection of our industrial system, globally, is necessary to transition energy production and other areas. This has happened in the past, during wartime, but never during peacetime and never on a planetary scale. What will it take to bring this about? That, dear reader, is a crucial question.

Planetary Boundaries

Probably the best effort to define the full parameters of our current ecological situation was made by the Stockholm Resilience Centre. In 2009, they brought together scientists and developed the planetary boundaries model. According to this model, there are limits in nine areas that humanity can't cross without endangering our own future as well as the health of the Earth.

'Anthropogenic pressures on the Earth System have reached a scale where abrupt global environmental change can no longer be excluded,' the scientists noted. The planetary boundaries are: global warming, reduction of biodiversity, nitrogen runoff, land use, consumption of fresh water, acidification of the oceans, thinning of the ozone layer, aerosol pollution and atmospheric toxins. Currently, we have crossed at least four of these: climate change, loss of biodiversity, ozone layer depletion, and nitrogen pollution.

Our situation is made more complex by the unanticipated ways these different boundaries interact with each other. For instance, there was a period in the last decades when global warming was slower than the scientific models predicted. Climate change deniers seized on this as evidence that global warming was a fraud. In all likelihood, this slowdown in warming was due to two factors. China massively increased coal production, leading to an enormous escalation of sulphur dioxide in our atmosphere. The phenomenon is called 'global dimming'.

Although sulphur dioxide temporarily reduces warming, since the particles reflect the sun's rays, these soot particles don't stay in the atmosphere for long and cause other forms of ecological damage. Scientists also found that the oceans have been absorbing more CO_2 than their models predicted. Once again, this is not something that will help us in the long term. Soon, the oceans will max out their capacity to absorb CO_2. At that point, like giant lungs, they will start releasing it, which may accelerate warming.

When we get into these types of fine-grained details of the mess we are in, we start to understand why James Lovelock believes we have already passed the tipping point which makes cataclysm inevitable. Lovelock is a highly esteemed scientist. He worked with microbiologist Lynn Margulis to develop the Gaia hypothesis, putting forward the theory that the Earth functions as a self-regulating system like a giant organism. In *The Revenge of Gaia*, Lovelock foresaw 'an imminent shift in our climate towards one that could easily be described as Hell: so hot, so deadly that only a handful of the teeming billions now alive will survive'.

He predicted that a maximum of only 150 million people will be left alive at the end of this century. He could be right. But it is also possible that, through globally coordinated action – if we apply our genius as a species to collectively beneficial ends – we can forestall this catastrophe and even thrive.

Above all, what the data on climate change – along with other aspects of the ecological crisis, such as species extinction and ocean acidification – tells us is that the fate of our world is at stake. This is not happening in the future. It is not happening decades or centuries from today. It is happening now and we must bring our focus to bear upon it.

Biodiversity

We are currently in the Sixth Great Extinction in Earth's history. Each day, an estimated 150 to 200 species disappear forever out of a total number of roughly 8.7 million. Doing the maths, this means we are losing something like 10 per cent of the remaining biodiversity every 10 to 15 years. The number is so high because we are currently polluting, over-settling, burning down and clear-cutting many of the most biodiverse places on Earth.

It can be difficult to explain to people why maintaining biodiversity is crucial for our own near-term survival. We have learned that eco-systems function as complex networks in which the different forms and varieties of life support each other – when any tier is taken away, the entire system may change dramatically. It may rearrange itself or become radically simplified, with only one or a handful of species proliferating.

People became alarmed, recently, by the collapse of the bee population, because bees, as pollinators, provide a crucial role in human agriculture. But other small organisms also have critical roles to play, down to the phytoplankton in the oceans, which are affected by ocean acidification. As I noted earlier, the speed of our industrial progress has been so incredible that we have not been able to reckon with its effects. It didn't occur to us, even twenty or thirty years ago, that we could empty the entire ocean of large fish – but that is what has happened. More than 90 per cent of the large fish are gone, and the massive trawlers which spread their nets in the seas have to go further and deeper out, collecting types of fish that would have been rejected as inedible a few years ago.

Ongoing loss of biodiversity may induce an abrupt change of conditions in the biosphere as a whole, which could revert back to a simpler state, no longer suitable for large lumbering mammals such as ourselves. When too many species are removed, an entire ecosystem may collapse. This can happen on a local or global level. The danger is that there is an unforeseen tipping point beyond which a rapid planetary shift could take place, and this could happen faster than we are able to react to it.

Global Warming

The climate change planetary boundary is the most well known – even so, even with marches and protests around the world, it doesn't compel the level of collective response that it should. It took science a while to catch up to the dynamics of global warming, but we now have a clear understanding of its underlying mechanisms. Before the Industrial Revolution, the climate was relatively stable for ten thousand years, a 'Goldilocks period' (not too hot, not too cold) which allowed human civilization to flourish. During this period, there were around 275 parts per million (ppm) of carbon dioxide in the atmosphere.

Decaying vegetable matter as well as the oceans emit a huge amount of CO_2, but the oceans are also able to absorb it naturally, in a cycle similar to respiration. The residue from our industrial systems – we currently expel 300 billion metric tons of CO_2 annually (more than a million tons per hour) – cannot be easily absorbed. It will linger in the atmosphere for a century, and accrue over time. We are now beyond 400 ppm of atmospheric CO_2. The last time there was this much CO_2 in the air, sea levels were 100 feet higher than they are today and temperatures were four degrees Celsius warmer.

Through studying the climate record preserved in ice-core samples, geologists have learned that the climate generally doesn't make a slow, incremental transition from one steady state to another. Instead, it tends to make a drastic lurch in a short timeframe. Glaciologists found that 'roughly half of the entire warming between the ice ages and the postglacial world took place in only a decade', writes Fred Pearce in *With Speed and Violence: Why Scientists Fear Tipping Points in Climate Change*, with a temperature increase of nine degrees Celsius during that time. In the past two centuries, humanity has increased levels of carbon in the atmosphere by about a third. Our continued tinkering runs the risk 'of producing a runaway change – the climactic equivalent of a squawk on a sound system'.

Already, global warming is drastically impacting on the planet far beyond what scientists imagined or projected even a few years ago. The three hottest years on record have all been in the last decade, with 2015 the hottest of all by a significant amount, and 2016 set to eclipse it by a large margin.

As Ramez Naam writes in *The Infinite Resource*:

> In Europe, half the mountain glacier cover seen a century ago in the Alps is now gone. In Switzerland, 20 per cent has disappeared in the last fifteen years. In Britain, researchers looking at the flowering of plants and the migration of animals find that spring is coming eleven days earlier than it did in the middle of the twentieth century. In the United States, researchers see spring plant and animal behaviour creeping three days earlier each decade, around twelve days earlier since 1970. Sea levels around the world have risen seven inches in the last century, and their rate of rise has doubled in the last ten years.

According to climate scientist James Hansen, humanity already faces the 'near certainty' of an eventual sea-level rise of five to nine metres. As subsurface warming causes the melting of the Arctic ice sheets, sea levels will increase by much as three metres by 2050. He notes it is 'unlikely that coastal cities or low-lying areas such as Bangladesh, European lowlands and large portions of the United States eastern coast and northeast China plains could be protected against such large sea level rise'.

However, even in the worst-case scenario, if sea levels were to rise 100 to 150 feet we would only lose 5 per cent of the Earth's landmass. There would still be plenty of room for humanity to live and thrive. It has been estimated that the entire human population could be settled in an area the size of Texas, and each family would still have room for a backyard garden. Similarly, the entire human population could stand, shoulder to shoulder, on an area the size of New York City. This shows it is not the size of the human population that is the problem. It is our massively wasteful use of resources. As we will discuss, we have the ability to design, build, even mass-manufacture, new urban areas and villages that are entirely self-sufficient, with food and energy produced on-site.

Over the next years, as climate change accelerates and we hit other ecological constraints, we will see escalating tensions between resource-starved countries, perhaps inciting wars, guerrilla insurgencies, terrorism, even nuclear conflicts. 'Climate change will kill people directly, but most will die at the hands of other people made desperate by climate change,' Stewart Brand predicts. Europe is already experiencing a refugee crisis as millions of desperate people flee Syria, a resource-starved country engaged in a vicious civil war. Drought in Africa has also resulted in migration to Europe. This is only the beginning of a process we will soon see unfolding across the world.

Take the country of Bangladesh where 157 million people live at zero to five metres above sea level. While many of us in the US and Europe have enjoyed lifestyles of luxury that require huge carbon emissions, the average Bangladeshi earns less than a thousand dollars a year and has a minuscule ecological footprint. As sea levels rise in the next decades, much of Bangladesh will become uninhabitable as fresh-water sources are infiltrated by the sea. India is already building a massive fence to keep out Bangladeshi refugees.

In a sense, one could argue that we in the developed world are no better than the worst and most barbaric regimes of the past. We have known for decades that our continued inaction on CO_2 emissions is a form of passive genocide committed against the most vulnerable populations of the Earth, but we remain wilfully unconscious about our impacts.

There is nothing we can do to change the past, but we can face the present. As practitioners of Huna, the spiritual discipline associated with Hawaii, put it: 'Now is the moment of power.' *Now* is the only moment – in other words – when we can accept our personal responsibility for the fate of our shared, imperilled world. *Now* is also the moment when we can choose to put aside petty concerns and to act, instead, as biospheric agents, conceiving our own lives as catalytic processes, applying our energies and intellect for the greater good.

Feedback Loops

Ecological disaster is being accelerated by a large number of feedback loops that amplify climate change and other problems as they are set into motion. These feedbacks are something like a snowball falling from a mountaintop, picking up momentum, causing more snow to fall, until it causes an avalanche. Many of these were not well understood or anticipated until recently. All of them point towards the necessity of rapid, coordinated action to ensure our continuity on this planet.

One feedback loop is the interaction between the loss of Arctic ice and what is called the albedo effect: the cooling of the Earth that depends in part upon the massive ice sheets that reflect the sun's rays, like a giant mirror. As the ice sheet shrinks and breaks apart, the albedo effect is diminished. Large areas go from white shiny ice to dark blue ocean. Instead of reflecting sunlight back into space, the Arctic absorbs more sunlight, which speeds up the warming process.

The Arctic is currently warming four times faster than the rest of the planet. Incredibly, in the winter of 2015, the Arctic reached a temperature that was over 30 degrees Celsius above its usual average – essentially, briefly reaching the melting point of zero degrees Celsius or 32 degrees Fahrenheit. While this was partly due to the natural warming cycle caused by fluctuations in the jet stream, it was still unprecedented, and – let's admit it – very frightening. In *The God Species*, Mark Lynas, a journalist who has travelled the world to write about climate change, admits he is astonished by 'the sheer rapidity of change already under way in the Earth system, changes I never dreamt I would see so quickly when I started working on this subject more than ten years ago'.

Despite Silicon Valley's euphoria over our capacity for innovation, we don't have any technological fixes for these runaway effects. We know, for instance, that the incidence of forest fires has been increasing for a number of years. A small amount of global warming is drying out the forests, making them more susceptible to fires. The forests act as carbon sinks, inhaling CO_2 and exhaling the oxygen we breathe. As they dry out and burn, releasing CO_2, global temperature increases, leading to more drying out of the remaining forests, which become even more susceptible to fire. This process, unfortunately, already seems to be cascading in the wrong direction.

In the autumn of 2015, the news was filled with reports of massive forest fires across the northwest of the United States, Alaska and Canada. These fires were unprecedented in size and ferocity. One blaze in Idaho engulfed 265,000 acres, while Alaska lost five million acres of forest, an area the size of Connecticut. With all of the fires across the Pacific Northwest and Canada, 11 million acres, 17,000 square miles, have been scorched – and the burning continues. As I write this, a massive forest fire in Alberta, Canada (where temperatures were twenty degrees Celsius above average for a few days in May) forced a mass evacuation of the entire population of Fort McMurray – 80,000 people.

In the past few years, the forests of Indonesia have been intensively assaulted and reduced by fire, with giant plumes of smoke visible from space. Many of these blazes are caused intentionally, so that forest land can be converted to palm oil plantations. The increased use of palm oil as an ingredient in many cheap processed foods has created an ecological disaster.

Somehow, we must rally humanity to protect the remaining forests, in particular our tropical rainforests, and engage in a cooperative process to reforest the planet. The tropical rainforests are estimated to produce as much as 20 per cent of the oxygen we breathe. Most of us would, I believe, like to keep breathing – even if Ray Kurzweil believes that nanobots in our lungs will soon do it for us.

Arctic Methane

We now confront the greatest – and, until recently, a totally unanticipated – danger of rapid warming, through the release of methane from under the Arctic. According to one estimate, there are 1,600 billion tons of carbon trapped beneath the oceans and locked in Siberian permafrost. Although it only stays in the atmosphere for ten years, methane is more than twenty times more potent than CO_2 as a greenhouse gas. If methane erupts in large quantities, this will accelerate the warming cycle, releasing more methane. 'If such a runaway event were to take place, it could occur within forty years or less, and would transform the earth into a biological desert,' notes Paul Hawken.

In 2007, 'atmospheric levels of methane began to spike', according to Bill McKibben. In 2011, Russian researchers found spumes of methane as much as a kilometre in diameter releasing from the Arctic. Scientists now understand that, in previous epochs, eruptions of thawing methane from under the Arctic induced mass extinctions. Unfortunately, a rise in temperature of two degrees Celsius above pre-industrial levels may pass the threshold at which the methane releases in vast quantities. Some scientists now believe a 1.5-degree temperature rise is the maximum we can handle.

To deal with the methane threat – probably the greatest danger now facing humanity, outside of nuclear war – we must severely curtail emissions, reduce the levels of greenhouse gases in the atmosphere, and get to carbon neutral or negative as quickly as we possibly can. At the same time, we must remove excess carbon from the air, and apply other non-invasive techniques to cool our planet. Some of these are so simple, it is absurd that we are not already putting them into practice.

For instance, we can paint all of our urban rooftops white to mimic the albedo effect. As Mark Hertsgaard writes in *Hot*, it is estimated that the average American household 'could counteract the ten tons of CO_2 it annually emits by retrofitting one thousand square feet of roof or sidewalk with reflective surfaces. Retrofitting all urban roofs and pavements in the world would yield emissions reductions equivalent to taking all the world's cars off the road for eighteen years.' As a global initiative, we could engineer mass plantings of forests, trees and gardens. 'The earth's plants and soils are not yet removing enough CO_2 to halt rising temperatures, but they could do much more with proper stewardship,' Hertsgaard notes.

Within the next few decades, assuming we want a future for humanity, we need to bring about a drastic reduction of greenhouse gas emissions, along with a global transition to renewable energies and low-carbon fuel sources. Since we have waited too long, this reduction must be as much as 8–10 per cent annually, for a number of years. Luckily, a great deal of our CO_2-producing activity is wasteful and unnecessary, and could be quickly eliminated once we find the will to do so.

Admittedly, we face what seems a socially impossible task. Although there is nothing stopping us, physically, from making the sudden changes in species-wide patterns of behaviour necessary to avert cataclysm, it seems inconceivable – culturally, politically and financially – that we will do so. Yet we must.

Who Do We Blame?

Many times, when I try to talk about the ecological emergency with prosperous neoliberal and liberal types, the quick answer they give me is that the world's population has grown too large. They either state directly or insinuate that nature will take care of this by wiping billions of people off the map. For the most part, I find, they don't include themselves in those billions who will be consigned to oblivion.

The inconvenient truth is that overpopulation is not our major problem. In fact, across the developing world, at least until recently, most people lived within sustainable limits, with a tiny ecological footprint. They farmed locally and ate their own produce. They didn't drive cars, waste polystyrene, wear clothes produced in Cambodian sweatshops, fly somewhere warm to relax for a spring break, or buy new computers and smart phones every few years. The reason we are rapidly approaching total ecological collapse is the consumerist lifestyle of America and Europe, which we have spread across the planet.

I cannot deny that it would be a good idea to taper off the rising population – I think this can and should be done in a humane and empathic way. Birth rates actually decline naturally as women attain a higher status, approaching equality with men, having more access to education and work opportunities. In other words, if we elevate the status of women everywhere, the global population will, gently and naturally, decline.

While 80 per cent of emissions are produced by just 20 per cent of the world's population, probably 50 per cent of emissions come from as little as 1 per cent of the population – the wealthy people of the developed world. But the prospect that this 1 per cent will voluntarily reduce their consumption – or be forced to do so – is never proposed or considered. It runs counter to our intrinsic sense of privilege and the cult of wealth that underlies the capitalist game. Or, in other words, it goes against everything our globalized society – our technophiliac New World Order – believes or stands for.

'We don't require the whole world to do something', notes Kevin Anderson, a UK climate scientist from the Tyndall Centre for Climate Research, 'we require a small proportion of the world to change what they do today for the next ten or twenty years while we put low carbon supply in place. Then we can go back to our old profligate lifestyles.' Unfortunately, the longer we wait, the amount of rapid reductions of emissions that we need to accomplish will increase, until the goal is out of reach.

Let's stop here for a moment. Let's think about this.

If it stings a little, let it sting.

I want to hold your attention, for a heartbeat or two, on that last comment Anderson makes about the need for a small proportion of the world to change their behaviour. Please realize that this is not just another idea in an ocean of nice-sounding ideas. What he is talking about is fundamentally necessary so that humanity as a whole – a group that includes our children, or, if we don't have kids, the kids of our friends and relatives, or if we have no friends, those little beings who occasionally smile shyly at us as they totter along – can survive and, eventually, thrive. What he is talking about requires that *you and I* change our behaviour and lifestyle.

Let's be brutally honest with ourselves: we can continue as we are now and watch our planet burn out, or we can change ourselves to change the world. If we prefer the second option, we must commit ourselves to a necessary task – a redemptive, spiritual mission. Our mission, if we choose to accept it, is that we work together to build a regenerative society, restoring the health of our biosphere for the long term. This project will be the work of future generations, also. What we can accomplish in our lives – the beginning of a great turning – will be our legacy to them.

I know it seems highly unlikely that the super-rich are going to swear off their private jets, their holiday outings in the Caribbean, their third houses in Ibiza, their ironically sumptuous (wink wink) Burning Man camps, their capital investments in new hotels and luxury high-rises. However, things can change. A lot of things are changing right now. They will be changing even more quickly in the years ahead of us.

Unfortunately, the wealthier people on the planet believe themselves likely to be the least affected by ecological catastrophe, figuring they can always fly off to some new still somewhat unspoiled place. While understandable from their perspective, this is stupid, short-term thinking. As I mentioned above, 20 per cent of the oxygen that we all, collectively, including the 1 per cent and the .001 per cent breathe, is emitted by the forests which are being slashed, burnt, mowed down to create more profit centres. If we lose too much biodiversity, the intricately interdependent web of life will crumble to dust, taking all of us down with it. Also, even the super-rich are running out of unspoiled places.

The ecological meltdown we confront, in fact, will eventually impact upon everyone on Earth. In the end, nobody is getting out of this one. Not Richard Branson or Donald Trump or the Koch Brothers – even if they happen to croak early, their kids and grandkids will have to face it. Perhaps there are bunkers deep underground somewhere for the Illuminati super-wealthy, outfitted with centuries of food, futuristic sex toys and other stockpiles. If so, I don't envy them that depressing, guilt-riddled future.

I have to admit – perhaps this reflects poorly on my character, but as I mentioned earlier I am no paragon of virtue and can, at times, be an asshole – that I didn't shed a tear when Harbin Hot Springs, epicentre of Northern California luxury hippie culture, burnt to the ground as forest fires swept the region. I almost felt this was a good thing, as a lot of transformational potential seems trapped in the Bay Area. The ecological, social justice and human potential movements all have West Coast headquarters. Maybe we need the progressive community to feel the heat – to get so uncomfortable they will break through whatever obstacles have kept them from challenging and changing the mainstream.

The consciousness revolution should, by now, have spread out from that area across the planet. But people fell into a smug, self-satisfied lifestyle. Instead of stripping themselves down in the quest for enlightenment, they stopped at what Chögyam Trungpa called 'spiritual materialism'. Perhaps the drought, the burning forests, and, now, the lack of hot springs where hippies can nakedly bathe and cavort will be enough to start an exodus.

The interesting thing about social behaviour is that it is extremely contagious. People tend to do what their peers do – and they can switch their beliefs and habits quickly, even immediately, when the reward structure changes around them. Malcolm Gladwell called this the tipping point. The maverick scientist Rupert Sheldrake proposes a more sophisticated model, based on something he calls morphic resonance, or the hundredth monkey principle. His idea is that when a certain small percentage of a species learns a new skill, that ability becomes easier to transfer to others – and can even transfer instantly, without direct contact, through some unknown mechanism, perhaps quantum nonlocality. Patterns of thought and action may create new fields of resonant potential that can become species-wide traits.

When you or I make a change in our behaviour, this affects and impacts upon the people around us directly and then the people around them, adding up to many more people. According to the morphic resonance theory, it may not be as difficult to effect large-scale change as we tend to think it is – particularly now, when we are so tightly linked together through networks.

Behaviour can change in a millisecond. I have seen examples of this at Burning Man – the festival functions as a laboratory for hedonic engineering and experimental paths to social change. Investment bankers, corporate lawyers, CEOs – highly intelligent people who tend to be motivated by personal reward more than abstract principles of ecological ethics – come to Burning Man and, in less than a day, they conform to a new set of social norms, responding to the cues around them. Their new behaviour patterns include 'leaving no trace', giving away stuff, hugging, smiling, building community structures, helping strangers put up their tents, sharing their drugs and so on. At Burning Man, wandering around in a pink tutu, saying '*namaste*', talking about your *chakras*, and picking up trash will gain you community acceptance and love. If being friendly, thoughtful and caring suddenly increases your status, gets you laid, brings you better drugs and makes you popular, then that is what you will do.

Interestingly, most of the changes we now need to make as a species so that we can all survive and prosper and our descendants can thrive would actually be beneficial for everyone, following an initial, awkward, admittedly uncomfortable period of adjustment. Today, for instance, many people live alone in small apartments, separated from their families and close friends. Bringing people together again to live communally in multi-generational compounds – as our tribal ancestors did – would be a powerful way to reduce consumption and waste. It would also make people happier, healthier and calmer.

I remember visiting Havana, Cuba, in 1999, where cars were rare, and people ride-shared and hitchhiked. This created a feeling of social cohesion and camaraderie – a sense that 'we are all in this together'. If ride sharing, and other forms of sharing, were encouraged or even (dare I say it?) enforced – systemically implemented using geolocating apps – it would have the same effect. Given a new incentive, life could become much better, not worse. People would have to learn to trust and care for each other once again.

The most luxurious vacation of my life was the week I spent at a retreat centre in Colombia without electricity. At night, torches would be lit. When they went off, we were bathed in starlight. I never saw so many stars. There was no use for our cell phones or laptops. When my brain discharged its static internal noise after a few days, I began to feel a level of natural peace and contentment beyond anything I had known for a long time.

We have been deluded by the momentum of our post-industrial society. We are taught to believe that progress only moves in one direction. The retreat revealed that many of the things our civilization believes to be necessary are actually just impediments that keep us cluttered and distracted. In the future, masses of people may realize that living with friends and family, in beautiful communities close to nature, where life is as self-sufficient and sustainable as possible, with minimal electronic interference, would be the ultimate lifestyle – and it is one that we can attain.

In any event, one essential point to grasp is that all of the changes in lifestyle and behaviour that we need collectively to adapt for our survival will have this side benefit: they will make the world kinder, gentler, happier, more cooperative, more loving. Living altruistically and cooperatively is closer to our basic nature as human beings than continuing our current state of alienation and competition. It is, after all, what we did for many thousands of years, as nomadic tribal people. Now we have to realize humanity as one unified tribe.

You may notice how all the solutions proposed in this book imply that we will be forced to live in a more responsible, truly adult fashion. In other words, there is something more in these practical solutions than just 'saving the world' – the same behaviours that support flourishing ecosystems will also force us to behave more wisely, carefully and compassionately – to act, ironically, as we've often wished we could, if we had the time or inner motivation to try.

Now let's return to the evidence – the terrible, heart-breaking facts about what we are doing as a species, out of our greed, hubris and stupidity. Please stay with me. The thing to remember is that – unlike sports statistics, news on Donald Trump's hair or Paris Hilton's sex habits, or myriad other titbits that whirl past us in the course of a day

– these facts about the planetary boundaries will have a direct impact on our lives, in the near future. They will be of great concern, soon, for all of our children. Quite likely, they will be the focus of attention for everyone within a few short decades.

Nitrogen

The third planetary boundary, nitrogen pollution, is also one we have exceeded. The exponential growth of the human population over the last century is often linked to the invention in 1909 of the Haber–Bosch process for synthesizing ammonia, which made it possible to add nitrogen to crops, by producing artificial fertilizer, using petrochemicals. An essential component of all proteins, nitrogen is in short supply in nature – nitrates are produced by lightning, and also by a number of beans and legumes able to fix nitrogen in the soil through a symbiotic partnership with microbes that live in their roots.

Nitrogen runoff – along with phosphorous pollution – from agriculture has created enormous dead zones in lakes, oceans and wetlands. There are over 400 of these dead zones across the world's coastlines. Some of them are enormous – like the one around the Gulf of Mexico, which swells to 20,000 square kilometres in the summer. Excess nitrogen reduces biodiversity and accelerates climate change, since the industrial process to produce it emits greenhouse gases. We must reduce the amount of nitrogen released into the environment by two-thirds, from 100 million to 35 million tons annually, even though this will be difficult, considering that the current food production system depends upon huge inputs of artificial, fossil-fuel-based fertilizer for agriculture. However, as we will discuss, we need to change our approach to producing food in any case.

Land Use

Currently, an estimated 12 per cent of the Earth's surface is used for arable farming, while as much as 30 per cent of all land is used for animal grazing. Scientists believe that 15 per cent is the maximum amount of arable farmland the Earth can tolerate. We haven't reached that level yet, but as drought conditions intensify because of global warming, the issue of land use is going to become a major one. This will be especially true if populations expand to an estimated 9 billion by mid-century, and if developing countries like China and India continue to demand more meat, which requires intensive inputs of water and grain,

The greatest species diversity – more than 40 per cent of plants and 30 per cent of animals – is found in a few dozen small areas that account for a little over 1 per cent of total landmass. We should seek to protect these areas, in particular. But many of them are under threat.

Malaysia, for instance, loses more than 5 per cent of its remaining forests every decade. Reasons for deforestation include demands for palm oil, urbanization, and various forms of clearing for agriculture. Mining is another factor as are hydropower and irrigation projects. Only about a fifth of Malaysia's original rainforest covering now remains, scattered in fragments across the region. Many developing countries are in similar straits.

The biologist Edward O Wilson proposes that humanity should set aside as much as 50 per cent of the Earth's surface area as a nature preserve. Although that sounds a bit extreme and unlikely, it is worth noting that, in the past, in many areas of the Earth, humans were actually caretakers and stewards of their natural environment. Evolution weeded out the ones who couldn't manage their local habitat – like the Easter Islanders, who left behind a number of enormous stone heads but no trees and few people. A good plan for the future might include reducing animal grazing lands significantly for reforestation, establishing larger nature preserves, and re-educating people so they become stewards and gardeners of their home rather than despoilers and extractors.

Fresh Water

Water may be the defining issue of the twenty-first century. Patterns of rainfall are changing around the world, as some areas suffer increasing monsoons while others enter permanent drought conditions. Global warming causes more ferocious floods as well as disastrous droughts. 'Drought is especially punishing for the hundreds of millions of subsistence farmers around the world for whom rain is the only source of water,' Hertsgaard notes. Within the next decade, it is estimated that the number of people living in water-stressed countries will increase from 800 million to 3 billion. We are already seeing 'water wars', although they are not generally billed as such.

According to the planetary boundaries group, human use of fresh water should not exceed 4,000 cubic kilometres per year, of which we use an estimated 2,600 today – still within the limits, despite the myriad other impacts of our hydro-engineering practices. Scientists from Stockholm University estimate we have already passed that threshold, consuming more than 4,300 cubic kilometres annually, with 70 per cent used for agriculture. According to one extraordinary statistic, over 15,000 litres of water are required to produce one pound of beef. Other estimates have us slightly below the boundary threshold. Around the world, humans have constructed around 800,000 dams that block the natural flow of water, fragmenting most of the world's largest rivers. Even so, over a billion people lack access to reliable sources of clean water, and 2.6 billion people lack proper sanitation.

According to Mark Lynas, these dams 'impound approximately 10,000 cubic kilometres of water – a quantity so substantial that it measurably reduces the rate of sea-level rise (by about half a millimetre a year for the last half-century) and even changes the mass distribution of the planet sufficiently to alter its axis and slightly increase the speed of its rotation'. Many scientists believe we should seek to reverse some of the changes we have made to the natural course of rivers and drainage basins.

Meanwhile, glaciers and icepacks are rapidly melting around the world. Mountaintop glaciers feed rivers, streams and aquifers in India, Tibet and Peru, as well as California, sustaining billions of people who settled in the valleys below these sources, which have flowed reliably for tens of thousands of years. Their disappearance will cause social dislocations on a scale we cannot yet imagine. There is potential for a rapid scaling up of desalinization plants, particularly if this technology is improved, and if it can be powered by renewables. In that case, we might be able to have as much abundant fresh water as we need. However, we are still far from prepared for the water scarcity we are confronting globally.

Ocean Acidification

Although less discussed, ocean acidification is another huge and worsening problem. Up to 85 per cent of the carbon dioxide we release into the atmosphere each year ends up in the oceans, altering their chemical composition. In the last 40 years, we have made the world's oceans 30 per cent more acidic, as they absorb excess CO_2 pollution like gigantic lungs. One major concern is that the oceans may soon reach the limit in terms of the amount of carbon dioxide they can absorb, at which point they would start to emit carbon, rather than storing it. This feedback loop would accelerate warming.

Coral reefs are largely made of calcium carbonate, which is extremely susceptible to acidity. As the oceans grow more corrosive, the coral reefs will first die, then dissolve, disappearing completely. This deterioration is already underway. Marine biologists at the Royal Society believe the coral reefs 'will be in rapid and terminal decline world-wide' by mid-century if not sooner. With them will go much of the ocean's biodiversity. We are already seeing the mass proliferation of species like jellyfish and squid, which are filling the ecological niches left vacant as fish populations crash.

As of now, I haven't heard of many plans of action that can address ocean acidification. There are some geo-engineering ideas, but they seem far-fetched. One scheme involves putting masses of calcium carbonate or silicate material into the oceans – essentially, like giving the oceans a gigantic antacid, a Tums. To make any kind of difference, this would require mining such a huge volume of rock that this effort would be highly improbable, most likely impossible. Google Director of Engineering Ray Kurzweil, in *The Singularity is Near*, proposes the creation of nanobots – minuscule robots – that can clean up the oceans for us. So far, this remains fantasy.

Environmental Toxins

The level of environmental toxins and pollutants the Earth can absorb has not been established as a set limit. We know that plastic polymers and other industrial compounds have infiltrated every ecosystem on the planet. They also concentrate through the food chain, and in our tissues, where they cause cancers, reproductive disorders and other adverse health effects. Chris Jordan has photographed dead birds on Midway Island – 2,000 miles away from the nearest continent – with their gullets full of plastic. Perhaps evolution – or future technologies – will find ways to make use of our synthetic polymers, but the process of breaking them down naturally will take millions of years.

Even so, industries continue to create new compounds, willy-nilly, and add them to the exotic bouquet of chemicals that is impacting on our fragile environment. Even where there have been studies of how individual compounds affect human health, there are no studies of the potential impact of multiple new chemicals when combined. A 2009 study of US drinking water, testing for pharmaceuticals and endocrine-disrupting chemicals, found 34 contaminants in just one sample, including atrazine (a herbicide), diazepam (Valium), risperidone (an anti-psychotic) and fluoxetine (Prozac).

Environmental contamination is considered responsible for the sudden enigmatic decline of some species around the world, including amphibians, butterflies and bats. Anecdotally, I am seeing many people I know developing strange allergies, chemical sensitivities, food intolerances and so on. This may be due to the chemical load we are all taking on, just by being subject to this strange laboratory experiment that corporations are subjecting us to out of a drive to increase their margins of profit.

Aerosol Pollution

The limit of the aerosols boundary is similarly unknown. Air pollution is responsible for more than 400,000 premature deaths each year in China alone. The developed world of the West has cleaned up its air over the last decades, largely by relocating factory production, mining and smelting to the developing world of the South and to Asia. In some cities in China, the air is barely breathable, and we see photos of Chinese people wearing facemasks as they go about their days. A Canadian company recently started selling bottles of fresh air to them. The soot produced by factories in the US, China and elsewhere ultimately drifts around the world, sparing nobody.

Aerosol pollution has a significant effect on the climate and the hydrological cycle. Globally, smokestack pollution from the North is thought to have contributed to a major decades-long drought in the Sahel region of Africa in the 1970s and 80s. Aerosol emissions are also causing a rapid decline in the monsoon season in India, Burma and Thailand, threatening the food production and livelihoods of a billion people.

Humanity nearly caused its own extinction by inadvertently trespassing into the ozone boundary, although we now have the situation under control to some extent. One man, alone, was nearly responsible for bringing our life as a species to an abrupt, sickening end: the American chemist Thomas Midgley, who worked for General Motors in the 1920s and 30s, developing non-flammable coolants for refrigerators, discovered chlorofluorocarbon (CFC) also known as Freon, a synthesis of chlorine, fluorine and carbon, which became widely used.

In the 1970s, scientists discovered that CFCs were circulating throughout the Earth's atmosphere, where they were breaking down ozone, causing a thinning of the ozone layer, which protects the Earth from dangerous ultraviolet radiation. In the 1980s, a major international effort led to the Montreal Protocol, which phased out the use of CFCs. Due to the ongoing circulation of gases already released, the ozone layer is still thinning, but at a slower rate. It is estimated that the ozone layer could return to its pre-industrial level of ozone concentration by 2075, barring further tampering.

The world's success in handling ozone pollution can be taken as a positive sign. It proves the human community does have the ability to come together and change our industrial practices, when necessary. If we did it with ozone, we can, in theory anyway, do it with CO_2 – not to mention nitrogen, factory farming, genetically modified organisms, aerosol pollutants and the other factors accelerating us towards global meltdown. Of course, CO_2 is a tough one, because it is so pervasive.

On the other hand, the threat to our species unleashed by CFCs is an example of the unintended consequences of new technological breakthroughs. We should think about this in relationship to nano-technology, biotechnology and other areas that the corporate elite promote as solutions to the hellish problems our industrial technologies have already unleashed. The past breakthroughs that were supposed to make everything great had tremendous negative consequences that were unanticipated. The new technologies – interacting with the processes of life and matter at a deeper level – could have even more destructive impacts. This doesn't mean we shouldn't develop new technologies, but we must do so within an ethical framework and an ecological worldview that considers long-term consequences rather than prioritizing short-term comforts and immediate profits.

What Do We Do?

Living in New York City, I see new buildings going up all the time. I don't see these buildings covered in solar panels feeding energy back to the grid, or vegetable gardens on their rooftops. We keep building luxury condominiums and hotels, not earth ships and vertical farms.

Young people still feverishly pursue careers in the art world, fashion, rock music, celebrity journalism, marketing; they get their degrees in old master paintings and French critical theory and so on – I look over their shoulders in East Village cafes to see what they are typing away on – but, honestly, if people understood what was coming, we would be applying our intelligence differently. Young people would pursue careers in ecosystem management, permaculture, wetland restoration, carbon sequestration. The best and brightest would be learning how to share and conserve resources, how to organize local communities to maximize resilience, practices of active nonviolence and so on.

Our system doesn't reward all of the work that desperately needs to be done now, and it over-rewards everything that shouldn't be done – such as using financial tools to extract money from the poor and middle class and funnel it to the wealthy, or marketing new trends that seduce people into buying more clothes, cars and gadgets. Financial world predators, unleashing global chaos from their computer terminals, make exponentially more than primary school teachers or nurses who take care of the old and sick. And we are all caught in this system.

A major problem is our culture's entrenched ideal of individualism. This is something we must supersede, even though it is hard to imagine how to do so. In reality, our independence as individuals depends on our interdependence – with each other and all of life. Our current social and economic system obscures this basic truth. We should, instead, devise systems, in alignment with nature's principles, that help us realize it.

What's coming may seem bleak and chaotic – but there are many amazing solutions already within our reach. Others are just on the edge of becoming feasible. Actually, the technical solutions are kind of the easy part, as we will see. The more difficult struggle will be to change our political and economic system so that we can implement the technical solutions rapidly. This requires that we bring about an evolution of consciousness in a short period. But even this – I believe, on good days – can be done. After all, we built a global communications infrastructure over the last decades that is like a central nervous system. The multitude can trade ideas and adapt new social tools instantly.

So far, many existing alternatives remain little known. We must act to change this situation as quickly as possible. We now know that renewable energy technologies can be exponentially scaled up in a few decades to supply the entire world's population with non-polluting energy. If we coordinate a global transition to regenerative, organic and no-till agriculture, we will be able to put a great deal of excess CO_2 back in the soil. That transition can also be combined with the rapid distribution of regenerative technologies, like biochar gasifiers and biodigestors that convert organic waste into fuel while sequestering CO_2. We can stop all unnecessary forms of industrial manufacturing while we establish networks for sharing and conserving our remaining resources. All of this, in fact, is what we need to do. But how can we do it?

Now let's consider how we will transform our technical infrastructure if we decide to change our direction as a species, beginning with energy.

Part Three

Regenerative Solutions

4

Energy

As the residue of millions of years of stored sunlight, fossil fuels were a one-time-only bequest from Earth to humanity. They gave us the opportunity to build a global machine-based civilization, in a few short centuries. Over the last 150 years, we have accessed an enormous quantity of cheap energy. Incredibly, just one gallon of petrol equals 500 hours of human work output. Granted this largesse, it is not surprising we became utterly dependent on cheap fuel.

'Cheap oil is not a useful part of our economy,' writes Bill McKibben, 'It is our economy.' The availability of cheap energy allowed for the production of inessential goods, impelling the growth of a mass consumer society over the last 200 years. 'Oil provides 40 per cent of all energy used by human beings on Earth, and it powers nearly all transportation in the industrial world. It's also the most important raw material for plastics, agricultural and industrial chemicals, lubricants, and asphalt roads,' writes John Michael Greer. According to *Peak Everything* author Richard Heinberg: 'Without petrochemicals, medical science, information technology, modern cityscapes, and countless other aspects of our modern technology-intensive lifestyles would simply not exist. In all, oil represents the essence of modern life.'

As predicted by the oil company geologist M King Hubbert, we have passed the critical threshold, known as peak oil, when most of the easily available oil has been extracted from the Earth. We have entered a new phase in which fossil fuels become more difficult and expensive to extract, following the downward decline of a bell curve. However, as I write this, the fact that oil has become more costly to extract is not reflected in market pricing – in fact, energy prices have been going down, and the market is glutted. There are many reasons for this. It is possible that oil-producing countries are keeping prices low to stall the development of renewables. There is also the fact that we are now extracting more fuel from non-traditional sources. But this is not a good thing.

As we run out of traditional sources of fossil fuels, energy corporations pursue, with ever-increasing fervour, procedures such as hydro-fracking for natural gas, mountaintop removal to access coal reserves, and extracting oil from the Alaskan Tar Sands. Their success in developing new processes for accessing these resources has contradicted the predictions of peak oil doomsayers. But this is only a temporary reprieve, and the ecological impacts of these practices are devastating.

The depletion of traditional sources also explains the recent initiative to mass-produce ethanol out of corn. A global rush towards biofuels resulted in global famines, as well as food riots in 37 countries, in 2008. In the future, the depletion of fossil fuel supplies, as well as the limits of our 'carbon budget', could make large-scale projects, requiring intensive development of new technology and infrastructure, increasingly difficult to achieve. That is another reason – besides accelerating warming – that we should be seeking to switch to renewables now, when energy is still readily available.

Jeremy Leggett, president of Solar Century, writes, 'Peak oil is not a theory. Because oil is a finite resource, it is an inevitability. The debate is all about its timing.' Saudi Arabia, and other oil-producing nations, have passed their peak of production. What follows could be a surprisingly quick decline. Eventually, even unconventional sources of hydrocarbons will run out.

Leggett reports that many experts and insiders 'think there will be a drop in production within just a few years, and we are in danger of that drop being so steep as to merit description as a collapse'. This collapse would affect not only manufacturing and transportation, but our food system, which requires massive inputs of petroleum to make fertilizer, and for long-distance transport. The average morsel of food in the US travels over 1,500 miles.

In the 1960s, Buckminster Fuller realized we needed to use our resources of fossil fuels to switch to unlimited, renewable sources. 'The fossil fuel deposits of our Spaceship Earth correspond to our automobile's storage battery which must be conserved to turn over our main engine's self-starter,' he noted. 'Thereafter, our "main engine", the life regenerative processes, must operate exclusively on our vast daily energy income from the powers of wind, tide, water, and the direct Sun radiation energy.' Unfortunately, society went in the opposite direction, burning massive reserves of fossil fuel without establishing a new infrastructure based on renewable energy.

As a side benefit, if we make a global transition to renewable energy sources, we will eliminate air pollution. 'The idea of a pollution-free environment is difficult for us even to imagine, simply because none of us has ever known an energy economy that was not highly polluting,' writes Lester Brown, the founder of Worldwatch Institute, in *Plan B 4.0: Mobilizing to Save Civilization.* 'Working in coal mines will be history. Black lung disease will eventually disappear. So too will "code red" alerts warning of health threats from extreme air pollution.' As an asthma sufferer, I can appreciate this happy by-product.

We have the technical ability to make this energy transition, but our time for accomplishing it is short. Whatever it takes, we must force our global civilization to put the brakes on its current momentum, and change its course. This requires a realistic reckoning with the urgency of our situation – far beyond the voluntary limits set by the 2105 Paris Climate Conference, also known as the 21st Annual Cooperation of Parties (COP-21), where 195 countries came together but were unable to make the UN Framework on Climate Change legally binding – and a rejection of meaningless half-measures. Let's take a look at some of the admittedly wonky details.

How Do We Transition?

The likelihood that we can make a rapid energy transition keeps growing due to technical innovations – such as Tesla's recent development of the Powerwall, a storage battery for renewable sources usable in private homes, or the ongoing development of the infrastructure for an 'Internet of Energy', maximizing efficiency, and allowing people to send extra power back to the grid. Germany is leading the way, particularly with solar. Solar now satisfies around 7 per cent of Germany's electricity needs – but on bright summer days this goes up to above 50 per cent. While the percentage of world energy needs supplied by solar remains relatively small, the amount has been doubling annually, revealing the potential for a rapid, exponential leap.

The Solutions Project, founded by Mark Jacobson, Director of the Atmosphere and Energy Program, Stanford University, mapped out a programme for all 50 US states to run on 100 per cent renewable energy by 2050. This envisions a rapid transition in energy infrastructure at the state level, with power coming from numerous renewable sources, including solar, wind, geothermal, hydroelectric and wave devices. To take the state of New York as an example, the Solutions Project proposes that 40 per cent of the state's energy could be generated by offshore wind turbines, with solar photovoltaic plants providing another 35 per cent. The rest would come from a mix of other sources, including solar cells on rooftops.

Similarly, in the UK, a report from the Centre for Alternative Technology at Machynlleth, *Zero Carbon Britain: Rethinking the Future* (2010), proposes that Britain could completely eliminate fossil fuels in twenty years, through a systemic transition in energy use, production, agriculture and land-use patterns. The report looks at the policy framework needed to drive such a rapid shift, as well as the technologies and lifestyle changes needed to make it a reality. *Zero Carbon Britain* points to a future where Britain has 'acknowledged our historical responsibility as a long-industrialized nation and made our contribution to addressing climate change by reducing UK greenhouse gas emissions rapidly to net zero'.

Through a coordinated effort and strategy, Britain could decrease greenhouse gas emissions by 95 per cent in two decades. Reductions would be made in every area, including households, business, industry and waste management. These reductions would depend on significant changes to industrial processes and patterns of personal use, as well as the diversion of waste from landfill, and the conversion of landfill sites to storage silos.

The report estimates that Britain could cut its demand for energy by about 60 per cent through energy-saving and conservation measures. Without a skilful marketing campaign that unites the population behind a common purpose, many of the proposed measures would be extremely unpopular – such as reducing the amount that people travel, as well as limiting the transport and manufacture of unnecessary goods. Within two decades, the authors point out, all power could be generated from renewable sources, reducing greenhouse gas emissions from the energy sector to zero.

The plan calls for reductions in the consumption of meat and dairy, plus changes in land-management practices, dropping CO_2 emissions from agriculture by more than 70 per cent. Another significant change in the British landscape would be a doubling of the area of forest. A larger proportion of this – almost a third – would be left unharvested, enhancing biodiversity and sequestering carbon. 'These changes to the way we use land, the increased area of forest, the restoration of 50 per cent of our peatlands, and the use of more plant-based products made mainly from harvest wood' would allow Britain to capture about 45 million tons of greenhouse pollution every year. According to the report, this systemic transition would produce millions of new jobs, as the country 'powers down' from fossil fuels such as oil and coal and 'powers up' on renewables.

In 2011, two American experts, Peter Schwartzman and David Schwartzman, at the Institute for Policy Research and Development issued a report entitled *A Solar Transition is Possible*. The Schwartzmans believe that, using current resources and known technologies, the world can engineer a complete transition to renewables over the next two or three decades. To achieve this, world governments would have to cooperate to build a new infrastructure that would focus on conservation. Developed countries like the US would agree to reduce energy usage as much as 25–35 per cent within a matter of years, not decades – a far greater level of reduction than that proposed by COP-21. The Schwartzmans' plan would require demilitarization, since industries related to defence are huge energy wasters.

They propose the construction of a 'new direct-current (DC) distribution network, as a means for moving solar-generated electricity around the country'. They believe this could be 'achievable and economically feasible' by 'using geothermal as base supply, wind at night, solar during the day, and hydropower at peak hours of need'. Solar, we know, is an intermittent power source. However, this can be compensated for by distributing wind farms and solar arrays across a wide area, while increasing storage.

As the amount of financial capital required to extract energy from the remaining supplies of fossil fuel continues to increase, the Schwartzmans predict that renewable energy will become more attractive as an option. The rise of solar power in the next decades will drastically decrease the demand for petroleum in the global economy.

Joining a chorus of academic voices, the Schwartzmans conclude that shifting to renewables is achievable, can fulfil the energy needs of humanity and can provide a higher quality of life for all.

Deep Decarbonization

Thinking along the same lines, The Sustainable Development Solutions Network, an initiative of the United Nations, is devising a plan for the entire world to eliminate CO_2 emissions over the next few decades. Their 2014 report, *Pathways to Deep Decarbonization*, led by the economist Jeffrey Sachs, focused on 15 countries, including the US, UK, Brazil, Japan, China and South Africa. According to the authors, 'deeply reducing greenhouse gas emissions and achieving socio-economic development are not mutually exclusive. Robust economic growth and rising prosperity are consistent with the objective of deep decarbonization. They form two sides of the same coin and must be pursued together as part of sustainable development.'

While I like the bold outlines of the deep decarbonization approach, I disagree with the authors in one crucial area. I don't believe that we can reduce global emissions – and avert catastrophic climate change – while continuing rapid economic growth. When the United Nations issued its Sustainable Development Goals recently, it forecast a 7 per cent annual growth rate, measured by gross domestic product, or GDP, for developing countries. This seems impossible, if not suicidal. At the moment, GDP is increasing at about 2 per cent annually, while global debt is increasing at 7 per cent. Even though a transition to a renewable energy infrastructure can create hundreds of thousands – even millions – of new jobs, a rapid reduction of CO_2 emissions to avert climate catastrophe will require strict limits on industrial production and development, at least during a transition period. Sachs is well known as a neoliberal economist, a proponent of corporate globalization. I think he wants to avoid the politically unpalatable realization that 'deep decarbonization' is only possible if we transition away from the current model of economic growth.

To stop our destructive momentum, we must transition our economic paradigm to promote a steady-state system, a 'degrowth' model or a 'post-capitalist' model, in the near term. I agree with Sachs, as well as the UN's recent Sustainable Development Goals, that we must do this while we enhance the living conditions of the world's poor. This requires far more than a reform of the global financial system. It requires a redefinition of many basic terms, such as work, value and happiness. It means we must change our behaviour, both individually and as a species.

Sachs's plan proposes three essential strategies: increasing energy efficiency and conservation, rapidly developing low-carbon sources of electricity, and switching to them for building, transport and industry. He believes that we can become carbon neutral by replacing all of the existing fossil fuel plants to generate energy from renewable sources, and then we can save an enormous amount of energy through conservation, applying the most efficient technologies in areas like urban design, home construction, transport, industry and so on.

The problem is that our current infrastructure was built for an age of limitless, cheap energy. Some experts, like Vaclav Smil – Bill Gates's favourite thinker – believe it will take a century, or more, to make the transition envisioned by experts like Sachs. Smil pessimistically notes that changing our fossil-fuel-based system is a 'gargantuan task'.

Our energy infrastructure, including 'coal mines, oil and gas fields, refineries, pipelines, trains, trucks, tankers, filling stations, power plants, transformers, transmission and distribution lines, and hundreds of millions of gasoline, kerosene, diesel and fuel oil engines – constitutes the costliest and most extensive set of installations, networks, and machines that the world has ever built, one that has taken generations and tens of trillions of dollars to put in place'. The annual throughputs include 'more than 7 billion metric tons of hard coal and lignite, 4 billion metric tons of crude oil, and more than 3 billion cubic meters of natural gas'.

It is difficult to conceive of human civilization simply abandoning this massive construction. For Smil, it seems impossible. He also notes that we have not yet *proved* that carbon-neutral energy sources such as solar can replace fossil fuels universally. However, there is no theoretical reason they can't be scaled, in the ways that Sachs and the Schwartzmans suggest. The difficulties in making a rapid systemic transition are financial and ideological. There are no physical constraints preventing us from doing it. If this transition became a central focus of collective human activity over the next few years, we would accomplish it. We do know from the past that ideologies, beliefs, social behaviour – as well as the economic systems that underlie them – can change quickly.

Focusing on averting a two-degree rise in global temperatures, the *Decarbonization* report warns that 'without a dramatic reversal of the greenhouse gas emissions trajectory – one that leads to a significant decline in greenhouse gas emissions by mid-century and to net zero emissions during the second half of the century – the world will not only overshoot the 2 °C limit, but will do so dramatically . . . Humanity faces catastrophic risks on our current path.' Unfortunately, recent scientific projections have reduced that 2 °C limit to 1.5 °C as the maximum before large-scale release of the methane from the Arctic becomes inevitable. This only serves to highlight the severity of our current emergency, and how quickly we must work together to avert the worst possible results.

The Solar Singularity

Although solar energy currently supplies only about 1 per cent of electricity globally, we are on the verge, potentially, of an exponential scaling up of solar power. This could happen so rapidly that solar will surpass fossil fuels as our principal energy source within a few decades. Energy analyst Tam Hunt is among many commentators who agree we have already reached the tipping point where solar becomes the cheapest source of energy and hence the default source: 'The cost of solar power has plummeted in the last few years by over 50 per cent and we are seeing solar power costs at or below the cost of utility power in an increasing number of jurisdictions already; this is generally known as "grid parity".' This is the case, even though fossil fuel companies receive all sorts of government subsidies.

A recent report found that Germany, Italy and Spain are now at 'grid parity' for solar photovoltaics, and many other countries are close. Grid parity means it is now just as cheap to use solar as other sources of energy. According to Deutsche Bank, 80 per cent of the world will reach grid parity by 2017. 'I call the next big step for solar after grid parity, the point at which solar power becomes the default new power source in a majority of jurisdictions around the world, the "solar singularity".

When this moment is reached, solar power will take off and become the dominant power source relatively quickly,' Hunt writes.

It is entirely feasible for solar to undergo a very rapid acceleration. One precedent for this is the rapid dissemination and penetration of cell phones and smart phones, which became ubiquitous more quickly than any past technology in history. In the US, the transition from horses to automobiles, early last century, took little more than a decade. If governments support the solar singularity with new subsidies and policies, solar could indeed become the world's dominant energy source within the next decades.

The potential for a rapid scaling up of solar power and other renewable sources has existed for a while now. Unfortunately, it has been blocked and subverted by governments, particularly the US and China. These super-powers have committed to fossil fuels due to entrenched interests and fixed ideologies. But for China, at least, this is now changing.

In 2000, the entire global market for solar power was 300 mega-watts a year. Since then, China's increasing commitment to solar has radically boosted the prospects for the industry: Jeremy Leggett, the founder of Solar Century, a UK company, believes we have now reached a point where solar's triumph is inevitable. Leggett saw the future when he visited a new factory in Shanghai, which can produce a thousand megawatts of solar panels annually. 'The machines stretch in ordered rows many football pitches into the distance', he writes in *The Winning of the Carbon War*. 'Hundreds of workers, dressed just like the touring party, attend them. A thousand people work under this roof, in alternating shifts, 24 hours a day, 7 days a week.' In 2012, the total capacity of solar photovoltaic panels crossed 100 gigawatts: 'This is equivalent to . . . 65 full-size 1.3 gigawatt nuclear reactors,' Leggett notes – and solar is continuing to grow, exponentially.

While China's totalitarian political system is not enviable as a social model, the Chinese might force a rapid conversion to regenerative practices in many areas. Instead of making disposable gadgets for the West, factories could be repurposed to produce rainwater harvesters, biochar units, storage batteries for renewable energy sources and so on. Similarly, China could undertake a large-scale retraining of its population to adopt conservation as well as permaculture practices. It could force its population to become essentially vegetarian.

The massive transition we need to ensure our continuity may be easier to manage under an authoritarian regime than under a liberal democracy, corrupted by special interests. The happiest outcome would be a worldwide metamorphosis, over a few decades, to both decentralized power grids and decentralized democracies.

The Internet of Energy

Making a rapid, global transition to renewable sources of energy requires the development of enhanced energy-storage capacities and the creation of what some commentators call 'The Internet of energy.' The economic and social theorist Jeremy Rifkin outlines this optimistic alternative in his book, *The Third Industrial Revolution*.

Rifkin believes this revolution will be based on a number of factors. Obviously, first and most pressing, is the transition to solar, wind, geothermal, hydro and other renewable sources. Second, we must transform our approach to building, so that we construct new buildings and retrofit old ones to act as micro-power plants, collecting energy on-site. The third is developing and deploying hydrogen batteries and other storage technologies to capture the intermittent power produced from renewable sources. Then, we must develop network technologies that transform the power grid of every continent and country into an 'energy internet' able to transmit power efficiently. This would require a decentralized infrastructure, like the Internet itself. Lastly, we must transition our transportation system – cars, trucks, trains, boats, planes – to run on renewable sources of fuel.

We can replace the current fleet of cars with electric plug-in and fuel cell vehicles – even though this would require a tremendous expenditure of energy. There are over a billion cars and trucks currently on the planet. Retrofitting them to run on electricity – or salt-water hydrolysis – might be less wasteful than junking them. We also might want to rethink the private automobile as our principal mode of transport. A ton of steel, raw materials and precious metals to move around one or two human beings is not very efficient. Cars are difficult to recycle. Once they cease working, they end up in dumps, leaking toxins into the Earth.

Rifkin, by the way, followed up his extremely optimistic book, *The Third Industrial Revolution*, with an even more optimistic one. In *The*

Zero-Margin Cost Society, he argues that humanity may be reaching a threshold where super-abundance becomes our natural state. We will avert the ecological crisis by rapid innovations, spreading sustainable solutions across the Earth through distributed manufacturing and open-source, peer-to-peer forms of collaborative production. We will be able to 'print out' solar panels and desalinization kits, for instance, ending our dependence on scarce water.

Other futurists believe such a direction is plausible if we can overcome our ideological blockages and stop the robots from pulling a *Terminator* on us. For instance, Paul Mason realizes, in *Postcapitalism*, 'Knowledge-driven production tends towards the unlimited creation of wealth, independent of the labour expended.' Mason believes we are approaching the potential for a post-capitalist civilization where a basic income or universal subsidy gives everyone the means to live decently, where we achieve 'freedom from work'. Once again, as Buckminster Fuller predicted, we seem to be on a seesaw teetering between polar opposites of utopia or oblivion.

Algae-based Fuel

One question is whether there are other forms of non-polluting renewable energy – besides solar, wind and geothermal – that we can access, which can speed our escape from fossil fuel dependence and help us reach carbon-neutral or negative, globally. While solar energy and other renewables could fulfil all sorts of needs, they are not effective for certain purposes, for instance air travel. It takes an enormous amount of fuel to power the world's current fleet of jet planes as well as giant cargo ships.

'One round-trip flight from New York to Europe or to San Francisco creates a warming effect equivalent to 2 or 3 tons of carbon dioxide per person,' states the *New York Times*. 'The average American generates about 19 tons of carbon dioxide a year; the average European, 10. So if you take five long flights a year, they may well account for three-quarters of the emissions you create.' For someone like myself, who doesn't drive a car, air travel is my biggest single contribution to warming.

Through my work, I get many opportunities to hop on a plane, which I love to do – although ironically, my work involves speaking about this very quandary. But I recognize that travel is a massive drain on the planet's resources.

For those of us in the privileged classes – not only defined by wealth, which I lack, but access to other forms of capital, such as 'culture capital' – our ability to travel freely around the globe, whenever we like, is considered an inalienable right, not something to be judged, censured or questioned. Every other week, friends of mine jet off to Nepal, Bali, South Africa, Indonesia, Japan, Siberia, Berlin, Costa Rica, Gstaad, expelling several tons of CO_2 with each puddle jump. They visit ski lodges, ancient temples, secluded eco-lodges and yoga retreats, and take selfies with native tribes sporting their picturesque penis gourds.

Many of us believe that our ability to descend on distant cultures – whenever we feel like it – is, somehow, beneficial for the world. We don't see it as a form of colonialist entitlement, or another addiction. One by-product of this incessant travel is that wealthy people don't develop a deeper connection with any particular place. They don't feel the need to deepen community where they are. Why should they, when they can always jet off to the next spot, as soon as things feel dull for them and they desire more stimulation? Perhaps we could start with a commitment to travel less, to invest in building community at home? For instance, if one million or ten million or one hundred million people agreed to restrict their air travel to once a year, or less, that could be shown to have measurable impacts in the amount of CO_2 and other waste produced.

If people continue to travel by plane all of the time, without regard for consequences, we are going to have to pray for some amazing, still-unimagined breakthrough technologies to arise – technologies that can suck carbon out of the atmosphere, and allow us to fly without emitting clouds of doom. One somewhat fanciful idea I entertain is the revival of airships – hydrogen-filled blimps (helium, unfortunately, is increasingly scarce). Imagine, particularly in a post-work society organized around the pursuit of what Oscar Wilde called 'cultivated leisure', airships being used as gigantic co-working and co-housing facilities, drifting slowly around the world, perhaps even containing some version of indoor aquaponics farms, producing their own food. They could become floating festivals. But I digress.

One tantalizing prospect for a new energy source for air travel and other forms of transportation is the use of algae as a source of biofuel. Algae is a non-flowering plant that uses photosynthesis to convert carbon and light into lipids and carbohydrates that can be turned into ethanol. Perhaps the most important organism on Earth, it is a major contributor to the stability, health and regenerative capacities of the biosphere, producing more than half of the oxygen that we breathe. Algae can be commercially grown in mass quantities, and then pressed – much the way olives are pressed into olive oil – to produce fuel, which, in theory, can power jet planes, ocean liners, as well as cars and home heating systems.

The path to a regenerative transformation of human society will require harnessing the restorative capacities of the oldest organisms on Earth, and applying our industrial techniques to scale up production and distribution. This will include working with plants and fungi, as well as anaerobic microorganisms called Archaea, ancient one-celled organisms with no nucleus, which can be utilized to transmute our waste products into fuel.

A number of companies are currently working on the commercial production of algae-based biofuels – and when they perfect the process, it presumably can be scaled up rapidly to be a replacement for fossil fuels on a large level. One of these companies, Algae Systems, based in Nevada, makes 'diesel fuel from algae by simultaneously performing three other tasks: making clean water from municipal sewage (which it uses to fertilize the algae), using the carbon-heavy residue as fertilizer and generating valuable credits for advanced biofuels'. The technology, according to the company, is carbon negative, removing more CO_2 from the atmosphere than it releases, but it is still a work in progress.

Nuclear Power

Currently, nuclear energy supplies an estimated 20 per cent of electricity in the US, and 14 per cent of electricity globally, without releasing CO_2. Without dismissing other sources of renewable energy, billionaires like Peter Thiel and Bill Gates, along with 'Neo-environmentalists' like Mark Lynas, Stewart Brand and Ramez Naam, promote nuclear power as a necessity – even after Fukushima.

Lynas writes that 'nuclear power is likely to be the most environmentally friendly technology of all, although appropriately sited wind, solar and other renewables are similarly benign and should be equally encouraged'. But to create enough power to satisfy the ever-increasing demand, while reducing global emissions of CO_2 by 50 per cent by mid-century, would require the construction of 12,000 new nuclear power plants. In other words, one plant would have to come online, every single day, for the next 30 years.

In *Eaarth*, Bill McKibben writes, 'Nuclear power plants don't seem as scary as they did a generation ago – not that they've gotten safer, but other things have gotten nastier . . . If a nuclear plant has an accident, it's bad news, but if you operate a coal-fired plant exactly according to the instructions, it melts the ice caps and burns the forests.' Nuclear plants are extremely costly to build and often involve enormous cost overruns. 'Bottom line: building enough conventional nuclear reactors to eliminate a tenth of the threat of global warming would cost about $8 trillion,' McKibben notes, and would run electricity prices 'through the roof'.

Plant safety and nuclear waste disposal remain serious concerns – not to mention the potential to turn radioactive byproducts into weapons. In the US, engineers are starting to fret about the potential of the ageing fleet of reactors to withstand the increasingly frequent onslaught of super-storms and earthquakes. Indian Point, near New York, where I live, appears to be leaking radioactive waste, according to news reports. As peak oil and climate change continues to intensify in the next years, large-scale projects such as building nuclear reactors will become increasingly difficult to implement. The construction of a nuclear reactor not only costs several billion dollars, but also adds an estimated 20 million tons of CO_2 to the atmosphere.

Energy companies are in the process of developing fourth-generation nuclear reactors – including some able to use already existing radioactive waste as fuel – but the technology remains untested and unproven. These new kinds of reactors, according to Peter Diamandis and Steven Kotler, could be 'so-called backyard nukes. These self-contained small-scale modular generation IV nuclear reactors are built in factories (for cheaper construction), sealed completely, and designed to run for decades without maintenance.' The timetable for these new reactors is vague, with the potential for a demonstration model of one kind to be running by 2020.

If it can be conclusively demonstrated that next-generation nuclear plants are safe and will help us stave off global warming, the technology should be considered. But the inherent problems with nuclear power remain severe. Even if the loss of life from Fukushima and Chernobyl was far less than initially feared, we still don't know what the long-term, even multi-generational, impacts of this radiation will be. Nuclear reactors cost a fortune to build and require a massive security infrastructure to protect. They reinforce the current model of centralized government and corporate control.

On the other hand, we know that both solar and wind work. These energy sources are getting cheaper faster and they are available now. Solar power has already reached grid parity, and will soon be far more cost-effective than fossil fuels. Renewable energy does not require a huge security apparatus, does not produce dangerous waste and can be installed in a decentralized manner. The only question, in fact, is how do we bring about their immediate adoption?

Cold Fusion, Zero Point

Other potential energy sources exist. Some of them are controversial and remain on the fringes, but if it can be proved they work reliably without disastrous ecological costs, they should be implemented. One of these is cold fusion, also called Low Energy Nuclear Reactors, whose viability is still being studied.

According to promoters, cold fusion technology is on the verge of producing 'zero carbon dioxide emissions, zero noise, zero radiation and zero toxins of any sort. In addition to being powerful and efficient, the technology is completely safe. It uses no radioactive materials, produces no nuclear waste, emits no radioactivity into the environment, and releases no pollution.'

On the scientific fringe, a number of other researchers believe we can draw an essentially unlimited amount of power by tapping quantum fluctuations from the vacuum, or the zero point field (ZPF). 'Zero point energy is the sea of energy that pervades all of space and every atom, often called the physical vacuum,' writes Thomas Valone. A tremendous amount of potential energy exists in every atom of space. According to Richard Feynman, a Nobel Prize-winning physicist, 'the energy density of the ZPF would be ten raised to the 108th power joules per cubic centimeter'. This translates into the theoretical ability to access enough energy to power the world – more than we will ever need – by accessing zero point in a tiny region of space.

Valone, among others, claims that engines applying zero point are almost ready for mass release. These engines would make use of the Casimir effect – the repulsion between metal plates at a micro-scale – to produce energy. 'Analysis of the Casimir engine cycle demonstrates its departure from hydroelectric, gaseous or gravitational systems', Valone writes.

One issue to consider is that, if we did access unlimited free energy from zero point or cold fusion before we attained a more advanced planetary consciousness, this might exacerbate other problems. With unlimited power, for instance, we might rapidly exhaust our resources, plundering the last fish from deep in the oceans, pulling out the remaining raw materials buried deep beneath the Earth. We might also create new super-weapons. The other question, of course, is whether these two technologies are, in fact, attainable. Mainstream scientists remain sceptical, but we should stay open to all options. After all, we have already accomplished many things that were once, simply, unimaginable.

Making the Energy Transition

I realize this chapter has included a lot of information. I know your brain may have switched off here and there while reading it. I often find, when I speak to people – non-specialists or non-fanatics – about the ecological mega-crisis, as well as specific solutions, such as these proposals for global energy (let alone macro-economics, which is coming up later), they reach a threshold where their eyes glaze over. They stare, vacantly, away from me, into the middle distance.

The essential takeaway is that we have a realistic capacity to make a complete overhaul of our global energy system away from fossil fuels, towards renewables. This doesn't have to take us a century. We can accomplish it in a few decades. This is not a pie-in-the-sky fantasy. It is something that can happen. As quickly as we can, we must impel our society in this direction.

In fact, nobody can say how fast we might bring this transformation about, once our focus shifts in this direction. Globally, civilization must break through political obstructions to engineer a rapid transition to solar and other renewable sources, focusing on conservation while we build new infrastructure. Unfortunately, the 2015 Paris agreements on climate change did not do the job – as Naomi Klein noted, COP-21 was 'scientifically catastrophic', like telling a patient with heart disease to cut down from five to four hamburgers a day and jog once every two weeks.

What humanity needs, as Lester Brown realized, is something like a Marshall Plan for the planet. We must act together as if we are facing a threat as dangerous as Soviet totalitarianism. The threat comes not only from the entrenched power of the fossil fuel companies, but also from social complacency – as well as consumerism and hyper-individuality.

Roy Scranton writes in *Learning to Die in the Anthropocene*:

> The problem with our response to climate change isn't a problem of passing the right laws or finding the right price for carbon or changing people's minds or raising awareness. Everybody already knows. The problem is that the problem is too big. The problem is that different people want different things. The problem is that the problem is us.

Scranton is correct. We therefore must seek to engineer a collective shift in values and behaviour, based on the understanding that individual and collective consciousness are, in the end, socially produced.

In the short term, we must radically reduce our use of energy and design and implement a system based on conservation, cooperation and efficient sharing of resources. As we will discuss, a 'carbon tax' – financially penalizing the production of CO_2 – might help. However, it won't be enough. We must engineer a structural transition in our socio-economic paradigm, away from growth.

Smil and other critics are correct in noting that our current fossil-fuel-dependent energy infrastructure represents a massive global apparatus, a huge 'sunk investment' made over generations. I realize that we confront a daunting task in switching over to renewable power.

Even so, this daunting task can be accomplished. The multitude must demand it, forcing the hands of corporations and governments. This will require a global movement of civil society, beyond anything we have seen to date. How such a movement develops – how it organizes itself to overcome the existing power relationships – is a question that I don't think anyone can answer fully at this point.

5

Farming

Carbon in itself is not our enemy. Carbon is the basis of life itself. All living things are carbon-based beings. The problem is the imbalance we have created through our ongoing, ever-increasing industrial activity. We must reduce the excess carbon we have already released into the atmosphere, as quickly as we can.

How do we remove CO_2 from the atmosphere in large quantities? One of the best ways to accomplish this would be to engineer a coordinated global transition from industrial agriculture back to ecological or organic farming. To do this, we have to reconnect people with an ecologically advanced, locally based, food system. In the US, this means accelerating the ongoing movement away from supermarkets, back to farmers' markets and community supported agriculture projects, where people buy directly from local farms. In some respects we need to return to older ways and traditions. More of us need to start growing our own food.

As the authors of 'Climate Change or System Change?', a paper produced by the Local Futures Institute, directed by Helena Norbert Hodge, notes, a lot of trade today is redundant, with goods 'sourced from thousands of miles away when an identical product is available next door'. Huge supermarket chains contract with massive industrial farms to stock their stores, ignoring local sources. Britain, for example, 'imports and exports 15,000 tons of waffles annually, and exchanges 20 tons of bottled water with Australia', while 'supermarkets on the Citrus Coast of Spain carry imported lemons while local lemons rot on the ground'. To save on labour costs, companies will transport produce across the world to be processed. For instance, the US company Trident 'ships about 30 million pounds of fish annually to China for filleting, and then ships the fish back to the US for sale'.

I admit I am one of the billions of alienated city people; I didn't grow up near a farm and rarely visited one. As a kid, I had no connection to where my food came from. I have barely managed to grow a few house-plants, in fifty years of life.

I feel deeply unqualified, therefore, to make proposals when it comes to farming. I admit my information is based on various reports and second-hand sources. I do know how different it feels to eat food grown organically rather than commercial produce. I can sense – as everyone can – that the food system has become more compromised, and more dangerous, as the Earth's population has swelled over the last half-century. Allergies, environmental sensitivities and food intolerances are a growing epidemic.

The growth of the organic sector – seen in the rising popularity of Whole Foods and farmers' markets – is problematic. Food has become another area where the divide between 'Haves' and 'Have Nots' keeps widening. Organic food is generally much higher priced, targeting a well-heeled clientele, while ghettos and poorer suburbs remain 'food deserts' where the only available food is cheap and low quality. Worldwide, food is a battleground in the struggle between the developed and developing worlds. Advancing corporate globalization, the World Bank, under US control, has used subsidies and unfair trade policies that force poor countries to accept subsidized produce from industrial farms, decimating healthy local industries.

According to estimates, commercial agriculture is one of the main contributors to climate change. The food industry as a whole generates an estimated 30 per cent of the world's greenhouse gas emissions, while the agricultural sector accounts for 14 per cent of total global emissions, most of which stem from the meat production industry alone. Livestock cultivation is also responsible for deforestation, nitrogen runoff and other ills.

Much evidence suggests that, if we return to earlier ways of farming, like no-till agriculture, this will substantially reduce CO_2 emissions. Traditionally, farmers will plough, disc or harrow land to form a seedbed for rows of crops, then use a mechanical cultivator to cull weeds. Turning the soil over and over in this way releases carbon dioxide. With no-till agriculture, farmers plant seeds into undisturbed soil. This kind of farming minimizes soil erosion and energy use while retaining water and carbon.

According to a 30-year study by the Rodale Institute, 'Organic farming is far superior to conventional systems when it comes to building, maintaining and replenishing the health of the soil.' The study estimates that conventional agriculture produces 40 per cent more greenhouse gases than its organic equivalent. One 2007 study, commissioned by the Pew Center on Global Climate Change, concluded that organic agriculture had the potential to sequester 11 per cent of the emissions for that year if put into practice globally.

If it is true that organic, ecological and no-till farming, where appropriate, can be more productive than industrial farming, requiring less artificial fertilizer and polluting pesticides, while sequestering carbon and having benefits for human health, then society should make a systemic return to these practices. Returning to older, more human-scaled systems will require a great deal of retraining, but it can be done. We have the tool we need for it – a planetary nervous system, in the Internet, that allows for immediate transmission of new ideas and traditional techniques. As a basic principle of the new planetary culture, we will reconnect people to their local ecosystems. We will support them to become gardeners, stewards of the commons (our land and watersheds), caring for biodiversity and for one another.

Meat

There is no doubt that we need a steep reduction of meat consumption to reduce CO_2 pollution. Humans kill, process and consume 100 billion creatures per year. Animal farming on this scale depends upon a vast global infrastructure of factory farms and soybean plantations. The amount of grain grown for animal feed is one of the largest contributors to the deforestation that erodes biodiversity and accelerates climate change. Consumption of meat is highly inefficient in terms of energy and water use. It requires an estimated 28 calories of energy to produce one calorie of meat. The meat-based diet of the average person in the United States requires an estimated 4,200 gallons of water per day, compared to 300 gallons a day for a vegan diet. Thirty per cent of the Earth's land surface is used for animal grazing. A great proportion of this land should be converted back into carbon-sequestering forests and wetlands.

A 2006 report prepared by the United Nations Food and Agriculture Organization found that our meat-based diets are responsible for emissions of more greenhouse gases into the atmosphere than either transportation or industry. According to estimates, the meat produced in factory farms around the world contributes between 14 and 22 per cent of the 36 billion tons of CO_2, or its equivalent, that is emitted every year by our industrial and agricultural systems.

According to the Worldwatch Institute, 'Serious action on climate change will almost certainly require reductions in the global consumption of meat and dairy by today's major consumers in industrial countries, as well as slowing the growth of demand in developing countries.' One way to bring about this reduction, they propose, is to put 'a price on livestock-related greenhouse gases, so that producers treat them as a business cost and thus have a direct incentive to reduce them'. Beyond enforcement through financial or legal means, an engineered shift in mass consciousness will be necessary to reduce or temporarily eliminate meat consumption.

Would it really be so bad if humanity put a moratorium on the consumption of meat as well as wild fish for a period of time, in order to allow the Earth to replenish and restore itself? A 'global meat fast' would be one of the fastest ways for us to make a significant dent in emissions, quickly.

While I know that some of you reading this are already vegetarian, I also know that many of you have contemplated it, perhaps attempted it, and decided it 'wasn't worth it'. Personally, I have been largely vegetarian for the last years, although I admit I fall off the wagon at times, depending on who I am dining with as well as other factors, including laziness and boredom. In many areas, I find myself a helpful test case, because I am typically slothful, slow to change, and not particularly good at maintaining habits. In all this, I am probably representative of many well-intentioned people.

My friends Sharon Gannon and David Life are ardent and exemplary vegans for moral reasons. For Sharon, animals are actually 'people' who deserve all the same rights as us. She has even written a book on how to prepare vegetarian pet food. I admit that I can't feel as passionate about this as she does. I tend to think that humans were designed to be omnivores; hunting beasts in the wild was a basic and essential part of life for a very long time. In the end, everything lives, eats and dies, and gets recycled by nature.

Having said that, however, I do find factory farming to be morally reprehensible. Like many of us, I consider the conditions so many animals face to be horrible. They are sentient beings that suffer misery and torture, a hellish existence.

Traditional people felt a deep relatedness to animals and all of nature. As Jack Forbes writes of Native American culture, in *Columbus and the Cannibals*:

> When a plant, tree or animal is to be killed, first, the need must be great; second, permission is asked for, if time allows; third, the creature is thanked; and, fourth, dances, prayers and ceremonies are used to further thank the creatures so killed and to help those that are alive to grow and prosper.

Indigenous people ask for permission to take an animal's life, and express gratitude for its sacrifice. Our meat comes from mass, mindless slaughter. I admit I also find something off-putting about our potential for creating bio-engineered vat-grown meat, although I can see why people would consider it an ethical advance over this endless global genocide.

We can all agree that animal farming is a multi-dimensional ecological nightmare. It causes deforestation, nitrogen runoff, CO_2 pollution and the overuse of antibiotics and so on. It is mass torture and degradation. If we have a spiritual viewpoint, we may believe this mass suffering has karmic repercussions – not only for those directly involved with it, and those who consume its products, but also for our society as a whole. Considering all the factors, a global transition towards a primarily vegetarian diet seems the only answer for humanity. If we want to be stewards and midwives of the global transition, then we should lead the way by making this shift, personally.

Beyond any personal commitments, we need a broad-based social movement promoting vegetarianism and veganism. A global campaign, using cutting-edge techniques of advertising and marketing, could educate people, asking them to give up meat for our children's future. Can we imagine the world's advertising, marketing and branding agencies joining forces for this project? I don't see why not: our future depends on it. We then must consider how such a project could be funded and supported.

What Can We Do?

Even in the best scenario we can envision, humanity is going to be dealing with a drastically destabilized climate over the next century. This will cause more floods, super-storms, droughts and so on. Growing food locally, using organic methods, is one of the best ways to make our society more resilient, helping to insulate communities from possible disaster in case supply chains get disrupted. It will also reduce transport, plastic packaging and CO_2 pollution.

In agriculture, as in many areas, the best solutions can be implemented fast if we make use of mass media and social networks to spread good ideas globally. This is already happening on a small scale. People learn how to sprout, pickle or can vegetables from YouTube videos or online courses. Progressive organizations like Bioneers – which has an annual conference in the Bay Area – have been promoting best practices for decades. Permaculture and gardening techniques can be taught through the Internet and even on mainstream TV shows, telling people what's happening while giving them the tools to help the world as well as themselves.

Sustainable technologies could be deployed on a global scale to accelerate soil regeneration and carbon sequestration. One of these technologies is biochar, which scientists learned about when they studied the ecological practices of tribal people in the Amazon jungle. Natives would burn organic waste slowly, in an oxygen-weak environment, and then use the residue to replenish local soil, adding carbon back to the Earth. Biochar is the industrialized version of this ancient practice. According to Mark Hertsgaard, 'If Biochar were added to 10 percent of global cropland . . . it would store 20 billion tons of CO_2 equivalent' – that is more than 50 per cent of humanity's annual greenhouse gas emissions. I don't know why we are not doing this already.

To break through current obstacles to changes in farming, a movement of civil society must build global alliances. The progressive and environmental community must partner with global institutions – for example, with the Catholic Church. Considering Pope Francis's environmental outlook in his encyclical, *Care for the Earth*, there should be a way to follow through on his principles and use the global network of Catholic churches as a ready-made social infrastructure for the transformation of farming. The community of the faithful could be trained in ecologically restorative and permaculture techniques, rooted in local conditions. Tangible ways to 'Care for the Earth' could be taught after the Sunday sermon, and in Catholic schools.

Over the last century, farm work became devalued as rural populations were forced to relocate to urban areas and find jobs in industrial manufacturing or the growing service sector. Where most people in the US were farmers a century ago, now only a small fraction of people work on farms. A great deal of our food is produced through industrialized agriculture, by big companies. We need to restore social prestige to farming and gardening and support people in growing on urban rooftops and in suburban yards at least some of the food they eat.

Designing agricultural systems that are decentralized and specialized would help to maintain and enhance the ecological and genetic diversity that is essential to the health of an ecosystem. Current mega-farms could, in theory, be divided into smaller, specially designed ecological, permaculture and agroforestry projects built around the contours, water availability and environmental quality of their sites. Smaller farms could be integrated into larger cooperatives, where social support, hardware and labour could be shared by the farmers.

Cuba's forced transition, in the 1990s, to a regenerative agricultural system in the face of crisis offers an encouraging model. After 1989, the country was forced to produce its own food due to the collapse of the Soviet Union, which cut off Cuba's main subsidies and supplies. Under great pressure to innovate, the Cubans developed a local food system that incorporated urban gardening and made it mandatory for most of the population to grow some of their own produce. Inadvertently, they created a model for self-sufficiency that could be replicated, particularly in the global South.

High- and Low-tech Innovation

Hopefully, we will see a growing movement away from industrial agriculture and the destructive aspects of the 'Green Revolution' towards ecological practices that will democratize food production and make organic food the normal standard again, eventually. Many different techniques can be applied, depending on particular circumstances.

These include permaculture, agroforestry, poly-cropping and so on. There are many ways we can assist nature in regenerating damaged and despoiled lands. The mycologist Paul Stamets uses mushrooms – fungus – to leach toxins out of the soil. Allan Savory's method of cattle grazing reverses desertification on grasslands. Many other techniques of bioremediation can be applied, depending on circumstances.

Permaculture was developed by Bill Mollison and David Holmgren in the late 1970s. The name stands for 'permanent agriculture' or 'permanent culture' – I have to admit, I'm not crazy about the term because nothing in nature is permanent. The term 'permaculture' has a built-in ideological bias, suggesting a kind of hippie Fundamentalism. However, as a design science applied to agriculture, permaculture offers many crucial ideas and insights.

One central principle of permaculture is to observe the land before interacting with it. Studying the local ecology and water sources, perma-culturists seek to understand what kind of development meshes with a site's innate contours and requirements, rather than making it conform to an abstract model. Instead of immediate profit, the objective is long-term resilience. A permaculture designer will ideally observe an area of land for a year before making any interventions or changes to it.

Permaculture is based on a number of beautiful and sensible principles. These include: 'Observe and interact'; 'use and value diversity'; 'creatively use and respond to change'; and 'use edges and value the marginal'. Implementing permaculture requires a long-range investment of attention, effort and care, along with significant training. Perma-culture advocates say that, given time, they can produce a much greater yield of food – several times as much – than commercial farms, while building topsoil; they can accomplish all this without using chemical poisons. Once again, it is important to realize that this approach – which seeks to build enduring reciprocity between human beings and their environment – requires a good deal of education, patience and careful attention. Even so, it is entirely feasible for our society to shift its focus in this direction; our future survival depends on supporting and enabling people to replenish the health of the Earth's ecosystems.

Some version of agroforestry has been practised by traditional societies for thousands of years. These cultures grow crops in a manner that mimics the interacting layers of a diverse, healthy forest. Examples can still be seen in the Western Ghats of rural India, on small-scale farms in Indonesia, and throughout the tropics. While agroforestry does not sequester as much carbon as old-growth forests, it helps to preserve forests by creating a buffer around them. Like permaculture, agroforestry is based on deep local knowledge and artisanal attention, rather than chemicals or machines.

Some developing countries with scarce resources are already being forced to adapt to climate change. They are innovating and creating new models. Mark Hertsgaard visited one of these farming communities in the western Sahel of Africa. The Sahel is a strip of savanna south of the Sahara desert which 'stretches like a belt across the width of the African landmass', marked by relentless heat. Hertsgaard learned that farmers in the region had begun to adapt their practices to deal with climate change. He was amazed by what he discovered:

> Using simple techniques that cost them nothing, millions of small farmers throughout the region have begun protecting themselves against the scorching heat and withering drought of climate change. Their methods amount to a poor man's version of organic farming: fortifying soil with manure rather than chemical fertilizer, growing different crops on the same piece of land (known as intercropping), relying on natural predators to counter pests rather than applying pesticides. In the process, farmers in the western Sahel have rehabilitated millions of acres of degraded savanna that was on the verge of becoming desert, thus increasing the amount of land available to grow food.

The success of this enterprise depends on the straightforward solution of planting and growing more trees in the fields. The practice of mixing trees and crops is called farmer-managed natural regeneration. 'The trees' shade and bulk offer crops relief from the overwhelming heat and gusting winds . . . Leaves serve other purposes. After they fall to the ground, they act as mulch, boosting soil fertility; they also provide fodder for livestock in a season when little other food is available.' In emergency famine conditions, people can also eat the leaves to stave off starvation.

Due to tree-planting initiatives in the region, water reserves have increased locally, to the surprise of scientists. According to one agriculture scientist, with the propagation of these simple techniques since the late 1980s, 'water tables in many villages have risen by at least five meters, despite a growing population'. If this is possible in the extreme conditions of sub-Saharan Africa, similar initiatives might have tremendous benefits in other water-scarce regions, such as, for example, California.

These are low-tech methods that could help us greatly, but there are also high-tech methods that could be crucial. For instance, let's consider vertical farms. Inventor Dickson Despommier has developed the concept of vertical farms for cities. He envisions the construction of 30-storey towers able to feed 50,000 people, in climate-controlled, pest-free environments requiring minimal use of water. One acre of a vertical farm could yield as much produce as 10 or 20 acres of land, he believes, through optimizing conditions and careful monitoring. Benefits of vertical farming would include year-round crop production, elimination of agricultural runoff from fertilizers, promotion of urban sustainability, and returning farmland to nature. Why don't we try this?

We can also reduce food waste significantly. According to Anna Lappe, of the Small Planet Institute, we waste as much as 30 per cent of all food that we process, because the current system is inefficient. When food waste is not composted, it releases methane as it decays. 'We know how to grow food in ways that cut emissions, create more resilient landscapes and ensure ample yields, all while reducing the use of non-renewable resources, fossil fuels, and land,' Lappe writes.

To make a systemic transition in farming practices worldwide, we would have to search out the most successful local initiatives, isolate the principles and techniques that make them work, then turn them into design templates that other localities can use and duplicate, in ways appropriate for their particular conditions. The Internet project Open Source Ecology provides one example. The project is 'developing a set of open source blueprints for the Global Village Construction Set – a set of the 50 most important machines that it takes for modern life to exist – everything from a tractor, to an oven, to a circuit maker'. Conceived by Marcin Jakubowski, a fusion physicist turned farmer, Open Source Ecology offers detailed blueprints and plans for building farm machinery such as tractors and mechanical ploughs. The designs of these machines are available, copyright free, to anybody who wants to build their own versions in their workshop.

I love projects like this one, where knowledge and expertise is freely shared. Another one is Windowfarm. Windowfarm's website defines it as 'An Open Source Community Developing Hydroponic Edible Gardens for Urban Windows'. Windowfarm builds systems for growing plants and vegetables out of plastic water bottles and other household objects. They share the blueprints for their systems on the website, so that other people can copy and improve on their designs.

Another model that can be copied is the 'polyface' agriculture system, designed by Virginia farmer Joel Salatin. Salatin developed 'a symbiotic, multi-speciated synergistic relationship-dense production model that yields far more per acre than industrial models', while 'being aromatically and aesthetically romantic'. According to Salatin, 'We haven't bought a bag of chemical fertilizer in half a century, never planted a seed, own no plow or disk or silo – we call those bankruptcy tubes.' Salatin's farm proves it is possible to develop closed-loop farming methods that are innately regenerative and resilient. Such methods could become widely distributed.

Even though we must reduce our consumption of animals globally, there are ways that farms benefit from integrating livestock, on a small scale. This includes making use of animal waste. Manure can be transformed into compost, on-site. Methane can be harvested from cow manure and turned into electricity, fuel and heat. Compost from manure can also be spread on grazing land to sequester carbon and enhance soil fertility. According to the Marin Carbon Project (2013), adding a half-inch-thick layer of compost to half of the current cattle-grazing land in California would mitigate an amount of carbon equal to the region's entire emissions of greenhouse gases.

Genetic Engineering

And then there is the genetic engineering (GE) in agriculture debate. The manipulation of the DNA of crops and other organisms to enhance their utility for human purposes remains a highly controversial, polarizing subject. While the United States leads the world in pushing for mass adaptation of GE crops, more than sixty countries, including those of the European Union, continue to prohibit or severely restrict the production and sale of genetically modified organisms (GMOs).

According to its proponents, which include neo-environmentalists and technocrats like Bill Gates, GE is necessary to feed the world's growing population. Genetic manipulation, they argue, can accomplish a number of crucial goals. By integrating insect-resilient and pesticide-resistant genes with plant DNA, it can reduce use of pesticides. Plants can also be engineered to be resistant to drought. Fertilizer is used to supply nitrogen to the soil, a nutrient that plants need to grow but one that is scarce in nature. Only a few beans and legumes create their own nitrogen – 'fixing' nitrogen in the soil. Potentially, through GE, many other crops may be able to produce nitrogen. Nitrogen runoff is also a major ecological problem, one of the nine planetary boundaries defined by the Stockholm Resilience Centre.

One major problem with GE, under the current system, is that its commercial development and application is controlled by a few for-profit corporations, who gain by increasing the sales of chemicals and 'terminator seeds' (seeds that must be bought anew each season, because they don't germinate), making farmers dependent on biotechnology. These companies also profit by being able to copyright genetic material and gain monopoly control over seed stocks.

At the same time, biotechnology and synthetic biology – the ability to create entirely new organisms – has become a technology available even to hobbyists and garage start-ups. The global community of biotechnology entrepreneurs recently launched a Kickstarter campaign 'to develop plants that glow, potentially leading the way for trees that can replace electric street lamps and potted flowers luminous enough to read by', noted the *New York Times*. GE seems to be a genie that has got out of the bottle. When I consider the unforeseen consequences of previous technological advances, I find this truly frightening.

There are many unknowns involved in transgenic crops. They may degrade biodiversity. They may have other negative impacts on human and ecosystem health, over generations. We simply don't know.

Paul Kingsnorth, founder of the Dark Ecology movement in the UK, believes our dependence on increasingly advanced technologies has created what he calls a progress trap: 'Each improvement in our knowledge or in our technology will create new problems, which require new improvements. Each of these improvements tends to make society bigger, more complex, less human-scale, more destructive of nonhuman life, and more likely to collapse under its own weight.' More troubling than the foreseeable problems are the unforeseeable ones.

We have already seen examples of this with GMOs. Some GE crops produce higher yields at first, but this leads the insect population to mutate as well, and within less than a decade, those gains can be eliminated or even reversed. This is similar to what the medical field has experienced with antibiotics, which are becoming less and less effective over time. If we keep trying to wage an arms race against nature, we will lose, because nature has been at this for billions of years longer than us.

We currently have an irrational system driven by market imperatives. The world overproduces food but wastes a great deal of it, while some countries face malnutrition and famine. It would be far more sensible to address the inefficiencies of the current system, which causes so much unnecessary suffering, before we seek to engineer new life forms which may degrade ecosystems – and have negative consequences that we can't even foresee – generations into the future.

GE may be contributing to the increase of allergies, food intolerances and drug resistances, which seem epidemic. Is there a correlation between these syndromes, as well as proliferating cancers and other maladies, with GMOs, as well as herbicides such as glyphosate that saturate genetically engineered plants? It may be so – but it might take decades, or more, to establish a scientific consensus. Millions of people may suffer and die in the interim, as we continue to degrade the health of our ecosystems. It took decades to link cancer to tobacco use. During that time, millions of people died from lung cancer and emphysema. The same difficulty makes it impossible to link any particular 'super-storm' or natural disaster to CO_2 emissions and climate destabilization. Our scientific method is failing us here.

To consider one of many examples of how GE could negatively impact on natural systems, geneticists are now developing new strains of a tobacco plant that are able to photosynthesize with much greater efficiency than normal varieties. Plants capable of 'turbocharged photosynthesis' would have a tremendous advantage over other plant species. They could proliferate in the wild, wiping out native species.

We are falling prey to the blind hubris of scientists and profit-seeking corporations.

In its fixation on linear growth, our industrial techno-culture – the technological society – makes the mistake of separating the world into separate, atomized parts, rather than seeking to understand, and enhance, the hidden connections between them. By altering the basic material of life, biotechnology has the potential to damage the complex ecosystems upon which we rely. Ecosystems developed over millions of years. Profit-seeking corporations think in terms of decades at the most.

On the other hand, we are facing a global ecological emergency, and if temperatures rise quickly, we may need rapid innovations in agriculture. If geneticists could engineer new heat- and drought-resistant crops, as well as vegetables able to store nitrogen in their roots (something that only a handful of legumes and beans do naturally), we might need these breakthroughs, as climate change intensifies.

Ideally, civil society as a whole should take control of genetic research out of the hands of publicly traded corporations. This research should be conducted transparently, as a public trust, based on an ongoing exchange. This would require a systemic change in the relationship of public policy and science. A people's movement is needed to take the initiative to learn about subjects impacting on all of our lives that we have mistakenly left to the 'experts'.

Biologists now recognize that life is characterized, at all levels, by web-like networks of organization. An organism cannot exist in a vacuum, but depends upon its environment. Any living being is, essentially, the organism plus the environment which sustains it. Stewart Brand is promoting the idea of 'deextinction', taking the genetic material from long-dead species like the woolly mammoth – as well as the millions of species we are currently driving out of existence – and using it to recreate these organisms in the laboratory. But, unless we also rebuild the ecosystems that mesh with these organisms, this seems little more than an eerie museum exercise. The better plan is to focus on conserving the species we have now.

Transforming the Food System

Just as we must build a decentralized system for producing energy from renewable sources that will make local communities more self-sufficient and less wasteful, we should establish a new global model for agriculture which is locally based, distributed, cooperative, and healthier for people and the planet.

While farmers' markets and community supported agriculture programmes take root and flourish, urban gardens could, theoretically, be established in every city, using vacant lots, suitable rooftops, parks and greenways. I have interviewed experts who believe that 80 per cent of the food needed by New York City could be grown on the rooftops using aquaponic methods.

Multinational corporations like Monsanto, as well as 'philanthro-capitalist' organizations like the Gates Foundation, promote the rapid scaling up of the Green Revolution. They believe the answer to feeding the world's still-growing global populace is to amp up industrial agriculture while we double down our bets on still-experimental technologies like GE. What we can do, instead, is make an intentional shift to local, ecological farming, using organic, no-till and permaculture techniques, as appropriate. A drastic curtailing of meat eating will reduce emissions, and return grazing lands to forests. A global campaign could educate and inspire people to change their behaviour for future generations.

We can change our approach to agriculture by subsidizing farmers to embrace methods such as permaculture; we can retrain the public to become part-time gardeners, to see themselves as stewards of their local bioregions. While it may sound difficult to bring about an evolution of cultural values, as well as a paradigm shift in how society operates, the result would be incredibly beneficial for humanity, on all levels.

6

Industry

What we now call 'poverty' is essentially a result of modern industrial civilization and colonialism. Before the eighteenth and nineteenth centuries, most indigenous and traditional societies knew how to operate within the limits imposed by their local environment. Then capitalism, with its developing technology, shattered the integrity of intact cultures, forcing them to grow beyond their means, to become dependent on foreign powers and industries. Take Hawaii, for instance: it was once a fertile, self-sufficient paradise. Now Hawaii imports something like 90 per cent of its food and exports nearly all of its waste. The same process has taken place all over the planet. We must reverse it.

In our current economic system, profit is generated by ever-increasing commercial activity. Because it is based on debt and inherently unstable, our economic system must grow constantly just to maintain itself. Our industrial system has a parasitic relationship with the Earth's natural systems. In essence, we generate wealth by subtracting from the Earth's natural capital.

Over the last decades, vast areas of the developing world, such as China and India, have adopted the Western model of industrial growth. These huge societies are beginning to come up against hard limits on their natural resources, much like the rest of the world. The challenge for us – the privileged elite in the highly industrialized societies, who have the leisure time to think about this stuff – is to develop a new model of industrial production, based on regenerative principles, then distribute it globally.

Corporations

For a corporation to survive, it must keep selling more and more goods and services, increasing its market share and profit margins. Therefore, its products – from electronic goods to sneakers to IKEA furniture – must be disposable and replaceable. They must be designed to last just long enough so that the consumer will be willing to replace them with the next new models, without getting so annoyed that they change brands. The system forces excessive over-production – and not just for corporations. For individual entrepreneurs, creative artists or designers to survive in this system, we must constantly produce new things – books, jewellery, toys, snazzy clothes, DVDs – that only add to the burden under which the Earth is already groaning.

We find ourselves in a bind created by our economic system. While some corporations actively promote initiatives aimed at sustainability and social responsibility, these efforts inevitability fall short of what is actually needed for real resilience. Publicly traded corporations, even the ones with good intentions, are programmed to generate waste and externalize environmental costs.

The rapid development of a world-encompassing 'technosphere' appears to have been a natural extension of the potential of our species – a necessary stage in our evolution. In fact, most people believe that our industrial system has provided extraordinary benefits, improvements in health and lifestyle, for billions of people. When it works properly, the technosphere functions like a hyper-organic extension of our bodies. What do I mean by this? Let's take an example.

When I visit my local cafe in the East Village, I find myself at the end point of vast, intermeshed systems of agriculture, manufacturing and transport; global networks of trade routes, supply lines, communications and financial data. The beans used to make my coffee come from Sumatra, Guatemala or Brazil. The cup might have been made in China. The oil used to transport the beans may have come from Russia or Alaska. In other words, the entire world is involved in the seemingly ordinary act of buying a morning coffee – an act we usually perform unthinkingly.

The invisibility of these vast networks that produce the objects of our daily lives is akin to the invisible cellular mechanisms that operate all of the time within our bodies, that maintain us in good working order. We don't have to meditate on our follicles for our hair to grow, or concentrate on our hearts in order to keep them beating. We are continuously sustained in our existences by vast realms of the invisible and the unseen, by networks of coordination all around us and by cellular processes within, although we generally only consciously recognize our dependence on these processes when they break down.

If it is true that we are on the cusp of realizing ourselves as a planetary super-organism, continuously reshaping the Earth, according to our collective will and intention, then we must also think of corporations in a different way – as the most powerful creations we have woven out of our social technologies.

A corporation is constructed of legal code, financial data, branding insignia, mission and vision statements. In the abstract, a corporation is a streamlined, hyper-efficient engine for taking ideas and transforming them into material form, then distributing those tools, products and services across the world, at high speed. The world-spanning successes of companies like Apple, Nike, IKEA and Samsung are a testament to that power.

Corporations can be seen as the nascent organs in the collective body of humanity. An energy company functions like the circulatory system, spreading blood – fuel, electrical power – through the body. A sanitation company is like the liver or kidney. A media company is like the organs of perception which take in sense data, decode it and transmit it to the brain, so it can make decisions.

Corporations are artificial life forms that human beings have created and programmed, giving them sets of rules they must follow. We have built these artificial life forms to compete in a game that we also concocted, called the stock market. Like the sorcerer's apprentice in *Fantasia*, whose misuse of a spell creates a situation where he has to fight off brooms multiplying to infinity, we have lost control over our creations.

The problem is that we made mistakes, errors of design, in the way we defined the rules of our game. We gave the corporations one prime directive: to increase shareholder value, to maximize profit, which they will try to accomplish, no matter what. In this sense, you can't totally blame a company like British Petroleum for the Gulf of Mexico oil spill (although we can still hold its managers culpable), or Occidental for the atrocities it has committed in the Ecuadorean Amazon, or Dupont for the Bhopal disaster, or Apple for using conflict minerals that unleashed African genocide, or H&M for its exploitation of adolescent girls and young women in Asian sweatshops.

When you give the corporation the single directive to maximize profit, then that is what it will seek to do, even if it means undermining ecological restrictions, condemning workers to slave conditions, or buying armies of lobbyists to corrupt the legislative process to its advantage. We programmed its underlying system, its game machinery, so that it must seek to dominate and grow. This often requires cutthroat tactics. It leads naturally to monopolization, cronyism and patterns of behaviour that make sense for a corporation's balance sheet but are destructive, sociopathic, for society as a whole. Glaring examples include the ways that tobacco companies obscured the evidence on lung cancer, or how energy companies have used massive campaigns of disinformation to hide the link between climate change and CO_2, which they may have known about for a number of decades. Now, for the sake of our survival, we must change the underlying rules of the game.

If we conceive of humanity as a planetary super-organism, then we must consider how the organs of a body work with maximum efficiency to support the health of the whole. If corporations are the organs of the super-organism, then they should be reinvented as transparent orchestrations, responding to ecological necessity as well as human desire. When I project into the future, I tend to think we will need to abandon the distinctions between a public and private sector, eventually. There is no private interest within an organism: it must function efficiently, according to a unified intention. As a super-organism, we must do the same.

It is possible that the ongoing movement towards collaborative production that is open-source and peer-to-peer could provide the new social model for our future. As Paul Mason writes in *Postcapitalism*, we are experiencing an increasing tension between 'non-market forms of production' and traditional capitalism. 'Technologically, we are headed for zero-price goods, unmeasurable work, an exponential takeoff in productivity and the extensive automation of processes. Socially, we are trapped in a world of monopolies, inefficiency, the ruins of a finance-dominated free market and a proliferation of "bullshit jobs".' The potential, Mason believes, is for 'the abolition of the market and its replacement by postcapitalism'. If this is going to happen without massive dislocation and mass violence, it requires a designed transition.

People will always require goods and services, but these could be provided for them by a new social infrastructure, based on peer-to-peer systems for distributed manufacturing and resource sharing. Through an intentional redesign of our financial system, corporations could 'evolve' into self-governing systems based on open cooperation and resource sharing, designed to bring universal abundance. They would maximize our potential as a species, while minimizing waste and internalizing externalities, such as CO_2 emissions.

Innovation or Transformation?

In *The Big Pivot: Radically Practical Strategies for a Hotter, Scarcer, and More Open World*, Andrew Winston looks at climate change and resource depletion as opportunities for businesses to evolve their practices without sacrificing their bottom line. Optimistically quoting billionaire entrepreneur Richard Branson, who has described climate change as 'one of the greatest wealth-generating opportunities of our generation', Winston sees the ecological limits as new stimuli that will 'propel innovation, new thinking, and new business models, which make a lot of money for the fast movers'. This is true, up to a point.

Winston outlines a number of strategies that will enable companies to navigate in a rapidly warming and ecologically deteriorating world. These include 'fight short-termism', 'set science-based goals' and 'inspire customers to use less'. He reviews the ecological data honestly, and advises companies to build in resilience, redundancy and other safeguards against increasing instability, making it clear that the landscape for industry will be radically transformed in the coming decades: 'Most companies and industrial sectors will change profoundly, or they will disappear. Without a "clean-coal" technological miracle, for example, the coal sector will be gone.'

The Great Pivot seeks to assure corporations that they can reinvent themselves for increasing profitability, even in a time of tumultuous transformation. 'Revamping our built environment, our transportation infrastructure, and our energy systems – as well as reworking consumption and what defines a good quality of life – will be multi-trillion-dollar endeavours with huge pots of gold for those who find the greenest ways to do it.'

Some corporations, like Unilever, portray themselves as leaders in this new transitional space. They study patterns of consumer behaviour, and build models on how these habits can be changed. However, the reality is that we require more than innovation in how businesses function. Fundamentally to transform the corporate system, mass consumerism and planned obsolescence must be replaced by different models. Eventually, we can generate abundance for all through regenerative technologies and cradle-to-cradle industries. This metamorphosis requires a paradigm shift in how value is exchanged, not just in how business operates.

The UN recently defined a new set of Sustainable Development Goals. Many of these goals are laudable – but there is a problem. One of the goals is 'sustained, inclusive and sustainable economic growth, full and productive employment, and decent work for all', hopefully resulting in a 7 per cent annual growth in the economies of the developing world. Unfortunately, considering our maxed-out resources and accelerating climate catastrophe, this seems impossible and even suicidal.

When I rack my brain for solutions to our current crisis, I keep returning to the belief that we must give up on the current model of sustainable development, based on ever-increasing GDP. At the same time, we can't give up the project of enhancing the lives of people in poor countries and regions. Our goal should be to establish human beings in healthy regional communities that will be as self-replenishing, resilient and autonomous as possible. Rather than seeking to fix a broken system, we need to design the transition to a post-capitalist society based on open-source, peer-to-peer collaboration, where everyone receives a basic income and shares scarce resources intelligently.

Development, by its nature, requires ever more inputs of energy and resources. Degrowth – a social and economic movement, launched in France – proposes that we reduce the scale of our activity in accordance with the limits of the planet. We would focus innovation on building systems that allow us 'to live convivially and frugally'. But how can we implement the model of degrowth? How do we reach a form of post-capitalism that completely contradicts the current political-economic system?

The Story of Stuff

In *Capitalism and the Destruction of Life on Earth*, originally published on Alternet, the left-wing critic Roger Smith argues persuasively that our capitalist industrial system is in a doom-spiral:

> The engine that has powered three centuries of accelerating economic development revolutionizing technology, science, culture and human life itself is today a roaring, out-of-control locomotive mowing down continents of forests, sweeping oceans of life, clawing out mountains of minerals, drilling, pumping out lakes of fuels, devouring the planet's last accessible resources to turn them all into 'product' while destroying fragile global ecologies built up over eons.

Smith sees our technical infrastructure as directly responsible for the crisis we have unleashed. It is hard to argue with him.

This much seems obvious: we are mortgaging our future to maintain an unsustainable, suicidal system, hyper-focused on maximizing short-term gains for shareholders. Even the best companies are guilty. Take IKEA, for instance. The Swedish company recently earmarked one billion dollars for climate change initiatives, which seems to suggest that they care. But IKEA's practices are, in themselves, environmentally destructive, and this massive bequest is also PR for them.

IKEA is the third-largest consumer of wood in the world, logging out forests from East Europe and Siberia. IKEA clear-cuts 1,400 acres per year of 200- to 600-year-old forest near the Finnish border, despite the protests of conservancy groups. IKEA succeeds by using the cheapest means of mass production, building disposable furniture out of particle-board, rather than durable, long-lasting items. Its business model – like that of almost every major corporation – is based on the ideal of producing disposable goods that must be frequently replaced. Planned obsolescence and extreme waste is built into the logic of their system.

As you may already know, the mining of rare materials for our smart phones and other disposable electronic goods has caused ecological and social disaster in West Africa, in the Congo and neighbouring countries. An estimated three million have died in wars and genocides fought over control of 'conflict minerals', to satiate the world's lust for these seductive gadgets. When Western colonialists discovered sugar, the entire European continent became addicted to the stuff. They created the slave trade to make sure they had a steady supply of it. Today, we are equally addicted to our electronic gadgets, and equally unconscious about the suffering we cause by our addictions. In some ways, nothing has changed.

The disposal of electronic goods is another environmental nightmare. Much of our trash ends up in dumps in the developed world, where it disintegrates, leaching toxins into the soil. We can't continue these practices. Our culture reveres Steve Jobs, posthumously, as a saint of technology, a kind of digital messiah. He was a brilliant man, but he was not a great humanitarian. He knew what was happening in West Africa – as well as in Asian factories with terrible conditions, where teenage labourers often committed suicide – but he didn't make it his mission to stop it. He allowed this destruction and misery to continue, because it fed Apple's profits.

Our industries currently threaten most forms of life on Earth. 'At present, global manufacturing and production processes consume more than 220 billion tons of resources annually, all taken from the Earth's "natural capital" – oceans, forests, plants, plains, soils, mines, and all other aspects of biodiversity,' note the editors of *Alternatives to Economic Globalization*, put together by Jerry Mander. Our current form of accounting considers depletion of natural resources '*beneficial* to gross national product (GNP) and gross domestic product (GDP) because they are indicators of increased economic activity. In fact, they ought to be considered negative factors, because they decrease the long-term ability of societies to sustain themselves.' The ecological damage, depletion of resources and toxic pollution generated by companies require massive clean-ups or remediation projects. Taxpayers rather than corporations generally end up paying the bills, as the health of the planet deteriorates.

The alternative is to make planned obsolescence obsolete. All goods should be made as durable, as long lasting, as possible. They should be designed so they can be easily repaired, not thrown out. Electronic devices should be made from components that can be replaced when necessary, when an upgrade comes along. All products should also be made in such a way that they don't contaminate the Earth. After reducing toxic emissions to a minimum, we will seek to eliminate them entirely. Companies can be made responsible for their products over their entire life cycle and be legally bound to recycle and reuse all of their elements.

What Do We Do?

An economy is, fundamentally, a way of shaping matter, energy and time, according to human intention. If we are going to survive our current predicament, we must redirect our intention, and reshape our financial system to move in a new direction. We need to stop overuse of natural resources, limit pollution, enforce an ethos of conservation and sequester carbon, and we need to do it now, before the situation becomes any more dire or irrevocable. As Roger Smith notes, we confront a stark choice between 'emergency contraction' and 'ecological collapse'. This means quickly cutting back on manufacturing, distribution, unnecessary consumption, pointless trends in fashion and gadgetry. We should comprehensively refocus our industrial powers, only supporting innovation that helps to salvage, reclaim, restore, replenish, regenerate, degrow and downshift.

The billionaire entrepreneur Manoj Bhargava, who invented the 5-Hour Energy drink, is one of many innovators currently pointing the way forward. Taking the profits from his company, Bhargava built a research centre near Detroit, designing new sustainable products to address current world problems. These products that could be distributed across the developing world include a stationary bicycle that generates energy – one hour of pedalling produces enough energy to power a house for 24 hours. Bhargava has also constructed a small-scale desalination machine, the Rain Maker, which can be placed next to wastewater treatment facilities. The Rain Maker might provide a partial solution to mega-droughts in California, Iran and India. 'The purpose of business, in the end, is to serve society,' he has said. 'I want to redistribute wealth in an intelligent way.'

We need more technocrats like Bhargava who are willing to use their capital to build sustainable solutions in all areas. At the same time, relying on wealthy entrepreneurs or 'philanthro-capitalists' is not a systemic or sustainable solution. One alternative model was explored by a group of young tech developers during COP-21 in Paris. 'Late summer 2015, we have joined forces in a stunning French castle to prototype the fossil free, zero-waste society. Our ultimate goal was to overcome the destructive consumer culture and make open-source, sustainable products the new normal.'

A collaboration between the OuiShare network based in Paris and OpenState from Berlin, they called it 'Eco-Hacking the Future'. Over five weeks, they developed 12 separate projects: new modular systems to provide solar power to remote events, zero-waste kitchens and easy-to-build wind turbines. Among their projects was 'snap-fit kits for urban agriculture'. The developers envision 'a city where grey walls, rooftops and balconies are transformed into living ecosystems'. Their kits include 'a chicken coop, vermicomposter, three plant beds, and two sorts of beehives'.

The great opportunity is to repurpose corporations, give them new goals, and use the incredible expertise and engineering genius they have amassed to address the social and ecological crises that may soon overwhelm us. One way to do this is to create innovations in corporate structures. The B Corp is a triple-bottom-line company that seeks to benefit people and planet while generating profit. Another new model is the flexible-purpose corporation, which is driven by its mission and doesn't need to generate profit at all. That mission could be to find, develop and implement solutions that can be scaled rapidly as we confront the ecological emergency.

The possibility of a society where technology would free humanity to cultivate its creative powers and individuality was foreseen by visionaries like Oscar Wilde and Buckminster Fuller. The stunning prospect is that, even as we confront the potential for our own extinction, we also have the prospect of engineering a rapid transition to a planetary civilization able to create universal abundance for all. In *The Zero-Margin Cost Society*, Jeremy Rifkin explores how the Internet has reduced the actual cost of reproducing non-material goods such as books, music, films and online education to zero. The same metamorphosis could take place with material goods and also energy. Renewable power could be reliably transmitted and stored through an Internet of Energy. Objects could be produced locally, via 3D printers, enabled by distributed manufacturing. At the same time, all industrial production could transition to a closed-loop model, where inputs lead to non-toxic outputs and all waste is recycled, following nature's principles.

In *Cradle to Cradle*, William McDonough and Michael Braungart, an environmental designer and a chemist, explore the necessary steps we would need to take to redirect our industrial system. The authors 'see a world of abundance, not limits'. They ask, 'What if humans design products and systems that celebrate an abundance of human creativity, culture, and productivity? That are so intelligent and safe that our species leaves an ecological footprint to delight in, not lament?'

As simple examples, McDonough and Braungart imagine producing compostable ice-cream wrappers, with seeds embedded in them, so they can be planted in the ground and produce a vegetable garden; vehicles might be constructed from hemp, or other materials that decompose naturally. They imagine all power provided by renewable sources, creating a virtuous circle where both people and nature would be able to thrive.

If we were to establish a worldwide industrial system that harmonized with nature, enhancing biodiversity and resilience, the super-organism of humanity would become a kind of 'supernature'. We should make it our mission to create a hyper-complex planetary civilization perfectly integrated with the Earth's ecology. If this seems impossible to achieve, perhaps that is because we are only now turning our focus in this direction. Many things that once seemed impossible have been accomplished by human willpower and imagination.

Inventing the Future

The prospect that we redesign all of our industrial systems following principles of biomimicry, imitating nature's zero-waste manufacturing, is a new idea – and a great challenge for our immediate future. Biomimicry seeks to learn from the methods that nature uses to overcome challenges, and replicate its systems and principles, in ways that support healthy ecosystems. For example, while the silk that spiders make is stronger than steel, it is manufactured in a 'biofactory' without the need for smelting or gigantic vats of boiling sulphuric acid.

According to Janine Benyus, author and founder of the Biomimicry Institute, nature can be copied, by human designers, on the level of form and function, as well as on the level of process. 'The truth is, natural organisms have managed to do everything we want to do without guzzling fossil fuels, polluting the planet or mortgaging the future,' Benyus writes.

Velcro, for instance, copies the burrs of the burdock plant, which sticks to fabric. A new moisture-catching materia used in dry regions of Africa to trap early morning fog, took its design from the shell of the local beetle, containing hydrophilic bumps and furrows that concentrate moisture from the air. In every area of industry, we can learn from nature's four billion years of research and development.

The mycologist Paul Stamets has pioneered the use of mushrooms for bioremediation, repairing the damage and pollution from industrial processes. Stamets calls mycelia 'the Earth's natural internet', because of its ability to exchange information over long distances. He believes that vast underground fungal networks function like the liver in the human body, recognizing toxins and learning, through trial and error, how to neutralize them, break them down and ultimately convert them to food. Stamets has demonstrated the ability of mycelium to break down contamination from petroleum, pesticides, alkaloids and polychlorinated biphenyls.

'Tomorrow's industry will eat, digest, and secrete the things we need not just in imitation of living beings, but through the actual cells of living beings,' write Alex Steffen and Jeremy Falludi in *Worldchanging: A User's Guide for the 21st Century*. 'With the help of biotechnology, we can create pools of hacked bacteria that spit out hydrogen, tanks of tweaked fungus that convert garbage into methane, and vats of tame microbes that allow us to design machines and structures with natural materials that resemble shells and spider silk.'

There is potential as well as peril in biotechnology's rapid advances. We must base the future development of such technology on a holistic, comprehensive approach, taking a long view of our relationship to the Earth. Learning from past mistakes, we must factor in the possibility of unforeseen impacts on the planet's ecology, which can degrade human as well as animal health. We need to become not just smarter, but wiser.

Eco-cities

As an urban bohemian who grew up in New York, I love my city's rich cultural history and the myriad worlds that overlap each other here. When I walk around Manhattan these days, however, I have the eerie sensation I am wandering through a gigantic sand mandala – like those intricate patterns laid out by Tibetan monks which get wiped away once the ceremony ends.

For Buddhists, life is an ongoing teaching on impermanence. The ecological crisis is going to emphasize that principle until it becomes a collective realization. Our current civilization is not built to last. The more we realize this now, the faster we can begin to turn our attention to reinventing the systems, technical and social, upon which we depend.

We don't know how long we have until sea levels rise to inundate many coastal cities. It could be as soon as a few decades. As we lose our urban centres, we will construct new 'eco-cities', to use the term of architect Richard Register. The cities of the future will have to be conceived as 'scaffoldings for living systems', according to ecological designer John Todd. Eco-cities will function as biodigestors and composters, places of self-sufficiency and abundance, where food is grown, energy is produced and waste is recycled on-site. Like coral reefs or beehives, the cities of the future should enhance the health, beauty and biodiversity of the local ecosystem. They should be designed for multi-generational communities, for bicycles and walking, for creative expression and participatory democracy.

We will face an ever-growing global refugee crisis in the next decades. We need to apply the hyper-efficiency of capitalist manufacturing and distribution – mastered by companies like IKEA, Walmart and Amazon – to an ecologically regenerative, systemic approach. We have the capacity to build durable, modular, carbon-negative housing units that can be shipped across the world, or potentially manufactured in each locality using 3D printers. In these instant settlements, people will need to grow their own food and produce energy on-site. A number of initiatives are already testing prototypes for modular houses that can be quickly assembled and easily shipped. One such project is ReGen Villages, pioneered by James Ehrlich, an engineer at Stanford.

ReGen Villages are self-sufficient communities. The houses come with renewable energy systems, battery storage units, composting toilets, rainwater catchments and insulation built into them. Food can be grown using aquaponic methods that preserve up to 85 per cent of water in a closed-loop system where 'ammonia created from fish waste is converted from nitrites to nitrates through bacterial interaction'. Such ready-made, self-sufficient towns could be mass-produced and shipped across the developing world, or produced on-site via distributed manufacturing. They could be supplied to refugees as populations find themselves forced to settle further inland.

Water and Waste

Much of the world is already suffering from a crisis of fresh water. Drought will become far more prevalent, and dangerous, in the next decades, as mountaintop glaciers cease to provide reliable sources of water for billions of people. Water use has tripled in the last half-century, and aquifers are running dry. To meet this crisis, we will require globally orchestrated efforts in water management plus a massive increase in desalination.

Desalination plants are proliferating across the world, with more than 15,000 of them now operational. However, as of yet, this technology is still flawed. Even Peter Diamandis and Steven Kotler, the super-optimistic authors of *Abundance*, admit that current desalination technology has fundamental drawbacks. The two main techniques – thermal desalination and reverse osmosis – require excessive energy and create toxic waste.

Thermal desalination boils water, and then condenses the vapour. In reverse osmosis, water passes through permeable membranes. 'Neither is the solution we need', note the authors.

> Thermal desalination consumes too much energy for large-scale deployment (about 80 megawatt hours per megalitre) and the brine by-product fouls aquifers and is devastating to aquatic populations. Reverse osmosis, on the other hand, uses comparatively less energy, but toxins such as boron and arsenic can still sneak through, and membranes clog frequently, reducing the lifetime of the filter.

Diamandis and Kotler look towards future developments of nano-technology – such as devices that will use nanoparticles to filter out toxic materials in water and make the desalination process less destructive.

As a new development in the conservation of water, Diamandis and Kotler point to a new computer-assisted irrigation system installed in Spain, 'designed to save farmers 20 percent of the nine hundred *billion* gallons of water they annually use'. The world is no longer unexplored territory; we now have the ability to follow the flows of raw materials and energy on a global scale.

Organic waste has a bright future. We have the capacity to develop no-waste processes based on nature's template. Regenerative technologies that can be industrially scaled include the conversion of organic waste into biogas, which can be used for energy. This conversion process happens through anaerobic digestion, in which microorganisms break down biodegradable material in the absence of oxygen.

Technologies based on anaerobic digestion convert manure, municipal wastewater solids, fats, oils and grease and so on into energy, burnt to generate electricity and heat, as well as natural gas and fuels for cars, trucks and planes. The residue includes nutrients that can be used for agriculture, as fertilizer. Sub-tropical countries – like Jamaica, and Haiti, where fast-growing vegetation produces large amounts of bio-mass – could generate their transportation fuels from wasted organic materials, without producing excess CO_2.

Industrial Design and Aesthetics

The noble mission of design, now and in the future, will be to package the rapid transition we need, at all levels. We must collectively conceive of this social and technological transformation as a seductive, hip, glamorous adventure for us as individuals and for human society as a whole. We can use our industrial systems to produce circulating, self-regenerating systems for transportation, energy, water and nutriments, for clothing bodies and building homes, for converting our waste back into energy and food. In order for humanity to graduate from parasitic pariah to planetary partner, we must not only learn to consume better, but consume far less.

To make matters more difficult, we will have to undertake this transition at a time when we face intensifying stresses from natural disasters and depleted resources, along with increasingly desperate refugee populations. We still find ourselves hampered by the moral blindness and self-serving cowardice of political leaders, finance capitalists, fundamentalist despots and other power brokers. We also have to confront our own expectations of what the future is meant to bring us, and accept that we are in a new situation. This requires a willingness to surrender some of our cherished hopes and dreams.

Personally, I don't think we can make effective changes until we understand how 'subjectivity' – the inner domain of human conscious-ness – is not something freely determined. Consciousness, identity, subjectivity are mass-produced by the corporate-industrial mega-machine. Those who are designers and media-makers must be willing to intercede in this process and produce new 'subjectivities', shaping new patterns of behaviour and new values for the multitudes. Design and aesthetics will be crucial tools for accomplishing this.

Aesthetics and ethics have a functional relationship which influences consumer choice and impacts on the direction of industrial manufacturing. Design creates objects of desire. Advertising assimilates humanity's collective yearnings for status, sex and success, and points them towards particular products and industries. The only way I can envision the type of systemic change of values, beliefs and habits that we need in a short timeframe is through the creation of a global marketing campaign coupled with, as Buckminster Fuller foresaw, a 'design revolution'. A massive media blitz can give people a new vision of the good, the true and the beautiful. We have to make conservation, degrowth, post-capitalism, self-sufficiency, sharing resources, food growing, generosity and the virtue of necessity glamorous and fun.

We are faced with a difficult, intricate, seemingly close-to-impossible mission. So let's accept it as our initiation, and even enjoy it in that sense. For a few decades, until we have converted to a regenerative society running on renewable fuels and closed-loop industries, people will have to find joy in self-sacrifice and contentment in having less. We must be willing to undertake difficult tasks for the benefit of the collective. To accomplish this transition, we need to overcome social inertia, break apart stagnant thought structures, and inspire the masses with new desires, values, habits and behaviours.

Summing Up

We find ourselves in a cliff-hanger. As the methane erupts and sea levels rise, a mass die-off could happen soon. On the other hand, if we change direction rapidly, the human family can reach a state of shared abundance. The goal is to build, distribute, scale exponentially and share new social and industrial technologies supporting resilience and local autonomy. Within a century, we could have rebuilt eco-cities and redesigned industries for future generations to live in harmony and in holistic communion with the planet.

I realize that many thinkers have argued passionately that our technological society has reached its apex – that it must give way to a new, more humane form of civilization that is, once again, smaller scale. 'The high-entropy journey humanity has undertaken under the illusion of growth and progress does not have a future,' writes Vandana Shiva, an activist who crusades against GMOs and for the rights of farmers in India. 'We will have to change the road we are on, and we will have to change our goals. The goals cannot be set by reductionist science, industrial technologies and neoliberal economies. The goals cannot be narrowly defined as economic growth or consumerism. The goals have to be the preservation of the earth, her diverse species, and future generations.'

Wendell Berry, like many deep and dark ecologists, believes that technologists are feeding a cultural delusion when they argue that ever-more advanced technology can save us from the ecological crisis that technology has unleashed:

> There is now a growing perception, and not just among a few experts, that we are entering a time of inescapable limits. We are not likely to be granted another world to plunder in compensation for our pillage of this one. Nor are we likely to believe much longer in our ability to outsmart, by means of science and technology, our economic stupidity. The hope that we can cure the ills of industrialism by the homeopathy of more technology seems at last to be losing status. We are, in short, coming under pressure to understand ourselves as limited creatures in a limited world.

I understand Shiva's pessimism, and I get why Berry dismisses our naive faith in futurist technologies, noting 'the work now most needing to be done – that of neighbourliness and care-taking – cannot be done by remote control with the greatest power on the largest scale'. And yet, at the same time, I think the only way we can deal with the mass scale of the problems industrial civilization has created is to redirect and repurpose the infrastructure of manufacturing and industry which now spans the world, as well as make use of the power of media, design and social technology to transform ourselves as a species.

In the same way that corporations and media apply many psychological techniques to create 'false needs' in the population, we can use the media and elements of the corporate system to create and then spread replicable models of community, alternative economic systems and local forms of participatory democracy. Factories can mass-produce and distribute regenerative technologies and techniques in agriculture, energy production and so on. My vision is that we resolve the antithesis between indigenous cultures that were small scale and Earth-honouring and postmodern civilization, defined by corporate globalization, in a new creative synthesis, where traditional values and holistic principles are mass-distributed using the efficient supply chains of global capitalism.

We can apply our technology to support ecologically regenerative practices on all levels and in all areas. For example, if we improve desalinization technology, and have these plants powered by solar, we can create enough fresh water for everyone on Earth. We can do this, even as the mountaintop glaciers disappear and as sea levels rise to make a great deal of ground water undrinkable.

Our mission is to engineer a transition to a post-capitalist society in which everyone on Earth receives a basic subsidy. This requires re-designing our factories so that the by-products of manufacturing are no longer toxic but feed back positively into the ecosystems, just as all the products of nature do. We can rebuild coastal cities as inland 'eco-cities', designed to be models of self-sufficiency. We can relocate and resettle large refugee populations in self-sufficient communities where they produce their own food and energy. The Internet and mass media become tools to train the global population in direct democracy, permaculture and bioremediation, so we become stewards of our local ecology.

If we want to maximize our chances for near-term survival, we must undertake a systemic transition towards renewable power distributed through a globally decentralized grid. We also must shift our agriculture system away from industrial farming that depletes soil and is dependent on fossil fuels. We must relocalize a great deal of our food production, and resettle some urbanites in rural areas, retraining them to be farmers – small-scale farming can be improved by digital technology which helps organize supply chains and distribution systems.

No matter what we do, we will confront increasingly severe ecological crises over the rest of this century. Realizing that our world is becoming more precarious, we can transition to a system that enhances local autonomy, resilience and self-sufficiency. This will be the best way to protect our human family from intensifying crises.

At the same time, we need to develop a healthy scepticism and probably reject many types of futuristic technologies that could cause more damage to our already damaged world, such as nuclear energy and genetic engineering. I personally think we must reject the idea of geo-engineering as a quick fix that will allow us to continue on our current path. The most well-known geo-engineering proposal is that we spray sulphur particles into the outer atmosphere to reflect the sun's rays back into space, artificially cooling the planet. This could wreak further havoc on the climate and cause negative consequences for human health. It will also have to be maintained perpetually, as temperatures would skyrocket again as soon as we stopped emitting sulphur. It is not a good plan.

I can't pretend the challenges we face are anything less than very intense. We may see the development of even greater forms of social injustice and wealth inequality, as automation eliminates millions of jobs while droughts and famines become endemic. Instead of this, we have the opportunity to take a different direction. We can establish a regenerative society that produces authentic security and is truly utopian, compared to what we have now. Increasingly, many thinkers see our potential to establish a new planetary culture based on ethically and ecologically viable principles, combining elements of capitalism, socialism and anarchism in a new political-economic operating system. This potential remains latent until we realize it.

Part Four

God, Love and Revolution

7

Mythology

One of my personal beliefs is that the kind of transition that may save us is only possible if it is accompanied by a transformation of planetary consciousness – a shift in worldviews. The secular materialism that pervades postmodern society is, in the end, a form of nihilism. People are told to believe that their lives are accidental, that consciousness is a peculiar epiphenomenon and that the universe is meaningless. In many sectors of our culture, to question that viewpoint is to open yourself to ridicule.

I agree with Albert Camus that, in the end, only two worlds can exist for the human mind. We must choose between the world of rebellion and the world of the sacred. I know it seems unlikely, but I think our civilization may be approaching a turning point – a polar reversal – where we break free of the consciousness of rebellion and return to the sacred. This shift is indicated by many long-term trends – some continuing for more than a half-century – that include the integration of Eastern mysticism and indigenous shamanic practices into our technological society.

If we are going to find the will, courage and tenacity to confront this oncoming catastrophe, we need to reconnect with a sacred, transcendent dimension. I believe we can build a bridge between the mainstream religions – Christianity, Islam and Judaism – with their billions of devotees and the cutting-edge ideas of contemporary explorers who use psychedelics, yoga, meditation, seeking heightened awareness. Ultimately, as the Dalai Lama has said, everybody wants a better life. If they are shown a way to get there, they will take it.

I find many people I know are living on the razor-edge of nihilism right now, skating the edge of the void. In my own life, I have lived through the eruption and the projection of my own shadow material, particularly around sexuality – and I see many people undergoing their own versions of this, in different areas of their lives. I can't help but see this as a perfectly appropriate and even necessary part of a process that could lead to our apotheosis as a species (the birth of the *Übermensch*, who, according to Nietzsche, represents the fusion of 'the mind of Caesar' with 'the soul of Christ') or our collective dissolution. It is exciting that this process seems to be happening within our current lifespans.

We lack a moral centre in our society as we rapidly plunge towards the abyss. It is extraordinary – in itself, miraculous – that the new Pope, Pope Francis, has shown up as one of the only people in our entire planetary culture able to speak directly to the needs of our moment – he calls for an 'ecological conversion', for shared sacrifice on the part of the wealthy elite, a new mode of empathic and compassionate action for us all. In the encyclical, *On Care for Our Common Home*, Francis writes:

> All-powerful God, you are present in the whole universe and in the smallest of your creatures. You embrace with your tenderness all that exists. Pour out upon us the power of your love, that we may protect life and beauty. Fill us with peace, that we may live as brothers and sisters, harming no one. O God of the poor, help us to rescue the abandoned and forgotten of this earth, so precious in your eyes. Bring healing to our lives, that we may protect the world and not prey on it, that we may sow beauty, not pollution and destruction.

Pope Francis could rehabilitate the Catholic tradition, which seemed utterly hopeless – corrupt and antiquated – and turn it into a progressive force for good. In fact, we are going to need a number of miraculous conversions and reversals such as this one if we are going to survive as a species, and learn to flourish together with nature in the short time before it is too late to do anything but undergo a universal, horrific meltdown – a Chod ritual, on a planetary scale.

In some ways, the infusion of Eastern metaphysics into the Western worldview is not helping. It may actually be exacerbating our current crisis of values. The popular Buddhist monk Thich Nhat Hanh has recently prophesied that within a hundred years, the human race may go extinct. His perspective is accurate, according to scientific predictions. With an accelerated warming cycle like the one that caused the Permian Mass Extinction, 250 million years ago, another 95 per cent of species will die out, including *Homo sapiens*. That is why we have to learn to touch eternity with our in breath and out breath. Extinction of species has happened several times. Mass extinction has already happened five times and this one is the sixth. According to the Buddhist tradition there is no birth and no death. After extinction things will reappear in other forms, so you have to breathe very deeply in order to acknowledge the fact that we humans may disappear in just 100 years on earth.

There is a kind of fatalism to much Buddhist thought that doesn't mesh with our Western approach to reality. Personally, I find myself resonating far more deeply with the Pope's call for a new spiritual mission that unifies humanity behind protecting life and nature than I do with Hanh's view, although I recognize the validity of his statement. We possess creative, empathic and imaginative capacities which seem be a divine power and dispensation. Instead of succumbing to Eastern fatalism or Western nihilism, we can choose to make use of our abilities to reverse the current direction of our civilization – to confront the ecological mega-crisis as a true initiation. Realizing what is at stake and what is possible, we can offer ourselves as vessels of this transformation.

Therefore, this current section will address what I think are some of the most powerful mythological structures we encounter as we undergo personal and planetary initiation: the quest for meaningful love and connection, spiritual awakening, and liberation through political revolution. As human beings, we are always forming mythologies. We can't speak, or even think, without building narratives, stories and interpretative frameworks. The problem is that we come to believe in the stories we create, or the ones that have already been created for us. We forget that an original, formless awareness precedes any words or ideas. Meaning is always something we make; it doesn't exist as an objective thing in the world. It is difficult to accept fully that we are responsible for whatever we choose to believe. Most people prefer to become entranced, hypnotized, by cultural concoctions, which easily turn into cults and belief systems.

Earlier, we explored the idea that the ecological crisis is actually a rite of passage for humanity, an initiation that will force us to become more compassionate, adult, decent, responsible, attentive and cooperative as a species – to spread our butterfly wings. Part of this metamorphosis will, I believe, be a mystical as well as a psychic unfolding or realization.

Until very recently, the modern belief was that only human beings possess consciousness. Increasingly, we find an alternative viewpoint emerging, which suggests that consciousness is an immanent property in all living and even non-living things. According to the emergent discipline of epigenetics, consciousness – awareness – is present at the boundary of the cell, which chooses what molecules it will incorporate into its metabolism, and which will pass through it. As its chemical sensors make this decision, the cell can produce one of many thousands of variants of genetic material.

Consciousness attains more complex expression, as life evolves into increasingly sophisticated forms. I think it makes most sense to see human beings – with our more developed sense of self-awareness, our larger brains allowing for more creativity and intelligence – as an expression of the total web of life on Earth, from which we are inseparable. We are less a single species than we are the cutting-edge of this planet's evolutionary process – our bodies and the structure of our brains encompass the entire history of life on this planet.

Humanity is part of nature, and nature wastes nothing as it continuously evolves. We are, most probably, undergoing a process with an underlying purpose and intention, just as foetal development leads to birth. We have woven a technical infrastructure around the planet – a sheath of industrial machinery and toxic waste – like a chrysalis or cocoon. We can use this cocoon of the technosphere to create a collective metamorphosis.

The planetary mega-crisis is both material and spiritual, physical and psychic. In fact, it supersedes those dualisms, revealing them to be false. The New Age spirituality that has permeated our culture since the 1960s is tainted by self-serving values. Its proponents directly or indirectly condone the privileged lifestyle of the developed world, which is responsible for the destruction of the Earth's ecosystems and the immiseration of the developed world. The next unfolding of our understanding will lead beyond it, as we realize our unity with our human family – the crew of Spaceship Earth, our planetary tribe – as well as the greater community of life.

The Elder Brother

In my mind, I often contrast the mythological worldview of the postmodern West – our inveterate faith in hyper-individualism, materialism and technological progress – with that of indigenous cultures I have visited. A few years ago, I helped organize two retreats with the Kogi and Aruak people, indigenous groups who live high up in the remote mountains of the Sierra Nevada de Santa Marta in Colombia. The Kogi and Aruak wear peaked caps and homemade white clothes, which they weave on their looms. With uninterrupted traditions going back thousands of years, they are autonomous, self-reliant and peaceful.

The Kogi call themselves the elder brother, and the modern culture of the West, younger brother. They only became known to the outside world a few decades ago, when they began to issue warnings about the potentially catastrophic consequences of our continued mistreatment of the Earth. The heirs of a pre-Incan civilization, they express a living philosophy that unites the physical and spiritual worlds.

The future leaders and shamans of the Kogi – called Mamas because they identify with the mother, the feminine principle of fertility, soul and soil – are recognized in early childhood. As children, these future teachers spend as long as nine years in dark retreats, never directly exposed to the light of day. They believe that the origin of everything that happens on Earth begins in the spiritual realm, which is darkness. Before they can become Mamas, wisdom keepers, they must know the darkness, the formless, and learn its ways.

Rooted in an ancient oral tradition, the Kogi and Aruak Mamas project great dignity, rarely wasting a word. According to ethnobotanist Wade Davis:

> When the priests, or Mamas, speak, they immediately reveal that their reference points are not of our world. They refer to the Spanish conquest as if it were a recent event. They talk openly of the force of creation, or Se, the spiritual core of all existence, and aluna, human thought, soul, and imagination. What is important, what has ultimate value, is not what is measured and seen but what exists in the many realms of meanings and connections that lie beneath the tangible realities of the world, linking all things.

For the Kogi, all life is sacred, a continuum. Seemingly simple actions have great significance. I found the Mamas to be the most centred people I have ever met. For them, every moment is ceremony; the only time that exists is sacred time.

The Kogi men chew bitter coca leaves out of a gourd, the poporo, which they mix with powdered seashells. They meditatively scrape the stick which they use to extract the white, chalky powder around the outside of the gourd. The gourd has a womb-like shape and represents the universe. The coca leaf, they say, helps them to speak the word of truth.

When the Kogi brought together the men in our group to try it for the first time, we sat together in darkness for over an hour. They asked us to contemplate its effects. Over time, I found that chewing the leaves induced a state of clarity and calm. I felt it connected my mind with my heart – so different from cocaine, which extracts the coca from the leaf and synthetically binds it with sulphuric acid to maximize a reptilian, robotic rush.

Over the course of a number of days, I listened attentively to the teachings of the Mamas, often conveyed through stories and allegories. I wanted to grasp the essence of what they came to teach us.

'Nature is a book that we learn to read by understanding its signs,' Don Leonardo, the Kogi Mama told us. By interpreting the signs, the Kogi communicate directly with the cosmos. He gave us an example of how a Kogi might walk past a dog with a butterfly in its mouth, on a path. From that encounter, he might know that his uncle, in a distant town, had passed away.

Their philosophy resembles Taoism, where the true man, who acts through non-action, maintains the balance between Heaven and Earth. The human being, in the worldview of the Kogi as in the Tao, is not accidental or contingent. We have an essential function in the cosmos; our role is to reflect its equilibrium and harmony, thus maintaining order. We support nature's continuity through our action and intentions – also through our prayers and meditations. Over the course of a week, the Kogi instructed us in ways to make 'payments' to the Earth. We imprinted the energy of our prayers and intentions into cotton balls, which they then buried in hidden, sacred places.

Through our translator, I asked if the Kogi and Aruak believe that the physical world is a direct reflection of our level of consciousness, or spirituality. Don Leonardo smiled. 'That is why we walked 25 hours down from our home in the mountain – to tell you that,' he said.

According to the Kogi, the reason we now experience increasing earthquakes, tsunamis, nuclear meltdowns, floods and other natural and manmade cataclysms across the world is ultimately spiritual. Industrial waste is a result of our low level of spiritual development; pollution reflects our lack of awareness of our interdependence with nature and cosmos. The world is in turmoil because we have failed to maintain a sacred, reciprocal relationship with Mother Earth: we lost our way. The nihilism of our culture reflects this.

The Kogi and Aruak see nature and man as a continuum. They believe our actions, and even our thoughts, influence the invisible spiritual worlds that express themselves in all natural phenomena, through the weave of synchronicity in which we are enmeshed. Our technological society perceives nature and the physical world as resources, devoid of spirit, which we can consume however we want.

Increasingly, the elites in our society drink ayahuasca and explore other aspects of indigenous spiritual traditions. But we have not integrated the humility and reverence for the creative forces of nature that we find in cultures like that of the Kogi. We have not yet understood that life itself is the prayer and the ceremony.

The Spiritual Worlds

Our thoughts, intentions and beliefs are very powerful. Just like indigenous people, we build stories, mythologies, out of our experience of the world. We have no choice but to create myths – it is part of who we are. We do it constantly. But we have a choice in what kinds of stories we create and choose to follow. We can live experiential mythologies that empower us to be great, or we can passively conform to cultural narratives that enforce cynicism, futility and apathy.

Our civilization has a number of myths and stories about the world which many people, unfortunately, believe are true. For instance, many people now believe that life is senseless and empty, that human consciousness is a meaningless blip in an accidental universe, that it doesn't matter whether we continue as a species or destroy ourselves, because the Earth can create a more intelligent species after us. Many people believe we have no power to change our situation, and it is pointless to try. Another idea is that we are incubating the robots who will take over. These myths reinforce the fatalistic view of man and the cosmos that has become prevalent. They provide us with excuses for inaction.

Personally, I believe we live in a multi-dimensional cosmos, inhabited by many levels of consciousness, and various forms of spiritual beings. There may be infinite dimensions, vast spider webs spanning subtle sub-quantum realms of consciousness, which we can discover and explore. In fact, I believe that the exploration of the psyche is part of our human birthright. It is one of the reasons we have been woven into this creation.

According to the mystical philosopher G I Gurdjieff, the universe follows the principle of 'reciprocal maintenance', where all beings consume and also provide sustenance to other beings. Human beings take in food, water and air, as well as the perceptions and sensations registered by our bodies. We transform these forms of energy into thoughts and feelings. Gurdjieff proposes that the subtle energy of our thoughts and emotions are also 'food' for spiritual beings who exist in subtler realms or other dimensions. Prayer and devotion are one kind of sustenance we can offer them. As we evolve in consciousness and sensitivity, the energy we provide also becomes more nourishing to the beings of the spiritual worlds.

As an emergent property of biological evolution, and of matter itself, human consciousness provides the necessary basis – the stable ground – for these spiritual and occult realms to make themselves tangible. We provide the raw material for the beings who are part of the spiritual worlds to learn, grow and evolve. According to Kabbala, our existence is necessary so that God can learn about Himself and give substance to His values. Without human beings, these values and principles remain purely abstract. According to these mystical ideas, our existence is not meaningless. Our work here on Earth is connected to vast realms and myriad dimensions of spirit. As we evolve ourselves, the cosmos evolves.

According to Rudolf Steiner, we inherited a 'cosmos of wisdom', where everything was perfectly formed. Our bodies, for instance, woven together from trillions of microorganisms, are masterpieces of design.

The planets orbit each other in complex geometrical relationships based on the Golden Ratio, also known as Phi. Our role as human beings is to transform the cosmos of wisdom we inherited into a 'cosmos of love' – a process that could take eons.

Just as there is an ecology of life forms on the Earth, there may be a vast ecology of astral and etheric beings who live in parallel universes or different dimensions. I believe we will, eventually, undertake an exploration and study of these myriad worlds-within-worlds. In the future, I believe, we will transition to what José Argüelles called a 'psycho-technical civilization' – a civilization that explores and develops our psychic nature. As part of this shift, we will learn from indigenous and traditional cultures around the Earth and develop a 'spiritual science'. A spiritual science does not contradict material science, but enhances it.

I do not think psychedelic substances are for everybody. I do believe they have an important, even a critical, function. Psychedelics open us to visionary, intuitive forms of perception. They give us access to otherwise invisible worlds and occult realms, and allow us to experience different aspects of time. They remind us that the universe is a dream-emanation of an infinite consciousness – an incredible art piece – of which we are all expressions and aspects. They reveal our separation as a temporary illusion.

We overly emphasize a particular kind of rational and analytical thought, with destructive consequences for our world. At the same time, this is all inevitable as part of our journey. It is one chapter in a greater story. I am not suggesting we reject rational, analytical thought for intuition. We need to find the balance, integrating reason and intuition, the psychic and the physical, masculine and feminine ways of knowing, to reach a new level of coherence, a new understanding of ourselves and our universe. I know this can seem an impossible task. Once we master it, however, it will become our habitual nature, our new baseline state.

In my earlier books, I wrote about DMT, which comes in two forms. One form, nn-DMT, reveals a hyper-dimensional other reality that is beyond the ability of language to describe. The other form is 5-meO-DMT, secreted by the glands of the homely Bufo toad, native to Mexico's Sonoran Desert and the American South-West.

A few years ago, I smoked 5-meO-DMT on a rooftop in the artsy, bohemian Condesa district of Mexico City. I was there to speak at a festival organized by a web magazine, *Pijama Surf.* My Mexican friends insisted I meet a young shaman who had been working with indigenous groups in the Sonoran desert, cultivating and milking the toad. I felt some fear, recalling previous trips. As many times as one takes DMT, I find there is still an innate terror and awe connected to the experience.

This time, as soon as I inhaled the powder, the world around me, and any sense of identity, vanished completely. There was only oceanic bliss, with no name or form or boundary. I can't say I was having this experience; there was no 'I' to have it. Subject and object did not exist. The closest I can come to describing the visual effect would be as a crystalline whiteness, a luminous mandala; delicate, feathery traceries, similar to the patterns found in Islamic art, extending in all directions, infinitely. But that is just an image. During the short trip (it can last from five to twenty minutes), you are not looking at this endless crystalline expanse from outside. You are all of it, dissolved into it.

As I came out of the trance, I recalled the boundaries of my identity. I felt great joy. In this limited Möbius strip of space-time that is life – my life, to be precise – I feel rushed, always fighting a deadline, unable to accomplish more than a fraction of what I would like. But I suddenly knew there will be time – endless no-time – for everything to happen, for every possibility to ripen, for every missed opportunity to be taken, in parallel dimensions and multiplex worlds.

My joy subsided, however, to be replaced by a slowly growing horror that seemed just as limitless. My mind recoiled from the direct experience of an ultimate reality – void, Nirvana – where mind could not exist.

'How else can one threaten than with death?' asked the writer, Jorge Luis Borges. 'The interesting, the original thing, would be to threaten someone with immortality.'

As I emerged from the void, I thought of all the projects I wanted to undertake – all the women I wanted to love. I saw how, given eternity, I would have the latitude to learn many languages, master lucid dreaming, compose symphonies, develop a superb three-point shot, write novels that would challenge Proust and Nabokov, master herbalism, study astrology, become a Tantric adept, DJ at Robot Heart. But as I felt the limitless expanse of time extending ever further, a coldness, a numb futility, crept over me. All of my ideas of what I would do seemed pathetic. I felt trapped between the mediocrity of my ego, which I desperately wanted to cling to, and that pristine Absolute where 'I' no longer existed, but all was totally safe, entirely at peace.

In *The Transcendent Unity of Religions*, the Sufi philosopher Frithjof Schuon draws a distinction between religion and mysticism, or the exoteric and esoteric paths to God. Religions, with their ornate rituals and hierarchical power structures, seek to indoctrinate – mind-control – mass populations. The priests establish a code of beliefs and moral laws for the faithful to follow. On the mystical path, priests have no authority. The goal is direct experience, which can be reached through many different techniques.

The Cosmic Illusion

Religions, exoteric cults, can't handle the more difficult revelations, the paradoxes, known to mystical philosophy. One of these, Schuon writes, is 'the doctrine of the cosmic illusion', the realization that 'the world is not only more or less imperfect or ephemeral, but cannot even be said to "be" at all in relation to absolute Reality, since the reality of the world would limit God's reality and He alone "is".'

When mystics encounter a personal God in their visions, they are only accessing one level of manifestation: 'Being Itself, which is none other than the Personal God, is in its turn surpassed by the Impersonal or Supra-Personal Divinity, Non-Being, of which the Personal God or Being is simply the first determination from which flow all the secondary determinations that make up cosmic Existence.'

The experience of taking 5-meO-DMT supports Schuon's view on the 'Divine Impersonality', as well as Buddhist and Eastern thought. In the *Tibetan Book of the Dead*, there are a number of different 'Bardo Realms', worlds or dimensions. Each Bardo is inhabited by different types of beings who are dominated by particular emotions. There is a Bardo of the gods, the demi-gods, the Hungry Ghosts, animals, and so on. Our human realm is one of the Bardo Realms. All of the Bardos are, ultimately, illusions. In a negative sense, they can be seen as traps. For the Tibetans, even the god realm is a trap – a god can live for many eons, have orgasms that last for untold *kalpas*, but gods eventually die. Even a god will have to be reincarnated in one of the lower Bardos, and undergo the whole cycle again.

Only humans, according to Buddhists, have the potential to attain enlightenment and exit the otherwise interminable cycle of rebirth. Our opportunity to do this comes after we die, when either we will reincarnate into one of the Bardo Realms, or we can choose to enter the Clear Light and merge with the infinite. Taking 5-meO-DMT, secreted from the glands of a homely desert toad, allows us to experience the Clear Light, Nirvana or the void for a few minutes of clock time that seem relatively endless, while we are still alive. Perhaps our evolutionary impetus is to merge with that infinite spaciousness while remaining embodied and individual.

We also find descriptions of the Clear Light, or Nirvana, in other traditions. Kabbalists use the term Ein Sof, 'the fullness of being and absolute nothingness': God prior to His manifestation as the universe – as anything tangible. Forgetting its origins in the infinite divine source, consciousness plunges into matter, into separation, to explore its creative capacities. As the poet Rainer Maria Rilke wrote, 'Although we may not like it, / God is growing.' God grows through us.

A number of occult cosmologies describe how humanity undergoes evolution or metamorphosis, passing through a series of stages of consciousness, worlds, dimensions, planetary incarnations. This may be true. At the same time, these stages or levels are relative, contingent and illusory compared to the non-dimensional zero point of absolute reality, without time or space, subject or object, where there is neither being nor becoming. Everything we experience as time has already occurred, from the perspective of a higher dimension.

Physicists postulate ten dimensions of space-time. As humans, we are embedded in the fourth dimension. We know one dimension of time – duration – and three spatial ones. It is difficult to conceive – the recent film *Interstellar* tried to depict it – but a being in a higher dimension would be able to pass through time as we walk through space. Our entire space-time – this universe – would be perceived as a sculptural object, which could be observed, played with, manipulated, from different angles.

The tenth dimension could be considered the loom of vibrating subatomic Super Strings, underlying any space-time manifestation. When we smoke 5-meO-DMT, we escape the limits and constraints of our personal identity and directly experience that luminous, resonating emptiness, realizing our original nature as unborn, uncreated, eternal and infinite. The experience directly supports the Tantric view, which realizes that Samsara – the transitory illusion of material reality – is Nirvana.

'The Tantric approach is to see all life experiences as the play of the same One', wrote Georg Feuerstein in *Tantra: The Path of Ecstasy*.

> Whether positive or negative, all experiences are embedded in absolute joy, the great delight (*maha-sukha*) of Reality. When we have understood that what we dread the most – be it loss of health, property, relationships, or life itself – is not occurring to us but within our larger being, we begin to see the tremendous humor of embodiment. This insight is truly liberating.

When we integrate this Tantric insight, we will be able to face the ecological nightmare and embrace the political and social mission our world needs from us now as our initiatory path. We keep running away from the heaviness and sadness of this world – the senseless suffering and unnecessary misery of multitudes, the global sex trade, the destruction of rainforests to produce McDonald's cheeseburgers and Doritos, the cynicism of CEOs and hedge-fund managers. We must turn towards it and confront it. But we must also realize – as DMT and other mystical experiences show us – that the entire drama is designed to bring about our illumination and awakening. We can find the joy and lightness, the divine play, in all of it.

We find ourselves now at the start of the spiralling return, from separation to unity, from unconscious ignorance to superconscious awareness, from all forms of physical, mental and spiritual constraint to the unobstructed liberation that we know in the deepest part of ourselves to be our original state. Humanity may undergo further transformations and mutations, as consciousness evolves. We might, ultimately, transition out of physical incarnation altogether, becoming multi-dimensional beings, self-created, formed from *akasha*, astral light or quantum substance. Anything is possible, really. Most likely, what lies ahead of us is more incredible than we can possibly imagine. But we are not ready to celebrate yet.

For Rudolf Steiner, the founder of Anthroposophy as well as Waldorf Schools and Biodynamic Agriculture in the early years of the twentieth century, the Earth itself, as well as individual human beings, reincarnates, again and again. We are currently in the fourth incarnation of the Earth, moving – speedily, inexorably – towards the fifth. Each time the Earth reincarnates, many human souls have not developed sufficiently to be able to handle the new conditions. Their evolution continues, Steiner notes, in other worlds appropriate for them, in parallel dimensions.

Steiner's mythopoetic language is difficult to grasp – he admitted that when he described conditions of existence in the far future as well as the distant past, he was discussing things far beyond the capacity of our language to express. He claimed to have 'supersensible' visionary abilities since early childhood – like a continual DMT drip – which allowed him to develop a spiritual science based on his psychic investigations.

I love Steiner's ideas, but I don't think any occult cosmology should be taken literally. The various occult philosophies can be counterpoised against each other, like musical compositions, themes and variations, to reveal underlying patterns and resonances. An esoteric Christian, Steiner believed that Christ's life had great significance – Christ didn't 'save our souls' through his sacrifice. He provided a model, a template, for how we must live, if we want our species to evolve and transcend its current condition.

Steiner deconstructed the biblical postulate of a singular devil. Instead, he proposed there were various occult forces working on us all the time, drawing energy from us and using us for their own purposes. He described two forces – necessary for our development but also dangerous, as they can pull us into deviation – as Lucifer and Ahriman. Lucifer means 'light bringer'; Luciferic spirits pull us up and away from the Earth, towards artistic beauty, genius, romantic illumination, but can also lead us into arrogance, hubris and pride. Ahriman represents the opposing force, or being, which drags us downwards, towards materialism and materiality, soulless mechanization, sterile technologies, nihilistic oblivion.

In Steiner's cosmology, there are also spiritual hierarchies, angelic and divine powers. We can commune with them through our higher cognitive faculties – intuition, imagination and inspiration – and align with them. As human beings, we are meant to work with the spiritual hierarchies to take a creative and participatory role in the cosmic unfolding.

Steiner foresaw that the twenty-first century would see the rise of Ahriman. Today, many occult thinkers believe that our current faith in technological progress – the Singularity theology expressed by Ray Kurzweil and others – represents Ahriman's attempt to make humanity deviate from its proper path of spiritual development. Ahriman seeks to make the human ego immortal through biotechnology and nano-technology, ultimately merging it with computer-based artificial intelligence to construct a synthetic, simulated universe that would be like an isolation chamber – a hell realm, an infinite hall of mirrors – cut off from divinity, from access to our spiritual source.

Philosophers and mathematicians explore the possibility that this universe is a simulation or simulacrum. The Cambridge philosopher Nick Bostrom, a transhumanist, argues that at least one of the following postulates must be true: '(1) the human species is very likely to go extinct before reaching a "posthuman" stage; (2) any posthuman civilization is extremely unlikely to run a significant number of simulations of their evolutionary history (or variations thereof); (3) we are almost certainly living in a computer simulation'. He leans towards the third option.

Bostrom uses terms taken from the tech world to propose something that is, in essence, identical to the Buddhist or Hindu view that the universe is Lila, divine play, and Maya, cosmic illusion. In Hinduism, this illusion is maintained by the magical, creative power of the Gods. The Gods could be seen as extra-dimensional programmers running our sublime simulation. The scientific, technological worldview is converging deliriously with mystical thought. We teeter on the verge of a creative synthesis, initiating a new paradigm.

Technology Is Consciousness

We can think about technology as an extension of our biological evolution. We evolved to be able to move through space, manipulate matter and explore the world around us. We use technology to extend our innate abilities in all directions. We augment our ability to move through space and transform matter by building cars, planes, bulldozers, rocket ships and so on. We enhance our thinking capacities through computers, media networks, search engines and the like. As human beings, we continuously seek to explore, to learn, to go further. That is part of our nature.

Even language is a kind of technology. Language originally developed so that human groups could coordinate their actions and intentions. As accidental by-products, the birth of language – the word, or the *logos*, which was 'in the beginning', according to the Bible – gave birth to conceptual thought, poetry, philosophy, culture, complex societies. As a tool-using and tool-making species, we constantly experiment and invent new technologies. These reveal new aspects of our being to us, and lead us to create, and iterate, the next set of tools. Technology and consciousness are so intimately related that they could be considered synonymous.

We currently hover on the brink of manifesting extraordinary as well as frightening possibilities, through science and technology, that may radically transform our species' capacities. For instance, soon we may be able to extend the human lifespan indefinitely, making people 'a-mortal', if not immortal. Scientists are uncovering the mechanisms that cause us to age and learning how to alter them.

As *Nature* magazine notes, 'Chromosomes have caps of repetitive DNA called telomeres at their ends. Every time cells divide, their telomeres shorten, which eventually prompts them to stop dividing and die.' In studies, mice were engineered to lack the telomere enzyme. They aged rapidly. When the telomere enzyme was replaced, they bounced back and de-aged, regaining youth and vitality. This suggests 'the possibility that normal human aging could be slowed by reawakening the enzyme in cells where it has stopped working'.

Scientists caution that ageing has complex causes. Even if we alter our telomeres, we would still die of cancer and other diseases, eventually.

Yet it is possible that breakthroughs in medicine and biotechnology will be able to address these conditions. We can currently print organs and body parts using 3D printers. Stem cell transplants may allow us to regrow damaged tissue. Our techniques for genetic engineering are also advancing incredibly rapidly.

If we were able to be 'vaccinated' against ageing – to have our cells rejuvenated – the vast majority of people would want that opportunity. Given the chance, I will be among them. I often feel life is shorter than it needs to be, and barely gives us time to explore a fraction of our potential. I consider the prospect of life extension as an opportunity to make a leap of species consciousness, towards a psychic realization that, even though the world may wear different disguises, our underlying reality is infinite bliss and ecstasy. After all, even if we lived for a thousand or a million years, it would be meaningless, insignificant, when we consider the billions of years of Universe Time – or the no-time of the Ein Sof.

We can foresee that new capacities – appearing in a period of rapidly increasing resource scarcity, mass species extinction and accelerated warming – will lead to new ethical quandaries, beyond anything we have confronted before. The only way to handle the deepening contradictions of our situation is to develop moral willpower, a core ethos of empathy and responsibility, strengthened through initiatory discipline and inner work. Before humanity can make the jump to any new condition of being, we must address the ecological and social catastrophes we have unleashed on our Earth. We must take care of all of our brothers and sisters who have been consigned to lives of squalor and ignorance, making a commitment to lift them up as equals and love them.

From where we are now, it feels, subjectively, like we have accelerated over the last decades. Things used to move in slow motion, now they are lifting off towards hyper-speed. We live in a science-fiction world that is getting incrementally trippier, with or without drugs. Every indicator suggests the situation will become more intense in the years ahead.

I believe there is an occult or esoteric reality, and this hidden dimension must be acknowledged. We must seek to know it, as much as we possibly can, permeate it with thought, and integrate what we understand into our lives. When we acknowledge the occult dimension, this also must influence our life's purpose and mission. Occultists tell us that the hidden reality expresses itself through symbols, signs, as well as the procession and pageant of historical events. If this is true, we will learn to interpret our world differently. If reincarnation is an occult fact, then we must change our ideas about the meaning and purpose of any individual life.

According to hermetic philosophy, whatever appears to us as 'out there' is, just as much, 'in here'. The physical universe, the material world, is a projection of the psyche, reflecting our current state of being. If the world is changing so rapidly, this means our inner being is also developing and transforming. Our technology – the technosphere – appears to be a ladder we must build and then climb, to reach what some have called the noosphere, the next level of consciousness.

Western mysticism talks about the *logos*, the underlying language that forms the world, that was 'in the beginning'. Science is revealing the *logos*, deciphering the code or language of nature, from the genetic all the way to the subatomic level. Once again, this reflects the larger process under way.

Whether we like it or not or feel ready for it or not, humanity appears to be evolving from a childlike relationship with the cosmos to a partnership with creation itself. As science opens to integrate the reality of the psyche, we may find new ways to express our connection to the sacred. If we make a quantum leap in species consciousness, religions will no longer be dogmatic or divisive. Instead, our human family will realize the essential truth – the core – of all traditions. We can transcend the current religious structures through our ability directly to experience mystical states which indicate the transcendent unity that is the source of all religions, despite the sectarian differences that have led to wars and caused global traumas. In a 'psycho-technical' civilization, based on devotional explorations of consciousness, we can merge science and spirit, welcoming all faiths in a new synthesis.

Some indigenous cultures talk about this age as the time when humanity 'dreams the world awake'. Where the reality we experience once seemed hard and unyielding, the world is becoming, incrementally, more mutable, mercurial – more responsive to our intentions. The gap between thought and manifestation is shrinking. This is a subtle phenomenon – hard to discuss without sounding crazy – but it is also something many people know to be true.

I think it is important to acknowledge the mystical or shamanic dimension of what's happening without negating the reality that our actions as a species are tearing the world apart – threatening us with civilizational collapse and even extinction. It is the collective burden of our unsustainable lifestyles that has unleashed this catastrophe on the Earth. The only way we can address this situation is to accept it as an initiation – choosing to go against the flow and fight the inertia, because that will strengthen and toughen our spirit.

As we undergo initiation, we discover that reality becomes, in gradations, increasingly psychic, translucent, malleable. William Blake wrote, 'The Eternal body of Man is The Imagination, that is, God himself.' The world is revealing itself, slowly, to be a total art form, what the original people of Australia call the dreamtime, an allegorical fable sculpted by the Poetic Genius, the Imagination, of which we are all aspects and expressions. As we realize we are the agents who create meaning for ourselves and each other, we discover we have the sacred, joyful task of defining a new mythology for our future unfolding together.

8

Love

We must accept from the outset that constructing a regenerative society will in all likelihood be a multi-generational task. That doesn't mean, however, that we can leave it to our children. We must undertake this mission ourselves – out of devotion, reverence and universal compassion. Learning how to operate Spaceship Earth, Buckminster Fuller noted, is humanity's final exam. If we pass, we graduate to the next level of consciousness as a species.

Unconsciously, we have been impelling ourselves towards planetary catastrophe. I believe we are doing this to end our alienation and ego-centrism – to reach a new intensity of communion. Because we no longer have rites of passage which create the same effect through intentionally guided ritual, we are inducing it through mass catastrophe. But the disasters we are unleashing could have the unanticipated effect of breaking open the collective heart *chakra*. Collectively, humanity can realize love and solidarity – universal, unconditional – as the basis for healing our world.

This may seem distant, theoretical and abstract, but I think many people already see reverberations of this process in their personal lives. For some, this is taking the form of a deep questioning of traditional relationship patterns – often, a rejection of them, as they seek to create something new. Culturally, the focus on transgendered people, gay marriage, the endless sex scandals tearing down politicians and public figures is all part of this unavoidable change.

We have inherited a restricted model of romantic and erotic love. Most people still believe that monogamy – exclusive partnership – is the only way to find enduring happiness and contentment. Of course, for some people, monogamy is the best option. But humans are not naturally monogamous, and the current system forces many people to act hypocritically, to deceive themselves and their partners, or to sacrifice their truth.

Deep in their hearts, many people feel permanently disappointed, sad, frustrated and angry because they have been unable to satisfy their erotic desires. Men and women lead lives of quiet desperation and compromise. An ambience of disappointment and frustration permeates our society, in overt and subtle ways. People seek false substitutes for true satisfaction. The insatiable lust for consumer goods is – I believe – a result of our failure to satisfy our deeper needs for love, erotic fulfilment, authentic communion.

'We are at war with our eroticism', write Christopher Ryan and Calcida Jethá in *Sex at Dawn: The Prehistoric Origins of Modern Sexuality*. After scouring evidence from anthropology and evolutionary biology, they point out that,

> Human beings evolved in intimate groups where almost every-
> thing was shared – food, shelter, protection, child care, even
> sexual pleasure . . . contemporary culture misrepresents the link
> between love and sex. With and without love, a casual sexuality
> was the norm for our prehistoric ancestors . . . human beings
> and our hominid ancestors have spent almost all of the past
> million years or so in small, intimate bands in which most adults
> had several sexual relationships at any given time.

Civilization constructed the institution of marriage, and enforced monogamy, to protect property rights, under a patriarchal regime which demonized female sexuality. The force of our repressed sexual instinct was channelled – or sublimated, in Sigmund Freud's term – into building civilization, creating culture and making war.

The curious fact about human nature is that it is not fixed, but changeable. This is something that makes us different from animals: we are the species that can reinvent itself, in many ways. However, some things are very resistant to change. The instinct towards sexual satiation, for instance, is hardwired into our biology. We are also unique among animals due to the incessant force of our non-stop, hair-trigger sex drive.

As Gerald Heard explored in the early 1950s in *Pain, Sex and Time*, we possess a tremendous surplus of evolutionary energy, far beyond what we need to sustain ourselves. This energy must find outlets for expression. Like Walter Benjamin, Heard believed we need to channel this force consciously, through ritual, initiation and training in special schools devised for this purpose. Otherwise, the excess energy continues to get discharged, through wars and violence.

'If our evolution is over,' Heard worried, 'if we have no further original outlet to our enormous and fretting energy, then the only choice is slow degeneracy through sex addiction or a conclusive end through homicidal mania.' The excess energy, the *kundalini*, driving us reveals something important about our destiny as a species. In other words, individually as well as collectively, we can choose to evolve and deepen ourselves, or decay and disintegrate.

Some people would say I am the wrong person to write about the subject of relationships. They may be right. I certainly don't recommend that anyone takes my thoughts and ideas on the subject as the final word or some kind of objective truth. I went through a difficult, painful struggle with the powers of Eros in my own life, a fall from grace related to sexuality that men in power positions often experience.

I didn't think I was doing anything wrong – I didn't deceive anyone. I was unconscious of how my behaviour was being seen by others, how it was impacting on the people around me. Angry at the restrictive rules of conventional society, resentful due to long periods of erotic frustration, I couldn't separate my own shadow from the collective shadow. What I learned from this gives me a good vantage point to consider the many aspects of our larger predicament – but my ideas remain radical.

Sexuality Is a Superpower

Sex energy radiates through every filament of our social structure. 'Sexuality is a superpower,' writes Dieter Duhm, one of the founders of Tamera, a 'free love' community in Portugal. 'Our attractions and repulsions, sexual signals and links, hopes and disappointments go through all of society like a nerve system, permeating every office, every shopping mall, every art exhibition, every conference, every group, every company, every political party.' He believes that any attempt to suppress this superpower only leads to negative outcomes – as with those Indian gurus in the 1970s who claimed to be transcendent masters, but couldn't resist the charms of their Western female disciples.

Duhm was the leader of a group of German radicals who tried to understand why 1960s leftist efforts to build a utopian alternative to capitalism ended in failure. He realized there were core issues around love, relationships and sexuality that people could not fully address yet or bring into their consciousness. 'The healing of sexuality is perhaps the most revolutionary step in the present healing work after thousands of years of suppression and neglect,' he writes. Because these issues were not addressed, the idealistic efforts to change the world imploded, instead. Communities and movements kept falling apart. Sex and love were the deepest *political* issues society could not confront or integrate.

'The most intimate questions of sex, love, and partnership, of faithfulness, trust, and community, of jealousy, competition, and fear of separation are political questions with global implications', Duhm writes. He and some like-minded people decided to step out of society to establish a community as an experimental laboratory. Their modest goal was world peace. They realized that peace on Earth would be impossible until we established peace between the genders – until we found peace in love. They courageously broke apart traditional structures and conditioning, seeking a holistic redesign.

I remember from my early years, my adolescence, how the cultural ambience around sexuality had a dark, shameful feeling. There was no sense that boys and girls – or men and women – might seek to collaborate for each other's sensual pleasure. That we might enjoy taking care of each other – that we could learn to be generous, compassionate, with each other. Eroticism was not part of our education. It was not something to be explored or studied, even as an afterthought – certainly not with the same kind of analytic rigour we brought to maths or physics, even though sex would be infinitely more important to our future lives than these academic subjects.

Our civilization applies tremendous reserves of intellect and capital to construct killer drones, virtual reality devices, surveillance systems – instruments of death, alienation and fear. Yet we believe that love and sexuality are not worthy of our conscious attention. We act as if they are outside the realm of logic, forethought and social design.

'Whereas the cerebrum is applied in war technology, in love man lives and thinks out of his spinal cord,' Duhm points out. When we channel more of society's intellect and resources towards the exploration of love and eroticism – freeing these areas from an antiquated and unrealistic morality – we will make rapid strides.

Just as we lack rites of passage to introduce us to transpersonal or visionary experiences when we are young – when we long, with our whole being, to experience a deeper intensity of communion, to access something greater than ourselves – we also lack for cultural traditions that would help young people to embrace their sexuality as something wonderful, as a great gift they can explore and share responsibly. We are still a subtly pleasure-denying society, despite Tinder, OkCupid, casual sex and the hook-up culture. Sexuality is considered a private matter, relegated to dark places like nightclubs and bars, which have an underworld ambience.

A lot of my early views on sex were shaped by Beat writers like Allen Ginsberg and Jack Kerouac, as well as their bohemian predecessors, Anaïs Nin and Henry Miller. Perhaps Henry Miller most of all. Miller described life in New York and Paris back in the 1930s and 40s as a seething erotic purgatory. The women were, on the one hand, yearning for sex – as he was, constantly – but passive, unable to voice their desire. 'I was lonely amidst a world of things lit up by phosphorescent flashes of cruelty,' he wrote. 'I was delirious with an energy which could not be unleashed except in the service of death and futility.'

With savage humour, Miller's novels contain numerous scenes that would elicit howls of outrage from feminists today, that would be seen as predatory or abusive. In one book, he describes standing on a crowded bus in rush hour, feeling up the woman who is pressed against him, pressing his fingers into her groin, convinced she is secretly enjoying it. His protagonist uses all sorts of sneaky means to overcome feminine resistance. 'What holds the world together, as I have learned from bitter experience, is sexual intercourse. But fuck, the real thing, cunt, the real thing, seems to contain some unidentified element which is far more dangerous than nitroglycerine.'

In my twenties, I was stricken with envy over men whom I felt were more successful than me, in their careers but, above all, sexually. I started a literary journal with two friends who were handsome, preppy, media darlings, writing short stories for *The New Yorker*. One of them had a huge family fortune. He cheated on his fiancée frequently, flying women to Paris for secret weekend affairs. His wealth, my other friend quipped, was like a giant invisible penis on his shoulder. Women reacted to it viscerally.

I longed to have the kind of sexual access his wealth provided him. I also felt angry at women, particularly beautiful ones, the ones I desired with such ravenous hunger. These ethereal goddesses almost invariably seemed to choose men based on their trust funds and bank accounts, or men who got rich by dumbing down the public or accelerating the destruction of the planet, or who triumphed in some superficial glamour field like pop music or fashion photography.

Later on, when I made it as a writer in my thirties, I didn't anticipate that other men would feel just as envious and competitive towards me as I had felt about my peers. I still saw myself as the adolescent underdog, the morose and envious twenty-something. Although I was exactly the same person as before – the one who felt rejected, under-appreciated by women – I was suddenly desirable. Often, after I gave a talk or went on a book tour, women – lovely, intelligent, sweet – approached me. Sometimes they would make it clear they wanted to connect with me.

All of a sudden I had an abundance of sexual opportunities. I'd never thought this would be the result of my books – writing them had been innocent, heartfelt efforts to communicate ideas, acts of service. I hadn't expected the gift would be reciprocated by the world in this way. I found it so beautiful. But the thrill of it became, quickly, addictive. Unfortunately, instead of feeling happy and satiated, I only wanted more and more.

Sexual hunger is quite different from the hunger for food, which is easily satisfied by a good meal, or even a mediocre buffet. Russell Brand became a raging sex addict who slept with up to eighty women a month at the height of his mania, or so he claims. Not only is Russell extremely charming and charismatic, he would also enlist people to help him in his quest to be 'shagger of the year', a title he held several times in a row. Eventually, he realized that this almost unbelievable expenditure of sweat and sperm was bringing him no lasting contentment, so he checked into rehab.

Russell may have gone a bit overboard. But my admittedly contro-versial perspective is that there is nothing wrong with having an abundance, even a super-abundance, of lovers and sexual partners –

whether for men or women – as long as this is done honestly and without coercion. Unfortunately, in our society, the pursuit of sexual desire tends to require all sorts of miserable deceits, lies and hypocrisies. Also, it is totally unjust and wrong that women still get put down for the exact same behaviour that society approves in men.

Sex at Dawn

I realize that just a few pages ago I was writing about occult cosmologies and our potential as a species to achieve unity with the cosmos through mystical experience and collective evolution, and, now, here I am considering what sounds like extreme erotic mania as something natural and okay. I am aware that for many people this may seem a jarring dichotomy, and admit I am taking a risk. But because our time for making our evolutionary leap or collective mutation is quite short – I am not certain I will have time to complete another manifesto before things start to blow up – I feel I must be honest and straightforward about what I think and why I think it.

I suspect some readers will feel I am promoting a hyper-masculine mode of sexuality. Of course, men are more biologically prone to seek multiple mates, but women also have the need to pursue various sorts of erotic adventures. In *Sex at Dawn*, Ryan and Jethá review studies that suggest there is an evolutionary explanation for why women make louder sounds during intercourse than men. These noises had a function in our early hominid days: the female was calling out to other males in the area to have sex with her in succession. In this way, the child's paternity would remain unknown. Also, sperm competition would occur in the uterus. The female orgasm also has a reproductive purpose, as the contractions of orgasm pull the sperm deeper into the womb. The male who elicited the most powerful orgasm would be the one most likely to fertilize her egg.

When it comes to sexuality, we have to accept how humans truly are, rather than how they are supposed to be, according to some imposed ideal. 'Monogamy is not found in any social, group-living primate except – if the standard narrative is to be believed – us,' write Ryan and Jethá:

If you spend time with the primates closest to human beings, you'll see female chimps having intercourse dozens of times per day, with most or all of the willing males, and rampant bonobo group sex that leaves everyone relaxed and maintains intricate social networks. Explore contemporary human beings' lust for particular kinds of pornography or our notorious difficulties with long-term sexual monogamy and you'll soon stumble over relics of our hypersexual ancestors.

The planetary mega-crisis is directly related to the problems we confront as a species in this area of love and sexuality. One primary urge driving many men to seek success – wealth or fame – is sexual access. Men – Alpha males, in particular – will do almost anything to attract women. The economic system tends to reward sociopathic behaviour. To succeed, people must climb corporate ladders, sell wasteful products, manage investment funds that transfer resources from the poor to the wealthy, promote vacuous fashion trends and so on. The system forces people to compromise their ethics and principles, or renounce them altogether, to get what they want.

My anthropological observation is that people – young people above all – waste an unbelievable amount of their life energy in the quest for sexual satiation. This energy that people expend in the incessant pursuit of sexual fulfilment is exactly the energy that we, the human community, need to redirect, channelling it towards our awakening, using it to enact social change and regenerate our planet's ecosystems.

Sex itself is not the problem. In our culture, for many people, the act of sex only consumes a tiny fraction of the energy expended in the pursuit of it. Also, sex can be nourishing, physically and emotionally. If there was no need to pursue erotic connections, to compete for mates, we could use that squandered energy to confront the ecological crisis we have unleashed as a species, and bring about a rapid cultural evolution.

If we can understand, and then fix, the flaws in our social design, our stale ideology and antiquated cultural programming, we will liberate a huge amount of productive energy for building a regenerative society. We will take a massive leap forward as a species. And we will do it quickly.

I don't think the answer is to restrict sexual behaviour, which will only lead to more frustration, repression, resentment and deception. I believe the solution is to consciously liberate Eros – not just Eros as it gets expressed through sexuality and romantic love, but also the various forms of love that bind communities together, including caring for children and old people. We must understand that the Eros that gets expressed through sexuality is not just an individual problem, but has a very large-scale social and political dimension. Men and women must be willing to cooperate for each other's happiness if humanity is going to have a long-term future on Earth.

Hollywood and the media idealize the nuclear family, which is the basic economic unit of our society. When individuals merge into couples, and particularly when these couples have children, they tend to direct all their energy and resources towards themselves. They lose interest – if they ever had any – in helping the collective. Instead, they seek to amass resources, playing the competitive capitalist game.

The problem in our culture is the atomization which forces individuals, as well as nuclear families, to fight for their own success and personal survival. We can now see that this system, enforcing self-interest as a survival mechanism, is not sustainable for the planet as a whole. It needs to change – since it won't change on its own, we need to change it.

'Deep conflicts rage at the heart of modern sexuality,' write Ryan and Jethá:

> Our cultivated ignorance is devastating. The campaign to obscure the true nature of our species' sexuality leaves half our marriages collapsing under an unstoppable tide of sexual frustration, libido-killing boredom, impulsive betrayal, dysfunction, confusion, and shame. Serial monogamy stretches before (and behind) many of us like an archipelago of failure: isolated islands of transitory happiness in a cold, dark sea of disappointment.

To maintain their relationships, many people find themselves forced to lie about or suppress their true desires. The vast majority of men I know who are in long-term partnerships have confessed they either feel an intense desire for other sexual contacts or have secretly satisfied some of those desires, through affairs or prostitutes – feeding the horrific global sex trade. Other people learn to dampen their sexual drive, but I don't find this a great outcome either.

I don't think it is an accident that so many creative artists and geniuses have been fascinated with eroticism and sexual love, pursuing the muse as she expresses herself in many embodied forms. Erotic love is a kind of fuel that makes people feel alive and inspired. Ideally, don't we want everyone to be as inspired and turned-on as they can be? Wouldn't we prefer a social system that supports everyone in exploring their deepest capacities for love, for erotic and ecstatic experience, as long as they are causing no harm to others?

There is a direct relationship between our corrupt politics and our failure, as a society, to handle love authentically. When people find themselves forced to lie to or deceive the person closest to them – their partner – about their desires, they are conditioned to accept corruption and hypocrisy in society at large. They can accept the half-truths of politicians and pundits because they are compromised themselves. We fail to care for the world as a consequence of our inauthenticity. After all, why would we want to protect and safeguard a world that has betrayed us at its core?

Eros Unredeemed

'The dream of a new world is not only a subjective wish, but also an authentic matrix for a different life, anchored in the structures of reality; it is an objective necessity and a possibility,' Duhm writes in *Terra Nova*:

> The concrete utopia is a latent reality within the universe, just as the butterfly is a reality latent within the caterpillar. It lies in the structure of our physical and biological world, in our genes, and in our deeper ethical orientation. Within the context of committed peace work, it is not the fixing of individual defects within existing structures that is required; what is required is a fundamental system change.

As part of the new story or myth of the near future, we will define a new vision of Eros – love and sexuality – which allows for the freeing of love, the fulfilment of desire, without exploitation or manipulation. This is not something that individuals can accomplish on their own, although I do know many people who have rewritten the laws in their own lives. All of the turbulence, bitterness and disappointment so many people have experienced points towards the need for a new social structure and a change of values. From what I have seen, Tamera, the community founded by Duhm and his cohorts, is the most advanced effort to work out the implications of our situation and construct a viable alternative.

Living in downtown New York, I find myself in the midst of a purgatorial, hyper-sexualized carnival. Nightclubs still radiate that old hipster attitude, replete with indie rock musicians, tattooed models, fashion world detritus, mostly clad in designer black, tooting cocaine and getting blotto, to the wee hours, until Babylon falls. There are also private, all-night 'play parties' in Manhattan, mixing the flotsam and jetsam of the Burning Man world with an uptown, *Eyes Wide Shut* crowd. This community engages in consensual sexual gymnastics, in townhouses and hotel suites, with collegial enthusiasm and peacock pride.

The next level of sexual liberation is happening now, along with the breakdown of old relationship models. It is unfolding in real time. Even as they are living it, most people do not think about it as a problem of system design.

Although it is a tentative step forward, the play party or swinger world is not the answer. Relationships remain shallow and immature, based on ego displays, physical attraction and self-centred hedonism. If we are truly going to liberate Eros, love and sexuality – in particular, female sexuality – we have to dig deeper. We need a new approach to community and, ultimately, a new social design that is holistic, comprehensive and secure. A truly liberated society must support long-term care for children. It must take care of old people. 'Free love', it turns out, requires a great deal of discipline.

A Healing Biotope

When I visited Tamera, a few hours south of Lisbon in Portugal, I was taken on a tour that included the children's centre. Past the age of two, most of the young children in the community live in a house together, where they are looked after by a few of the adults. They can go and see their parents whenever they want, but their parents – in particular, their mothers – have their time freed up for other pursuits.

Cooperative childcare is a simple but crucial design solution. Lacking a community support structure, the nuclear family model is a cumbersome way to raise children. It causes many psychological problems. Even worse is the single-parent model. Much of the anxiety in our culture has to do with this situation. Women must compete with other women, seeking a mate who can offer them long-term support, through the decades-long process of raising kids.

'How would the prevalence and experience of jealousy be affected in Western societies if the economic dependence trapping most women and their children didn't exist, leading female sexual access to be a tightly controlled commodity?' ask Ryan and Jethá:

> What if economic security and guilt-free sexual friendships were easily available to almost all men and women, as they are in many of the societies we've discussed, as well as among our closest primate cousins? What if no woman had to worry that a ruptured relationship would leave her and her children destitute and vulnerable? What if average guys knew they'd never have to worry about finding someone to love? What if we didn't all grow up hearing that true love is obsessive and possessive?

These are exactly the issues that Tamera has addressed.

Men and women find themselves trapped in mental webs of jealousy and fear, seeking to protect their investments of time and money, their possessions and property. In Tamera, they say, 'jealousy is to love as asthma is to breathing'. The only way to change this, they believe, is by building community. In a community, people can learn to cooperate to satisfy both short-term and long-term needs. They can work it out, because they are committed to staying with each other. In cities like New York, relationships tend to be extremely transitory by comparison.

Many aspects of Tamera amaze me. Duhm, Lichtenfels and their partners founded the community nearly 40 years ago in southern Germany and then moved their project to Portugal 20 years ago, establishing a vibrant community on an initially barren property of

330 acres. It has expanded, slowly, to its present population of 170 people, the majority of them Germans and northern Europeans. The older women are a major force in the community, much like the elder women in tribal societies.

Over the past ten years, the community has done a great deal of landscape restoration work, turning an area of dry land into an abundant oasis. The key to this was establishing a system of lakes (and other installations) to retain rainwater on the land and to replenish the aquifers. They call this a 'Water Retention Landscape', an effective way for overcoming desertification and assuring water and food self-sufficiency for decentralized communities.

The Tamerans see a link between how a community treats its water and how it handles love. They believe that both water and love need vessels of containment, along with opportunities to flow and expand. They believe, in fact, that love's natural tendency is to expand and to flow – that the monogamy model is an artificial constraint.

Many community members have primary partnerships, but most of them also have a 'love network' of other connections. Over time, Tamera has developed a set of social technologies which allow the community to process issues, such as jealousy, as they come up. They take everything that is normally hidden in our culture and make it explicit, transparent and visible to all. Benjamin von Mendelssohn, one of my friends who lives there, talks about the 'community super-soul', which is greater than the sum of its parts. Very little is hidden or private.

One of the social technologies Tamera developed is called Forum, which the whole community participates in, every day, in groups of 30 or 40 people. During Forum, everyone joins in a circle. People take turns going into the centre, where they speak about or act out their relationships and experiences with other members of the community. Tamerans then give feedback, 'mirrors', speaking about them in the third person. The goal is honesty.

During one Forum, a young woman spoke in the centre, dancing expressively as she discussed her past and ongoing relationships with men in the community. After her performance, one of the older men, in a position of authority, said, 'I appreciated what Martha had to share today, because I have always felt she was attractive, but I didn't feel I would ever be able to approach her for a sexual contact. After what she said today, I did feel it was possible that, at some point, I might approach her in this way.' I was impressed that his comment was so unadulterated. He said what he was thinking, with no effort to make himself look good, or try to impress the woman with some insight or advice.

Life is a process of learning, and learning is often painful. When I got famous, and women suddenly wanted me in a way they hadn't before, I became intoxicated by my new power. Consumed by the free love ideology I had absorbed from the Beats, particularly from Allen Ginsberg, I made the mistake of seeing almost any woman I found attractive as a potential sex partner.

If I had lived within a community like Tamera, I would have received constant reflections and mirrors back from the people around me that would have helped to correct my dissolute tendencies. Instead, lacking feedback, I developed negative patterns, sometimes hurting and offending women by my behaviour, which could be thoughtless and callous. I didn't possess the tools to understand or address it. Other people saw me as someone in a position of authority or leadership, while I considered myself an apprentice. I still feel I am learning, continuously changing and hopefully improving.

Tamera conceives of sexual satisfaction as more than the individual's problem. They consider it a community responsibility – and a sacred one. They have a house on their land which is called the Temple of Love. Certain members of the community undergo training in 'love service', to become priests and priestesses of the Temple. They make themselves available for other members of the community who desire connection. You might find, for instance, an older woman in the community seeking an experience with one of the younger or middle-aged men. Or a young man might have his first encounter with an older woman.

My friend Martin, for instance, moved to Tamera as a teenager. He had his first sexual experience with a woman in her thirties, when he was 16. They made a ritual out of it. The community gathered around the Temple to celebrate his initiation into sexual love. If something like that had happened to me at the age of 16 – if I had been part of a community that cared to make sure my awkward yearnings were satisfied, rather than suppressed – I think I would have developed a much healthier approach to love.

'We need a revolution whose victory will create no losers because it will achieve a state that benefits all,' Duhm writes. 'Eros and religion need to come together again so that we human beings can rise up to the source from which all of life originates.'

Communion

When we envision the transition to a post-capitalist, post-work society, we must have a plan in mind for redirecting the productive and creative energies of humanity as a whole. I think this ideal of a liberated Eros provides the basis for it. If we can create communities that allow people to have deep partnerships rooted in truth, along with other lovers if they desire them, we would no longer feel cheated by a world that seems to deny our deepest desires and yearnings. As labour becomes more automated, we will have more time to explore the communion of souls, as well as bodies, that our deeper nature seeks. We will restructure our society to enable this.

In many parts of the world, women are still horribly oppressed – in Muslim countries, in African cultures that are based on male power and even mutilate female genitalia through circumcision. Then there is the global sex trade, Internet porn – the massive industries that exploit women around the world. Equalizing the status of women, globally, is the quickest path to positive social change, on many levels. When women's power and access to education approaches that of men, the birth rate falls below replacement levels.

The scientist Rupert Sheldrake developed the idea of morphic resonance. He theorizes that the 'laws of nature' are not fixed and immutable. They are habits or patterns that become more coherent over time, until they seem permanent. This happens through a resonance on the level of form, shaped through holographic principles. As an example, once a first crystal forms when a certain group of molecules come together, it makes it more likely that another crystal will appear, given those same conditions, since a new morphogenetic field for crystal formation has been created. As this happens a few times, the morphogenetic field strengthens, stabilizes, and crystals form reliably. But the pattern could change, given new information.

The same process happens with social ideas and systems. New ideas, techniques or social arrangements create new morphogenetic fields, which make it easier for more people, as well as society as a whole, to adapt and innovate. Potentially, a few communities that have defined a new ethos of partnership and cooperation can create a new field of possibility. As it strengthens, the new pattern could become available – quickly and then suddenly – to the human community as a whole. As we know, spontaneous remissions – miraculous healings – do happen, from time to time. Just as there could be an exponential scaling up of new energy systems, so there could be a rapid spread of new social technologies and community models that shift humanity into a new framework of cooperation and empathy.

When I consider the ecological data, I can't help but feel humanity will need something like a miraculous healing through the coalescence of a new vision, a new consciousness, defined by regenerative practices and social habits. Rather than taking incremental steps, we may make a rapid evolutionary leap from our current suicide system to one that honours life and establishes a foundation of secure love and trust between the genders. Only this will give us the courage to deal with the onrushing tide of ecological decimation, and the social dislocation it will cause.

I realize such idealism may seem impossible and ridiculous to many readers. I know almost everything in our culture seems to support the alternate view that nothing will change – that the situation is hopeless, out of our control, and it is already too late to change course. Even so, when we look back through history, we have seen movements arise that took everyone by surprise. This was the case with the fall of the Berlin Wall, the Arab Spring, the civil rights movement, the French and American Revolutions, and so on. We never know what is possible – and we are more than observers. We are evolutionary catalysts who continuously influence what can and will occur.

9

Rebellion

All through my early life, I had the eerie feeling of being subject to a sinister, overwhelming power. The enemy was a degraded, corrupt authority, much like the court in Kafka's *The Trial*. The centre was nowhere and everywhere at the same time. My distant nemesis could neither be targeted nor opposed.

Self-expression, humour and art seemed the only meaningful way to fight back against such a foe. Even as adolescents, my friends and I knew our enemy had already won the decisive battle. Since we had lost, the best we could do was to carve out a private realm of artistic and personal freedom where we maintained some illusion of control.

When I was five, I remember lying on my grandma's red upholstered couch, watching the saga of Watergate slowly unfold on her black-and-white television. I wanted cartoons, but she was determined to follow the hearings from beginning to end. Watergate was a mind-numbing drone. It was obvious to me that nobody was speaking directly or truthfully. The dull bureaucrats had mastered the art of shirking responsibility and passing the buck. Everybody seemed embalmed, speaking a dead language.

Watergate set the tone for my future disengagement from politics. As I grew up, I saw the system as a rigged spectacle of manufactured consent, compelling compromise or capitulation to the special interests who pulled the puppet strings of power. Once in a great while, I flicked a voting lever or joined in some protest march. But these gestures seemed empty, degrading. They did not feel like meaningful forms of participation. The sensation was one of being conned and gypped. I knew this system could never represent my values or ideals – even if I didn't yet know precisely what my values and ideals were.

By the time I came of age in the late 1980s, my Generation X had surrendered without a fight. Overwhelmed by Reagan, Iran-Contras, the global success of the neoliberal agenda, we believed we were powerless to change our society. We turned away from politics or economics.

We identified as bohemians, marginal outsiders. We focused on art, film, literature and the avant-garde. Taking our cues from the culture, we greeted any attempt to discuss the ecological crisis or America's procession of endless wars with derision and cynicism. The suicides of Kurt Cobain and David Foster Wallace seemed to sum up Gen X's ambience of hopelessness.

I now feel that contemporary art and culture are a bit problematic. Even when art, films or music seems to have a dissident viewpoint, they often serve to legitimize the prevailing system. Anything seditious, rebellious or seemingly disruptive actually feeds energy to the post-industrial capitalist mega-machine, which thrives on disruption.

Contemporary society has the ability to absorb, assimilate and neutralize almost anything that seems to threaten it. Media critic Thomas de Zengotita calls the method through which any potential alternative or threatening idea gets 'covered', swallowed up, by the mass media, the Blob: 'What must be covered is any event or person or deed that might challenge the Blob with something like a limit, some-thing the Blob cannot absorb, something that could, in resistance or escape, become the one thing the omni-tolerant Blob cannot allow, something outside it, something unmediated – something real,' he writes in *Mediated*.

When we understand the mechanisms of post-industrial capitalism, we can use its techniques to potentially subvert it or accelerate its metamorphosis. If we apply our cunning and creativity effectively, it is quite possible we can transform this system peacefully from within. We don't have to 'smash the state'. We can supersede it. We can feed the Blob the antidote that will force it to dissolve.

Although I consider the contemporary art world is a nightmare, a black hole of ego and pretension that sucks a huge amount of excess capital and intellect into it, I believe art has a crucial role to play in our post-capitalist future. The German conceptual artist Joseph Beuys came up with the term 'social sculpture'. 'Only art is capable of dismantling the repressive effects of a senile social system to build a SOCIAL ORGANISM AS A WORK OF ART,' Beuys wrote. We can consider many human-made constructs – financial systems, festivals like Burning Man, intentional communities, even governments – as social sculptures, which we can intentionally design to change ourselves or enhance our powers.

We have new tools at our disposal that could allow us to accomplish what was once impossible and unthinkable. Ironically, yet appropriately, these tools are products of the system itself, which is revealing ever-more glaring inner contradictions. Art could find its proper function in helping to bring about this redirection. It would no longer be an ornament of post-colonial empire. In fact, if we are going to have a system after this one, art will play a far more integral role in it.

I believe many people feel deflated, defeated and disempowered by the system so early in life because of the failure of our world to provide us with access to anything transcendent or sacred. We are also wounded, in adolescence, by a sadness around love – by the sense that men and women are somehow at war with each other, that our deepest erotic desires are somehow shameful or wrong, and can never be met. When we understand the programming, we can consciously over-write it.

Instead of initiating people into adulthood through an act of visionary courage, our civilization indoctrinates and programmes us in many subtle and brutal ways. This is the residue of our Judaeo-Christian heritage, which denigrates direct experience, or gnosis, promoting received ideas and obedience to distant authorities. In my generation, we got the impression that whoever was hiding behind the curtain – the priest, the rabbi, the expert, the technocrat bureaucrat – possessed power over our world, and that we were exiled from it.

It was only after I published my first books that I realized I needed to explore social theory. It wasn't enough any more to believe the government sucked and the media was a sham – to reject the establishment, like some angst-ridden punk rocker. I needed to work out a sophisticated, reasoned critique. I needed to know what kind of alternative I believed in – something that had nothing to do with being a Democrat or Republican. I knew our society was approaching a tipping point that might lead to catastrophic breakdown within a few decades, but I didn't know what I would put in its place, or how this might happen.

Occupy

To define a political philosophy for myself, I undertook a brain-straining, labyrinthine course of study. I pitted Hannah Arendt's *On Revolution* against Lenin's *State and Revolution* and surveyed Marx,

Trotsky and Mao. I juxtaposed Rousseau's views on power against Machiavelli's, tried to understand the concepts of sovereignty and the general will, pitted Antonio Negri's ideas of 'immaterial production' against Slavoj Žižek's postmodern Marxism. I analysed social ecologists like Murray Bookchin, post-collapse theorists like John Michael Greer, anarchists like Kropotkin, liberal environmentalists like Bill McKibben and Gustave Speth. Years passed as I got more and more lost in a seemingly endless tangle of theories.

Suddenly, it was the autumn of 2011. Occupy Wall Street appeared on my doorstep. By the time I visited Zuccotti Park, the carnival was in full swing, with lines of police facing the young, cheerful, under-washed horde that had turned the tiny square into their motley home. The first reports from the media made it sound squalid and chaotic, a useless gathering of neurotic losers, with nothing better to do. As I found, this was far from the actual state of things.

For David Graeber, an anarchist and anthropology professor who helped inspire the movement, Occupy was the local expression of a 'wave of resistance sweeping the planet', part of a global response to imperial control and financial corruption. The plan, he writes in *The Democracy Project*, was to create the model for a 'genuine direct democracy' which would expose the charade of the current representational system. The Occupiers did this by launching the General Assembly. Meeting at the front of the park every day, by a tall orange metal sculpture, they made all their decisions transparently and collectively. Anyone who turned up could immediately participate.

Occupy applied Gandhi's tactics of nonviolent activism. These tactics had not been successfully used in the US since the civil rights movement in the 1950s – other uprisings had attempted to apply them but were quickly stomped out. For whatever reason – whether it was because it was the lucky or right moment or they needed a new story, or because mainstream journalists sympathized with the radicals – the press flocked to Occupy, giving it copious attention, which provided it with some protection from police aggression.

As I toured the bustling park, I was amazed by the quality of people's discussions, and the passion everyone expressed. It felt surreal – as if all of the conversations I had been holding inside my head with long-dead philosophers were suddenly being performed publicly, witnessed by a crowd of engaged participants. Everyone who attended the nightly General Assemblies had the same opportunity to debate, discuss and contribute to decisions that impacted on the movement as a whole.

I saw passers-by – office workers and labourers – recruited to help build a new democratic society. I watched their faces light up, as they realized they were being invited to participate as equals in this process. There was electricity in the air – a sense of renewed possibility.

I remember, at one midday teach-in near the library, hearing two young women with matching dreadlocks and wire-frame glasses – they had dropped out of college to join the occupation – talk about what they were learning by living in Zuccotti Park. They called it a process of internal 'decolonization'. They were freeing their minds, step by step, from the trance of empire. They said there were no experts in what they were experiencing, as they lived in the thick of it. Many Occupiers had a deep understanding of our political-economic system, and the planetary crisis. They knew the situation required a seismic shift and were willing to risk their lives for it.

Graeber notes that Occupy was, at its heart, a 'forward-looking youth movement'. Its primary constituents were young people who had tried to make it in the mainstream, only to find the system rigged against them. They 'watched the financial class completely fail to play by the rules, destroy the world economy through fraudulent speculation, get rescued by prompt and massive government intervention, and, as a result, wield even greater power and be treated with even greater honour than before, while they are relegated to a life of apparently permanent humiliation'.

Reform or Revolution?

The handling of the 2008 crash radicalized a generation of young people smart enough to realize the current system is in a doom-spiral. They are willing to transform what we have – to replace it with something truly humane, just and ecologically sustainable. During the 2016 US Presidential Campaign, the Occupy demographic emerged, for the first time, as a political force, impelling Bernie Sanders to prominence. Despite the efforts of the government, the media and the financial sector to confuse the matter, millions upon millions are awakening to realize that the system we have is not working for them but is engineered to serve the interests of a small, elite group. We will probably see increasing polarization in the next years, as authoritarian movements also gain traction.

Graeber believes the distinction between reform and revolution has vanished in the United States over the last decades. Since the 1960s, the US has transitioned from a manufacturing-based economy to one based primarily on the sale of financial products and services. Financial products and services have no intrinsic or tangible value, since nothing is produced by them. Products like bonds, as well as 'junk bonds', can yield tremendous rewards – but these rewards actually amount to a re-appropriation of resources. Wealth is extracted from the poor and middle class and transferred to the elite group of speculators and hedge-fund managers at the top of the pyramid, who control the money supply through the Federal Reserve and other central banks.

As a result of this systemic transition, the US economy became 'little more than an elaborate system of extraction, ultimately backed up by the power of the courts, prisons, and police and the government's willingness to grant to corporations the power to create money', writes Graeber. At the top of the pyramid, financial, corporate and government interests collude to maintain a rigid, centralized system that works against the interests of the debt-burdened multitude. 'In America, challenging the role of money in politics is by definition a revolutionary act because bribery has become the organizing principle of public life.'

In 2008, we witnessed the meltdown of the global financial system due to the collapse of mortgage-backed securities. While millions lost their homes, the US government bailed out the banks and financial institutions, creating an ever-ballooning burden of debt that can never be repaid. But rather than addressing the underlying flaws in the system, the government committed 'American taxpayers to permanent, blind support of an ungovernable, unregulatable, hyperconcentrated new financial system that exacerbates the greed and inequality that caused the crash, and forces Wall Street banks like Goldman Sachs and Citigroup to increase risk rather than reduce it',' journalist Matt Taibbi wrote in *Rolling Stone.*

Virtually none of the money given to the banks in the various stimulus packages and bailouts went to the homeowners or small businesses who were impacted by the system's malfeasance. 'Instead of liquidating and prosecuting the insolvent institutions that took us all down with them in a giant Ponzi scheme,' Taibbi points out, 'we have showered them with money and guarantees and all sorts of other enabling gestures.' The initial $800 billion bailout was only the beginning. Up until recently, the Federal Reserve has created, *ex nihilo* – out of nothing – $85 billion a month, using this credit to buy Treasury Bonds and mortgage-backed securities.

What this amounts to, according to journalist Chris Hedges, is the failure of the constitutional state – the checks and balances which were part of the original government of the United States have been over-ridden by financial interests, who control the levers of power. 'The collapse of the constitutional state, presaged by the death of the liberal class, has created a power vacuum that a new class of speculators, war profiteers, gangsters and killers, historically led by charismatic demagogues, will enthusiastically fill,' Hedges writes. 'It opens the door to overtly authoritarian and fascist movements.' As I write this book, Donald Trump has stepped through that door. There may be worse to come.

What has money become in our day and age? Money is a collective agreement that money is worth what the banks say it is worth. It has no intrinsic value, nor is it linked to anything tangible. The bankers and the administrators of the Federal Reserve and other central banks speak a complex technical language, difficult for most people to understand or follow. This is intentional. If the situation was made clear, people would, in all likelihood, rise up against it.

I meet a lot of people who claim to be 'spiritual'. They have impressive yoga practices, visit shamans deep in the Amazon, attend raw food retreats, ten-day silent meditations, spend megabucks on all sorts of workshops to heal themselves and develop their inner self. Personally, I found many of the twenty-somethings living in tents in Zuccotti Park, hanging out at local fast-food restaurants to get warm and eating donated pizza, to be more truly 'spiritual' than the people from the yoga, post-New Age or transformational festival scenes. The Occupiers were not just talking about unified consciousness and justice as some abstract ideal. They courageously risked their lives and their future to protest about our unjust society, seeking to build something better.

Occupy at first had a festive, numinous quality to it – like the last stand of the Mohicans, or the opening of a portal into another dimension. With Zuccotti Park, the Occupiers found an acupuncture point at the solar plexus of empire, just a few blocks from Ground Zero, across the street from Wall Street, the iconic capital of world greed, and punctured it. The brave act of a handful of youthful anarchists garnered global attention, sparking hundreds of copycat occupations across the world, summoning forth a Dostoevskian cavalcade of the wise and wounded, lost and disoriented, enraged and cogent. It was raggedy Buster Keaton pitted against a grim-faced army of RoboCops.

Friends from various stages of my life in New York and my years at Burning Man resurfaced as regulars at Occupy, working in the kitchen, running the library or cheerfully pedalling the bicycle generators that powered the media centre's laptops and cameras. Some friends went out at night to project anti-capitalist slogans on skyscrapers or joined in morning actions where dozens of protestors, dressed as janitors, brought brooms down to Wall Street and swept it out.

Democracy and Anarchy

When commentators criticized the movement for lacking clear demands, they were missing the point. Occupy was not, in its essence, a protest movement. It was a process movement. The Occupiers were seeking to build a new political system, based in direct participation, to supersede and replace the twisted version of pseudo-democracy we have now. Their goal was not reform. It was revolution – an anarchist revolution, giving power to the people.

As Graeber and other writers note, anarchy tends to be misunderstood. Anarchy is actually the most direct and egalitarian form of democracy, based on building consensus without coercion, recognizing the autonomy of everyone involved. Anarchist writers are often brilliant at summoning up their vision of a truly liberated society, what it would feel like and how it would operate. Instead of supporting institutions that become rigid, hierarchic and corrupt, anarchism would inspire continuous flux and immediate participation. What's interesting is that our new communications tools could facilitate such a system in a way that was never possible before.

Pyotr Kropotkin, a Russian prince who lived in the late nineteenth century, defined anarchism as 'the most complete development of individuality combined with the highest development of voluntary association in all its aspects, in all possible degrees, for all imaginable aims; ever-changing, ever-modified associations which carry in themselves the elements of their durability and constantly assume new forms which answer best to the multiple aspirations of all'. An anarchist society would be one 'to which pre-established forms, crystallized by law, are repugnant; which looks for harmony in an ever-changing and fugitive equilibrium between a multitude of varied forces and influences of every kind, following their own course'. For Kropotkin, who was a biologist, such a society would be based on nature's principles.

Gandhi, similarly, looked towards a future condition where there would be no political power – no machinery of the state: 'Representatives will become unnecessary if the national life becomes so perfect as to be self-controlled. It will then be a state of enlightened anarchy in which each person will become his own ruler.' Gandhi thought the ideal state would have 'no political institution and therefore no political power'. The ideal state, in other words, would be the one that no longer exists. I find this an exciting prospect.

The commonly held belief is that we need government and the state to prevent terror and chaos. Do we really know this to be the case any more? History reveals the state to be guilty of endless dark deeds and scorched-earth policies. The US government has laid waste to whole nations, causing the death and dislocation of large populations in Vietnam, Cambodia, Afghanistan and Iraq, using napalm, Agent Orange and shells of depleted uranium to further its geopolitical aims. Could no government do any worse?

Thinkers like Albert Camus and Hannah Arendt draw a sharp distinction between rebellion and revolution: 'Rebellion's demand is unity; historical revolution's demand is totality,' wrote Camus. The tendency of historical revolution is to demand the 'absolute negation' of its subjects, leading to ideological purity, mass murder and slavery without limit. The communist revolutions of the last century obliterated the individual, turning people into puppets of the state, forced to fulfil the inhuman dictates of a mega-machine. Camus preferred rebellion as a model.

Today, the radical reinvention of society – by global insurgency, mass awakening, spiritual intervention – seems necessary. It is something we must demand and enact. If we don't, there may be no future for humanity. But the models provided by past revolutions are outmoded, old hat. They won't serve us any more. So what can we do?

I don't think we can simply dissolve the governments we have now, as that would create chaos. But is it possible that we might engineer a peaceful step-by-step transition from governments controlled by wealthy elites where participation is limited, to a peer-to-peer system where local communities have autonomy, where power is decentralized, where we peacefully dissolve nation-state borders, where the people are free to be? I know this seems impossible. But so did a smart phone, 3D printer or neutron bomb until somebody built the thing.

Why don't we at least make this thought experiment? Until now, our focus has been technological progress, not social innovation. Our society has been focused on making things that make profit, not on reinventing our social system to support the greatest level of happiness, self-knowledge and freedom for all. What would happen if we changed our focus?

Our networks of communication could be used to orchestrate a worldwide campaign of education. As we teach the people of the world about what's happening ecologically, we will also train them in participatory democracy, as well as ecological restoration. We know that the collective consciousness is shaped by the media. Therefore, we can feasibly use media to point people in a new direction – one that allows us all to thrive. What I am proposing as the ideal is something like a holistic anarchism, where we apply the existing tools of post-industrial society – the tools of media, communication, industry and manufacturing – efficiently to construct a unified, peaceful planetary culture based on principles of ecological restoration and decentralized, local autonomy.

In actual fact, the United States has never experienced true democracy, except on a small scale, in townships. The American political system from the outset was carefully orchestrated to maintain wealth, privilege and elite control through a system of representation. In the Declaration of Independence, America is not defined as a democracy, but, explicitly, as a republic. James Madison wrote: 'In a democracy the people meet and exercise the government in person; in a republic they assemble and administer it by their representatives and agents. A democracy, consequently, must be confined to a small spot. A republic may be extended over a large region.' The US government became the model for other nation-states to follow over the next centuries.

Madison, like most of the Founding Fathers, argued that true democracy would lead inevitably to mob rule, factionalism and despotism. He feared what he called 'the horrors of democracy'. Given the power, the multitudes would undermine the structure of elite privilege and private property that the Founding Fathers, as landholders and legislators, wanted to maintain – and that their descendants have held to this day.

I agree with the Founding Fathers: if we establish a direct democracy where all people have an equal say, elite power and privilege will be dissolved, eventually. There will no longer be such extremes of wealth inequality, and everyone – including the super-rich – will be much happier because of it. I don't think a planetary democracy would disintegrate into mob rule or despotism, or some grim form of communism. As Rebecca Solnit discovered when she visited former disaster zones, when governments collapse the vast majority of people act more altruistically and compassionately towards others. They come together organically in communities and local democracies. This pattern is repeated again and again.

We seem to be quickly approaching that threshold where, as the social ecologist Murray Bookchin warned, our world 'will either undergo revolutionary changes, so far-reaching in character that humanity will totally transform its social relations and its very conception of life, or it will suffer an apocalypse that may well end humanity's tenure on the planet'. This process will only be finished when humanity no longer exists on Earth, or when we have established a just and humane society, liberated from artificial scarcity and free of domination.

Occupy represented the emergence of a new social organism, based on direct democracy and consensus. Like a windblown seed from a hothouse flower, Occupy infiltrated the control zone of imperial power, found a crack in the concrete, took root and suddenly blossomed. During the occupation, Zuccotti Park functioned as a new social organism.

The chaotic appearance of the park as a shanty town or tent city masked a well-defined order. In a short period of time, the Occupiers turned their temporary autonomous zone into a tightly organized command-and-control centre with sectors designated for particular functions. Within its small radius, Occupy included areas for public debate, education, communication, drumming, meditation, waste management, rest and so on. It was much like a cell, with internal functions, maintaining a permeable boundary with the world around it. Occupy Wall Street constantly incorporated new molecules – in the form of curious strangers – from the outside. Either visitors would circulate out again, or they would find their function within the cell's metabolism and stay put.

Spontaneous Evolution

Let's consider what's happening – and what we might make happen – through the lens of evolutionary biology. Long ago, the trillions of cellular entities and microorganisms that make up our bodies were competing with each other, devouring each other, as they blindly sought to grow and reproduce. Through a series of crises – through an evolutionary process of trial and error – they found they could further their interests by cooperating with each other. They learned to devise more complex structures, like eyes, bones, muscles and skin.

Spontaneous Evolution is a collaboration between Bruce Lipton, a cell biologist, and Steve Bhaerman, a political philosopher. They believe we are being impelled towards our next stage of planetary civilization, marked by interdependence. We will learn to coordinate our functions within the symbiotic super-organism made up of humanity as a whole in a harmonic relationship with the Earth's ecology.

As an analogy, they consider the process of the caterpillar becoming a butterfly. In the chrysalis, the caterpillar doesn't just sprout wings. After it has devoured all of the food surrounding it, the caterpillar's entire body melts down into a biotic goop. The code for the trans-mutation of the organism is held by a handful of 'imaginal cells' that begin to propagate as the caterpillar dissolves. At first, the dying caterpillar's immune system attacks the imaginal cells, but this only strengthens them. As they multiply, they install the operating code for the transforming organism.

'When provided with a new awareness,' write Lipton and Bhaerman, 'the cellular population that comprises the deteriorating larva collaborates to restructure their society in order to experience the next highest level of their evolution.' We have to hope that at the inevitable end of the metamorphosis of human society, we will have a live butterfly, not a dead moth – or an army of robot flies.

Biology reveals a pattern of fractal self-similarity on different scales and levels of complexity. Immature ecosystems are characterized by competition and aggression, while mature ecosystems are based on cooperation and sharing: our own bodies provide an example of this. They follow the same principle defined by the United States' original slogan: '*e pluribus unum*' – 'from the many, one'.

Evolution does not happen incrementally. Crises induce sudden mutations and rapid leaps. These leaps represent 'an evolution of increasing levels of communal complexity and interrelationships'. Theoretically, humans are on the verge of making a jump to collective harmony, modelled on the coordinated activity that happens within our bodies, which work together to support the success of the whole without wasting or hoarding energy. That is what the pattern of evolution suggests.

Unless we wipe ourselves out entirely, I think it is inevitable. The only question, actually, is the time-scale and the amount of destruction that will occur before we make this transition. It could take hundreds or thousands of years (which are tiny segments of time, compared to the millions and billions of years of evolution), during which the human population may crash drastically due to ecological catastrophe – perhaps down to a few hundred million or less. A better option is that we use our current infrastructure to bring about this change in our current lifespans, sparing our human family untold misery and suffering.

What we will see in the future is not a further biological evolution of individual humans – we won't suddenly mutate to be able to breathe methane and eat plastic – but a social evolution, facilitated by technologies and social technologies. Breaking through the current obstacles posed by governments, the financial system, the cult of profit and hyper-individuality, we will learn to build durable communities. A community is an assembly of individuals sharing the same interests and seeking the same goals – which can be as simple as a peaceful, happy life. Just like the microorganisms in our bodies, which gave up some degree of autonomy to become integrated within a greater whole, we will form communities to gain increased self-awareness and resilience – to enhance our happiness.

In *Non-Zero: The Logic of Human Destiny*, Robert Wright similarly proposes that evolution reveals a direction, pointing towards humanity becoming a harmonic planetary super-organism, a holon made up of nested holons. We are, inexorably, becoming a planetary community that orchestrates itself in an ever-more harmonic and unified way. 'As technology continues to shorten economic distance, the logical scope of supranational governance could conceivably become the whole planet,' he writes. Where I differ with Wright is that the kind of 'supranational governance' he envisions seems like the neoliberal New World Order taken to the next level. Instead of more corporate globalization, we can choose to reinvent our political and social systems to support local autonomy and bioregionalism within a truly planetary framework.

According to the postmodern worldview, as alienated individuals, we fight to maximize our personal advantage in a cutthroat world. The reductive scientific paradigm sees the universe as mechanistic, with genes as the master molecules determining our fate, but the new vision from biology is one of interdependence and symbiosis instead of cutthroat competition.

Much like single-celled organisms hundreds of millions of years ago, we find ourselves at a threshold where we must overcome our sense of separate identity to evolve new social organs. To survive, we must overcome limited self-interest and learn to cooperate for the benefit of the whole. This requires a change in our social nature.

As a new paradigm, epigenetics overturns the mechanistic ideology, presented by Richard Dawkins and others, that sees DNA as 'the selfish gene' or the 'master molecule' which controls the organism's behaviour. The DNA code within a cell can produce tens of thousands of proteins. How genes express themselves, what proteins they produce, depends on the cell's relationship with its environment, as the cell chooses, in a sense, what to incorporate into the cell's metabolism through its permeable membrane, based on cues it picks up from its surroundings. In other words, instead of being helpless captives of our genes, we have great power to influence both our health and our environment, if we can reckon with the subconscious programmes that guide much of our behaviour.

If we are going to make a leap to a new state of consciousness and social system, we must overcome the subconscious beliefs that distort our perceptions of our world and ourselves. At the moment, a great proportion of our behaviour is controlled by invisible ghosts, phantoms from the past. These ghosts limit people's awareness of their innate potential – their capacity to see their world clearly, heal themselves and work together for humanity's collective benefit. This is another reason that our self-transformation requires a spiritual evolution, an opening of consciousness, not just a political change.

Occult Conspiracy

So far, I have tried to be as honest as possible about what I personally believe is happening to our world. I have suggested we can see the ecological crisis as an initiation and also as a necessary stage in our evolution as a species. To me, it seems that nature has not abandoned us, but has orchestrated this transition. The best I can do is give you my best efforts to understand our situation, holding nothing back. As I said earlier, you don't have to agree with me about everything.

I have been primarily focused on the material and tangible aspects of our plight, but I think we should consider also the occult or invisible forces that may be involved, without overdoing or belabouring an examination of this question. Some writers, such as David Icke or John Lash, believe that humanity is currently controlled by off-planet or extra-terrestrial forces. This is also discussed or alluded to in many ancient works.

The Gnostics are often thought to be a sect of Christianity. In fact, the Gnostics were not Christian heretics. They carried the knowledge of the ancient Mystery Schools, which were brought to an end when the Roman Empire adopted Christianity in the fourth century AD. The Gnostics thought this world was an illusion – much like the simulated reality of *The Matrix* – constructed by deviant spirits, which they called the Archons, ruled by a cruel, deranged Demiurge. The Archons sought to compel humanity to believe in them, and to deny the existence of a true reality that we can only find through our personal efforts. In the Gnostic Gospels, Christ says, 'Open the door for yourself, so you will know what is.' But as Christianity merged with the Roman Empire, it enforced faith and obedience, rather than self-knowledge.

According to Lash, the Gnostics recognized the rise of Christianity as a deviation from spiritual truth. They believed it was devised by the Archons, who wanted to maintain control of humanity. When the Gnostics tried to educate the people and sound the alarm, they were killed – brutally assassinated, burnt at the stake. The priests used methods of indoctrination to control the people, in place of initiatory techniques.

David Icke believes that humanity was manipulated by extra-terrestrials at some point in our past. We were intended to be a slave species. These aliens either interbred with, or perhaps performed genetic experiments on, our primate or hominid ancestors. He thinks the ruling families – many of whom can trace their family trees back to early Roman emperors – are focused on bloodlines, because they can trace their genetic descent back to our alien, reptilian overlords. The trace of this heritage is the combination of genius with sociopathy. I find this an interesting thesis, but too literal and one-dimensional.

The alchemical philosopher Patrick Harpur looks at our situation differently. He questions the basis of modern, mental–rational conscious-ness. We have an inveterate tendency to believe that things must be either literal or imaginary, true or false. We are trapped in either–or dualism. Traditional and aboriginal cultures don't share this bias.

'Traditional societies do not distinguish between myth and history in the way that we do. Mythical events were not thought to have literally happened; yet in another sense they were true, as if they had,' Harpur writes. He quoted an ancient author, Sallust (86–34 BC), who wrote: 'These things never happened; they are always.' I believe we will attain the next level of consciousness as a species – overcoming the limits of mental–rational postmodernity – when we integrate the scientific worldview with this traditional perspective. We will transition from a dualistic viewpoint to an integral realization, accepting the paradoxical nature of reality.

Even our belief in a linear cause and effect is ultimately an act of faith. The universe might be organized on principles that are quite different from what we understand or imagine. The effect might precede the cause, as Nietzsche noted. 'History is that mythical variant we have chosen to take literally,' Harpur asserts.

By gaining initiation into the spiritual worlds, people realize the world is a cosmic illusion, ultimately a dream, as Tibetan Lamas remind us, as 5-meO-DMT directly reveals. Paradoxically, this doesn't make the world any less important or 'real'. The dream we are in is our precious opportunity for learning and awakening, for evolving spiritually. As it is in dreams, time may not be as linear or as straightforward as we believe it to be. There may, indeed, be other forces – powers or principalities – who seek to manipulate humanity, as the Gnostics believed; who play with us through history. But these forces are also, in the end, projections of our psyche.

Pronoia

If only one consciousness unfolds its creative capacities through all of us, then everything we experience as a nemesis or an opponent is actually a helper or a teacher in disguise. We have more reason to be 'pronoiac' than paranoiac. Pronoia is a concept developed by the astrologer Rob Brezsny. He thinks the universe is actually conspiring, at every step, to give us the most amazing experience we can handle at that moment.

I tend to agree with Brezsny, but I also think pronoia only makes sense – the world seems more pronoiac to a California dreamer than a Somalian refugee – if we also integrate Eastern ideas of karma and reincarnation. According to these wisdom traditions, our souls pass through many lifetimes; our actions in one lifetime determine our opportunities in future lives. Physics has demonstrated 'quantum nonlocality', where particles remain connected, even across vast distances, indicating that time itself is an illusion. Perhaps as we extend our knowledge of the quantum world, we will gain deeper ways of conceiving phenomena that are now considered mystical, such as reincarnation, or the *chakra* system.

If space and time are tools of our animal understanding, if they don't exist in reality – a reality defined by quantum nonlocality – then what we call a 'past life' might be more like resonance with an energy cluster. A particular set of experiences, feelings and thoughts might leave an imprint or remain connected through the quantum world. The subtle bodies and esoteric energy centres could have substance through consciousness itself, held in a morphogenetic field.

What some left-wing critics call 'empire' is a projection of our collective ego. The ego seeks control and solidity and can't admit these are illusions. In *The Wizard of Oz*, Dorothy discovers that a frightening spectacle of omnipotence is created by a little man hidden behind a curtain. We are in that situation today. The little man represents all of our fears and inadequacies, our lack of faith in our own powers.

In our society, a tiny group – the ruling elite, dubbed the 1 per cent by Occupiers – run the financial institutions, the mass media, the energy corporations. Seeking to maintain their power and control, this group employs experts in persuasion and propaganda, neurolinguistic programming and social psychology. It has inherited a whole structure of empire that is based on indoctrinating people, controlling them through artificial scarcity and violence, and keeping them ignorant, divided, disempowered, acting against their own interests. Now this control system is reaching its limit, confronting an obstacle which it can't control or assimilate.

I could go much further down this rabbit hole. I could look at the connections between the Bavarian Illuminati, the Freemasons, the Yale secret society Skull and Bones, and so on. I could consider the nihilistic worship of power as something occult and, in Steiner's terms, Ahrimanic. I don't think it will be helpful. Conspiracy theories have a hypnotizing, fixating quality. They can be profoundly disempowering.

I do not doubt there are many levels of conspiracy and complicity among those in power. Some of them may have an occult understanding of our situation. Some may be literal Satanists. Some may believe they have contacts with entities, Gods or grey aliens, that are not from this world. Whether this is true or not, it doesn't mean we can avoid our responsibility or abdicate our agency.

I recognize there are very strange, sinister worlds relegated to the cultural margins. These range from well-documented satanic rituals of child abuse among British Members of Parliament to semi-credible reports on treaties and technology transfers between the US government and extra-terrestrials. But these levels of subterranean connection and conspiratorial shadows are nothing compared to much more unbelievable facts. Among these is the fact that we exist at all (on a planet spinning around a star at 67,000 mph, as that star spins around the centre of the Milky Way at 450,000 mph), that the moon and the sun appear to be the same size in the sky and form perfect eclipses, that the relationships between the orbits of our planets weave perfect harmonic patterns according to Phi-based ratios, and so on.

Previous civilizations such as the Aztec, classic Maya and Egyptian understood that dark and light were complementary principles and both needed to be honoured and recognized. They created initiatory paths for those innately attracted to sorcery, malevolence and cruelty, as well as those who used ritual magic for benevolent ends and healing purposes. Mesoamerican cultures had temples dedicated to Quetzalcoatl or Kukulkan – a creator deity who protected life – as well as places to worship Tezcatlipoca, the god of black magic and the jaguar. In this way, those with innately destructive or sociopathic tendencies were integrated into the social order. By denying this polarity, monotheistic religions like Christianity actually empowered those with sociopathic tendencies to become leaders of society as a whole. If we are going to restore the sacred dimension to post-postmodern civilization, we will have to find a way to acknowledge the power of darkness, but place it within a system that allows the benevolent forces of light to guide, guard and rule.

In the transition from ancient myth-based societies to modern civilization, we lost ceremonies and rituals of initiation, while the priests and ruling elites designed a social structure based on hierarchical control and indoctrination, which kept the power in their hands, forcing the masses into obedience. In order for humanity to survive and eventually thrive, we must bring about a polar reversal of this system by creating a new synthesis, using its tools and techniques to bring about our freedom. As we will explore, there are many reasons to believe we can engineer this transformation.

10

Revolution

When the spirit of revolution arises in the people, it promises to change not only the outer world but also the inner domain of thought, dream and desire. The desire for revolution is the yearning for the decisive event that separates dream and reality – the threshold when suffering is redeemed, when freedom is gained, here and now.

The wait has been a long one. 'Man is born free, and everywhere he is in chains,' Jean-Jacques Rousseau observed, back in the eighteenth century. 'One man thinks himself the master of others, but remains more of a slave than they are.' Rousseau's ideas ended up shaping the French Revolution.

The cry for freedom has been the persistent undertone in the music of the oppressed, those who sing for Kingdom Come, the rising of the new sun, for whom history is an unfinished melody or a call that awaits its response. The dream of revolution is a secular version of the monk's desire for religious ecstasy, which erases the separation between subject and object, and, like fire, purifies as it scalds, transmutes as it consumes, creates as it destroys.

The Frankfurt School philosopher Herbert Marcuse found civilization haunted 'by guilt over a deed that has not been accomplished', the deed of 'liberation'. My psychedelic journeys made this so clear to me. We had got caught in an incessant tape loop of deferral and delay, an interminable 'not yet', in our agreements about reality. We betrayed the promise of past revolutions by building new prisons around ourselves – banking systems, governments, malls, corporate structures. We lost ourselves in a labyrinth constructed by the human mind.

From past revolutions, we know that 'we, the people', have the power to remake or reinvent society when it no longer serves us. This remains a strange and dangerous idea. Our civilization seeks to maintain the illusion that it is solid and permanent. Architects decorate banks and government buildings with Doric columns, imitation Roman statues and friezes that convey the sense of an ancient pedigree. All of this display is designed to fool us into obedience and complacency.

Revolution awakened the consciousness of mankind. People found, to their great surprise, that they were 'the people', historical actors: the subjects of history, not its passive objects. 'That all authority in the last analysis rests on opinion is never more forcefully demonstrated than when, suddenly and unexpectedly, a universal refusal to obey initiates what then turns into a revolution,' wrote the political philosopher Hannah Arendt. That is the lesson of our past. We discovered it again in 1989, when the multitudes tore down the Berlin Wall, destroying at the same time an antiquated ideology.

Until the late eighteenth century, the vast majority of people believed in the Divine Right of Kings. They didn't think of social systems as expressions of human intention, or as artefacts that could be changed or redesigned. The French and American Revolutions – deemed 'the vindication of the honour of the human race' by Alexander Hamilton, or 'the grandeur of man against the pettiness of the great' by Robespierre – were a shock to humanity. The people rose up to overthrow oppressive, corrupt, autocratic regimes. Through trial and error, the revolutionaries established the model of liberal democracy we know today – imperfect but a great advance over monarchy and feudalism.

Never-ending revolution remains our ideal in art, fashion and tech. Commercial society today requires continuous disruption, rebellion, the shock of the new. Capitalism is brilliant at absorbing anything that might threaten it. Che Guevara becomes a face on a T-shirt. The anguish of young black men is packaged as Gangsta Rap. Social outrage is turned into cultural product, more distractions to assimilate. The energy of dissidence and rebellion feeds the system and keeps it running.

The incessant onslaught of pop culture kitsch confuses and entrances people. We forget society is broken, that it needs to be changed, and we are the only ones who can change it. Made to believe we are powerless, we forfeit our power. It is easy to forget – until some problem leads to a crisis, and the crisis reveals a design flaw in the operating system that cannot be addressed by any reform.

Our society has revealed a number of severe design flaws that cannot be fixed within its current operating system. One is the grotesque, ever-growing increase in wealth inequality. Economists like Thomas Piketty have shown that the accelerated accumulation of capital by a few is built into the system. As the middle class collapses, we are experiencing something like the return of the *ancien régime*, a regression to a two-tier society of serfs and overlords.

Bill Gates and other billionaires promulgate their belief that the world is getting better for everyone. Depending on how we look at the evidence, this belief seems hard to sustain. For instance, in the US the number of children living in poverty has increased in the last decades, to almost one-third of all children. Corporate rulers and financier plutocrats are the new aristocrats, floating above the rule of law, whether they gather in secretive meetings in Switzerland to determine the fate of the world or preen in *Road Warrior*-esque costumes and gobble psychedelics at the Burning Man festival.

It is true that living standards and life expectancy have gone up in some areas of the world, while poverty has increased in others. We've managed significant gains in some areas, but this has come at quite a cost in others. We've managed only a few centuries of rapid industrial progress and we've accomplished this feat by over-exploiting the natural world, squandering finite resources that accrued over millions of years. At the same time, the advantages of our global industrial monoculture are somewhat ambiguous, at best. The desperate poverty we continue to see around the world is a direct result of industrial civilization and corporate globalization.

The second problem, of course, is that we are careering towards ecological meltdown. These design flaws are, I believe, linked. We can't solve one without addressing the other. I agree with the social ecologist Murray Bookchin that 'The private ownership of the planet by elite strata must be brought to an end if we are to survive the afflictions it has imposed on the biotic world, particularly as a result of a society structured around limitless growth,' as he wrote in *The Ecology of Freedom*.

We therefore need some kind of revolution, but it can't be anything like the revolutions we have seen in the past. We need one, to quote Dieter Duhm again, 'whose victory will create no losers because it will achieve a state that benefits all'. We must also make it a peaceful revolution – a gentle superseding of the current political-economic system, not an explosive insurrection against it. We need a revolution that is, at the same time, evolution and revelation.

The United States – guarding the global empire of disorder – has turned into a massive surveillance society, armed to the teeth, looking for opportunities to flex its police and military might. It has killer drones, biological weapons, neutron bombs, FlexiCuffs, Guantanamo Bay, 'extraordinary rendition', and myriad other forms of intimidation, torture and death at its disposal. Any effort to oppose this kind of force directly will only end in failure. With hindsight, we can see that many of the protest and radical movements that fought 'against' the system only ended up feeding and energizing it. A different approach is called for.

What we can do, instead, is use the current infrastructure to bring about a systemic transformation, much as the imaginal cells reprogramme the cells that make up the body of the dying caterpillar. Later we will consider how this can be done in more depth. Despite its military might and seeming solidity, the empire is fragile. Our global economy is floating on air, as central banks create money out of nothing and debt skyrockets faster than gross domestic product, which is a terrible indicator in any case.

The Promise of Politics

What lessons should we take from the revolutions of the past? According to Arendt, human beings have an innate political ability which modern society – empire – actively suppresses. Arendt was one of the most celebrated political philosophers of the twentieth century. Born as a Jew in Germany, she studied with the philosopher Martin Heidegger, who was also her lover. A brilliant phenomenologist, Heidegger became a Nazi Party member. In 1941, Arendt immigrated to the United States, narrowly escaping the Holocaust. As a thinker, she was extremely subtle, astonishingly wise.

Arendt published her first major work, *The Origins of Totalitarianism*, in the early 1950s. She outraged left-wing critics by equating Stalinism and Nazism, seeing them as equally destructive expressions of modern society. She coined the phrase 'the banality of evil' while reporting on the trial of Adolf Eichmann for the *New Yorker*. In her work, Arendt sought to rehabilitate the idea of political action as something that gives dignity and value to human life – action that is necessary, if we wish to have an ethical society.

Arendt changed my understanding of politics. She noted that the word 'politics' derives from the word '*polis*', the city-state in Ancient Greece. In a *polis* free citizens gathered to deliberate, debate and make decisions together. Arendt believes that democracy – human freedom – needs a public place where it can be practised, as the Occupiers demonstrated with the General Assembly in Zuccotti Park.

'Without a politically guaranteed public realm, freedom lacks the worldly space to make its appearance,' Arendt wrote:

> To be sure it may still dwell in men's hearts as desire or will or hope or yearning; but the human heart, as we all know, is a very dark place, and whatever goes on in its obscurity can hardly be called a demonstrable fact. Freedom as a demonstrable fact and politics coincide and are related to each other like two sides of the same matter.

By seeming to separate freedom from politics, modern society plays a trick on us. As long as we think of freedom as a purely private and personal concern, we remain unfree.

Arendt realized that Western philosophy denigrated and rejected political thought and action. Over 2,000 years ago, Western thinking turned away from politics – from action in the world – when Socrates was accused of 'corrupting' the youth of Athens and executed because of his constant inquiry. The impact of this was profound for Western civilization. It was like an original trauma, causing the split between thought and action that continues. Today, we still conceive of personal liberty as freedom from politics, rather than freedom to participate as authentic political beings.

Jonathan Schell wrote on Arendt:

> Among the difficult things she came to understand was that the great thinkers to whom she turned time and again for inspiration, from Plato and Aristotle to Nietzsche and Heidegger, had never seen that the promise of human freedom, whether proffered sincerely or hypocritically as the end of politics, is realized by plural human beings when and only when they act politically.

Philosophy became its own specialized realm, while politics became the path for those seeking power in the world.

What Arendt called the promise of politics begins when we understand that our power as political beings is a living force, rooted in our solidarity with one another. Electoral politics tends to be a sad spectacle of compromise and capitulation. But that is not the real essence of politics. It is a corrupt aberration. We are inherently political beings. Freedom is something we create, in collaboration and communion with each other.

When she studied the history of revolutions across the modern world, Arendt discovered, over and over again, 'the amazing formation of a new power structure which owed its existence to nothing but the organizational impulse of the people themselves'.

Once centralized authority disintegrates, the people establish assemblies, neighbourhood councils, cooperatives and working groups. They take over factories and schools and run them themselves, without bosses. They practise the direct, consensus-based decision-making found in many indigenous cultures.

The disintegration of state power inspires the immediate creation of local democracies. Arendt called them 'spontaneous organs of the people, not only outside of all revolutionary parties but entirely unexpected by them and their leaders'. Decisions are made by public referendums, arrived at through consensus. The people suddenly demonstrate 'an enormous appetite for debate, for instruction, for mutual enlightenment and exchange of opinion'.

The first time I felt this electric surge of possibility was during the General Assemblies at Occupy Wall Street. Recently the United States witnessed the promise of a redeemed politics, based on candour and compassion, in the campaign of Bernie Sanders. His campaign has proven that the energy expressed by Occupy is still vital, seeking new outlets.

Revolution is not the cause of social and political disintegration, Arendt noted, but a consequence of it. This was true in the socialist and communist revolutions of the nineteenth and twentieth centuries, and even in the neoliberal 'counter-revolutions' of the 1990s, which helped Putin gain ascendency in Russia. In *On Revolution*, she wrote, 'The outbreak of most revolutions has surprised the revolutionist groups and parties no less than all others, and there exists hardly a revolution whose outbreak could be blamed upon their activities.'

The revolutionaries would be hanging out in the demi-monde, skulking in the cafes of Zurich or Paris, writing their manifestos and screeds. Suddenly, social breakdown would start in their home country. They would return – Lenin was actually transported on a private train through Europe, to help accelerate Russia's collapse – to foment, infiltrate and take over. The professional revolutionaries' great advantage, Arendt noted, was not their intellectual theories or organizational talents, but 'the simple fact that their names are the only ones which are publicly known'.

Arendt believed that the professional revolutionaries, full of ideological zeal, often destroyed the rapid evolution of participatory democracy that had started, as if it were a natural phenomenon, as soon as government was gone. Given power, the revolutionaries immediately established new forms of authoritarian rule or dictatorship, following abstract principles from Marx, Rousseau or Mao. When they gained control, they crushed the new assemblies established by the people. They identified these democratic organs quickly as the greatest threat to their control. When 'the people in the sections were made only to listen to party speeches and to obey', Arendt wrote, 'they simply ceased to show up'.

Historians before Arendt 'failed to understand to what an extent the council systems confronted them with a new public space for freedom which was constituted and organized during the course of the revolution itself'. This pattern has recurred, again and again, in modern and postmodern times. In France, a citizen's government formed during the Paris Commune of 1871. In Russia, local councils emerged across the country during the early days of the revolution in 1917. For Arendt, councils and workers' assemblies were the embryonic forms of an entirely new system of government based on continuous, passionate participation that could have made the gains of revolution permanent.

When the Argentinian currency collapsed in 2001, the people gathered in schools and factories to organize their neighbourhoods. Workers took over the factories and continued production, forming cooperatives without overseers. Roughly a third of the Argentinian populace participated in General Assemblies, organizing locally to maintain systems for healthcare and food distribution.

Most recently, in Iceland, after the financial crisis of 2008, the people rejected the draconian dictates of the International Monetary Fund, choosing instead to evict the bankers responsible for the country's financial crisis. Using the Internet to hold a public referendum, they wrote a new, open-source constitution, declaring their country a haven for free information.

Crisis Is Opportunity

It is possible that the next revolution will never come. Although we are in a massive, out-of-control civilization barrelling towards ecological breakdown, the current system is also intricately interdependent and hyper-defended. While the underlying mechanism of the global financial system is broken, while shadowy webs of conspiracy and corruption extend everywhere, while billionaire financiers toast their own cleverness as millions lose their homes, while the planet's eco-systems buckle and collapse, it may be the case that our global oligarchy will manage to hold it all together for a while yet – like Major Kong in *Doctor Strangelove*, with a final 'Yee haw!', riding the bomb all the way down.

On the other hand, some series of unforeseeable events may create an opportunity for a massive, sudden change. Social experiments currently proliferate all over the world. They are happening in many countries, often as a result of the extractive practices and domination of empire. In southern Europe, where countries like Greece, Spain and Italy have undergone financial collapse, new political parties are emerging, based on grassroots activism. Finland is testing out a basic income. Many movements around the world, from La Via Campesina (the landless peasant movement in Brazil) to the Zapatistas in Chiapas, are starting innumerable local actions, from time-banking systems and worker-owned cooperatives to community farms. The hundreds of thousands, if not millions, of small-scale actions, occupations and resistance movements around the world could weave themselves together, causing the spontaneous emergence of a new social being.

We therefore need to understand what is at stake, and what is possible – even at the furthest edges of possibilities. If we don't have a plan or a new model ready, a social breakdown or series of disasters may only lead to new forms of despotic control and intensified repression, which will ensure further ecological breakdown.

Milton Friedman, the leading neoliberal economist, understood this. 'Only a crisis – actual or perceived – produces real change,' he wrote. 'When that crisis occurs, the actions that are taken depend on the ideas that are lying around. That, I believe, is our basic function: to develop alternatives to existing policies, to keep them alive and available until the politically impossible becomes the politically inevitable.' In the 1970s and 80s, Friedman and his fellow economists developed their model of intensive privatization, arguing that 'free markets' created the greatest benefit for all.

When the Berlin Wall fell in 1989 and the Soviet Union collapsed, economists and advisers from the US rushed into the void. Inspired by Friedman's ideas, they enforced privatization on a mass scale, convincing governments in eastern Europe and Russia to sell off state-owned resources and institutions to the highest bidder. A tiny elite appropriated the shared wealth of the commons, creating an oligarchy that led to the dictatorial rise of Vladimir Putin.

Radicals can learn from the Pyrrhic victory of Friedman and the neoliberals. Rather than stumbling blindly forward, we must define, in advance, the outcomes we desire – much as the Wright Brothers worked towards an aeroplane, or Steve Jobs organized Apple to produce the iPhone. Then we must define a strategic plan to attain our goal.

What we want, I believe, is to launch a social infrastructure that supports participatory democracy to grow and take root organically, without getting snuffed out by ideologues of the right or left. We also want to devise a system where resources are shared far more equitably. The goal should be a post-capitalist society where distributed manufacturing, renewable energy, participatory democracy, efficient cooperation and conservation combine with a universal subsidy or basic income to guarantee everyone on Earth – our human family as a whole – the opportunity for a good life, free of unnecessary insecurity and pointless suffering.

Revolution 2.0

As it widens the 'metabolic rift' between humanity and nature in its insatiable quest for more profit, for endless growth, capitalism has revealed a fatal design flaw. There is nothing in its internal logic to interrupt its momentum – to stop it eating its way through our planet, and ultimately collapsing our global ecosystems. Therefore, we must intervene and redirect it. The only way to do this is to make the global population aware of the dilemma, while those with the technical and creative capability design, field-test and distribute a functional alternative.

I find it helpful to look at the problem – as if we are seeing it from outside, like space aliens observing the Earth from an observatory on a moon of Jupiter – through the paradigm of design. When designers want to make something new, they expect they will have to build and field-test a series of versions and prototypes. When the first model breaks down, they build a second version. When that version fails, they create another. They keep iterating until they get it right. Artists similarly experiment in their studio, destroying or painting over their failed attempts until their vision emerges.

When it comes to building a social, or a political-economic, system, humanity has followed these steps – experimenting, building a prototype, field-testing it, discovering where the model breaks down, developing a new prototype, experimenting, field-testing, watching it fail and so on – over and over. Unfortunately, however, when the current version of society crashes, it doesn't happen in the laboratory or studio. It takes place across the much broader canvas of nation-states and civilizations. It tragically utilizes human beings – swarms, masses of them – as its Jackson Pollock-like splatters and drips.

Perhaps the greatest systems thinker of the twentieth century was the design scientist Buckminster Fuller. Fuller combined two strains of American thought, transcendental idealism and pragmatism, in a long career. He was a prolific inventor, mathematician and visionary. He passed through his own initiation as a young man, contemplating suicide at the age of 32, after the death of a beloved child. He decided that, rather than kill himself, he would dedicate his life to accomplishing the greatest good for humanity, without thought or consideration for personal gain. Fuller wrote many books expounding his philosophy, including *Synergetics, Critical Path, Operation Spaceship Earth*, and *Utopia and Oblivion* – they remain very relevant today.

In the 1960s, Fuller foresaw only two possible outcomes for humanity: we would either continue our current social and political arrangements and soon destroy ourselves, or we would undergo a design revolution in every arena. As part of this design revolution, we would apply our technical powers to allocate resources efficiently, working together to elevate everyone on Earth to a high standard of living and education. Even a half-century ago, he saw that we already possessed the technical means as well as the resources to do this. But the opportunity has been blocked by the inertia of our out-of-date political and financial arrangements, as well by as the ideology behind this antiquated system.

'All who are really dedicated to the earliest possible attainment of economic and physical success for all humanity – and thereby realistically to eliminate work – will have to shift their focus from the political arena to participation in the design revolution,' he wrote.

Fuller believed that the current model of work would be abolished in a truly rational society. I wholeheartedly agree with him. Deep down, nobody wants a job to occupy so much of their time. People want a mission that inspires them – that compels them to dig deep to apply their reserves of creativity, cunning, compassion and courage. Fuller noted that most of the work people do is a drain on the Earth's resources. All around the world, people are driving in cars to offices, using computers, toner cartridges and polystyrene packages. All of this is costly from the perspective of the planet's ecology (apparently the words 'ecology' and 'economy' have the same root).

It would be much more economical and efficient, Fuller reasoned, to subsidize people so they could live in self-sufficient communities where they produced their own food and energy. He proposed giving everyone on Earth who didn't already have a mission, a 'research grant for life', in whatever subject interested them. I love this idea.

Oscar Wilde, who was also a brilliant social thinker, arrived at the same conclusion over a half-century before Fuller. Instead of the current system, Wilde believed, we need some form of socialism, where people share property and reduce government to its most basic utilitarian functions. He thought that attaining a liberated society required developing our machines so that they could do all of the depressing and miserable labour – the drudgery – freeing people to develop their unique individuality. Wilde saw 'cultivated leisure', not work, as the ultimate purpose of human existence.

I find it significant that the field of robotics is developing quickly, reaching the point where machines can in fact do all of the horrible, dehumanizing tasks. Depending on what kind of society we construct for ourselves, we could liberate ourselves from meaningless labour, within the next half-century. For this to happen, we need a new vision of human purpose and possibility.

Buckminster Fuller made one error: he believed that the design revolution could happen without a major transformation in the political arena, forgetting that social systems are also artefacts of human design. As Arendt recognized, Western thinkers have tended to ignore our political and social system, which has developed through trial and error, experiment, failure and innovation. Also, it seems obvious that the only way we can address these areas is by changing the underlying beliefs, values and ideology that make up the consciousness of the collective.

In this book, we are exploring three areas: the technical infrastructure, which includes agriculture, energy, industry and so on; the social or political-economic system; and consciousness – the beliefs, values and ideology that are reinforced and reiterated through media, laws and education. These three main areas all work together, like three wheels with intermeshed gears that turn each other. When our technology changes, for instance, it opens new possibilities, which can change the social system as well as the collective consciousness.

As an example, we can look at the evolution in media technology, which has profoundly reshaped society over time. There would never have been far-flung empires like Rome's without a written code of laws, which could be disseminated across its territories, homogenizing how people behaved. The modern nation-state, our current form of liberal democracy, would have been impossible without the printing press, which allowed people to stay updated with regular news, so they could participate in elections as informed citizens. Following this logic, the interactive media we have developed over the last decades should also lead to a profound social transformation, beyond what we have already seen.

Karl Marx developed a model of how the technical, social and ideological areas supported each other as part of a whole system. He named them base, structure and super-structure. Marx also realized that the eighteenth-century revolutions had been incomplete, because they supported a false mode of individuality, protecting each person's rights (including the right to property) against those of other people.

The revolutions of the eighteenth century degraded 'the sphere in which man conducts himself as a communal being'. They enshrined 'the freedom of egoistic man . . . Man was therefore not freed from religion; he received religious freedom. He was not freed from property. He received freedom of property. He was not freed from the egoism of trade, but received freedom to trade.' The revolutions therefore led to the commercial society we have today, where people protect their interests against each other.

'Workers unite: you have nothing to lose but your chains,' Marx and his collaborator Friedrich Engels wrote in *The Communist Manifesto*. They wanted a worldwide revolution to liberate the proletariat – the urban workers, the industrial underclass – which they romanticized as the true subject of history. Their goal was to establish a stateless, classless society without privilege, private property or hierarchy, where the workers would own the means of production, and all aspects of social life would be centrally controlled.

Marx and his followers believed a worker owned society would mean liberation from domination and servitude – it would be the end of history. In practice, it didn't work out that way. Communist revolutions led to totalitarian regimes and dictatorships. Communism became a disgraced philosophy in the West.

To give Marx credit, he believed the communist revolution could only succeed if it started in a highly developed, fully industrialized society. Once a country like the US or UK developed a successful model, he believed, it would spread across the world. Instead, communism took root in underdeveloped countries like China and Russia, where ironically it accelerated a brutal transition from agrarian neo-feudalism to modern industrial societies. In the future, humanity may still choose to build a global civilization essentially without classes, states or private property – even if the system that results has a different name or no name at all.

The Venus Project

The Venus Project, developed by the millenarian Jacque Fresco, promotes a high-tech upgrade of communism. Fresco and his collaborators foresee a 'utopian' future based on a 'resource economy' without money or political parties. What the Venus Project envisions is not a democracy or communism or socialism – it is a world run by super-computers. Technology would be applied rationally, to create a world without social divisions, where goods would be mathematically distributed as needed. The Venus Project looks towards complete automation and computerization to liberate humanity from all forms of drudgery. Popularized by the Zeitgeist Movement, an outgrowth of Peter Joseph's *Zeitgeist* documentaries, which became Internet sensations, the Venus Project gained many adherents. While it offers an accessible utopian programme in which shared abundance is guaranteed to all, it envisions this happening through a totalitarian system that sounds nightmarish.

The Venus Project envisions futuristic cities, geometrically symmetrical, floating on the oceans, with a bit of Flash Gordon flair. 'Over time, automated machines would intelligently manage the earth's resources and ultimately free humanity of all unnecessary laborious tasks,' one proponent writes. 'All of the world's resources would be held as common heritage, and all people would have unhindered access to any resource, good, or product available, without the use of money, credit, barter, or any form of debt or servitude.'

In my head, I contrast my imaginary vision for our future with other models I encounter. The Venus Project comes close in some ways – Jacque Fresco and his collaborators envision an entirely equitable world, without need of money, where we have mastered technology to support ecological health – but I find the model they propose off-putting and dehumanizing, even though the Venus Project definitely owes a great deal to Buckminster Fuller's work. But their combination of design science with ideals of purity seem too similar to communism. And I think a world run by computers would be a boring, sterile and unhappy one. If we are realistically going to undertake a redesign of our social operating system to create a functional utopia, we don't want a world without eccentricity or nonviolent conflict.

The Venus Project rejects any kind of religion, mysticism or spirituality as antiquated and atavistic. Without an understanding of the psychic aspects of reality, its vision seems flat. It is unclear what people are meant to do in that sterile future state, once they have become appendages of a flawlessly computerized hive mind. The whole thing feels more dystopian than utopian to me. Without the prospect of a psycho-technic evolution, where people apply the tools of art, science and shamanism to explore the inner dimensions of consciousness, honing their telepathic abilities and psychic powers, I don't see the point.

According to the Venus Project, there will be no politics of any sort in the future. Super-computers will decide humanity's fate. Marx had the same idea, believing a communist victory would create a world without politics or struggle. I disagree with Fresco's team and agree instead with Hannah Arendt that political expression is part of our human essence. Politics doesn't have to be a corrupt puppet show. In an authentic society, the activity of politics – debate, discussion, decision-making – would be part of the fun. We would engage with it as something beautiful and true, an expressive form that combines art and ethics. We don't want to surrender our political agency – not to the 'dictatorship of the proletariat', and certainly not to a super-computer or silicon AI.

Permanent Revolution

For a number of reasons – perhaps because it was far more extreme and therefore more glamorous – the French Revolution tends to get studied, and celebrated, much more than the American Revolution. As Arendt saw it, the French Revolution was, in the end, a failure. It led to mass guillotining, the rise to power of a despot, and the Napoleonic Wars.

In fact, the French have kept trying to have another revolution to make up for the mess of the first one. Every few years, it seems, there are mass riots and occupations across the country. As I write this, another rebellion, Nuit debout, is under way, with actions in over 30 cities across France. Just as the original revolutionaries renamed the months – Messidor, Thermidor, and so on – today's rebels are following a new calendar, seeking to overthrow capitalism's temporal order.

The American Revolution – however imperfect – established successful, enduring institutions. But from my perspective, the failures of the American Revolution are as glaring as its achievements. The new government not only perpetuated slavery, denigrating Africans to subhuman status, it treated the native people on the continent as non-humans, who could be removed or killed without compunction.

At the same time, for the white settlers, the new system of government represented progress over the system of monarchy it replaced. The people were given some voice in their government, through the right to vote, and other rights were protected. Before the Enlightenment and the revolutions of the eighteenth century, the idea that 'All men are created equal' did not exist. This idea certainly represented progress, even though, in practice – from the early years until today – there continue to be two systems of justice, one for the rich and a quite different one for the poor.

Arendt explored the paradoxes inherent in the American Revolution – or any revolution, once it succeeds: 'The end of rebellion is liberation, while the end of revolution is the foundation of freedom.' To give a stable foundation to freedom requires institutions, rules and legal codes – and these, ironically, often limit people's freedom, in different ways. The Founding Fathers discovered an intoxicating joy in designing the new social system that their descendants would follow. They realized, however, that this delightful 'public freedom' they had found would not be passed down to future generations, who would be forced to follow the rules they made.

Late in his life, Thomas Jefferson realized that it had been a mistake, a design flaw, to end the revolution – to establish, in other words, per-manent and fixed institutions. An ongoing insurrection would have been preferable. During the revolution, local townships had tremen-dous autonomy – Jefferson called them 'elementary republics'. But this autonomy was taken from them once the federal government was established. He realized, too late, that he actually wanted a system where everybody is 'a participator in the government of affairs, not merely at an election one day a year, but every day; where there shall not be a man in the State who will not be a member of some one of its councils, great or small, he will let the heart be torn out of his body sooner than his power be wrested from him by a Caesar or a Bonaparte'.

Arendt discovered that, between the fall of an old regime and the rise of a new state, something new was always seeking to be born. This self-organizing had gone on time after time, as soon as government disintegrated. Worker's assemblies and neighbourhood councils had been, as Jonathan Schell also points out, 'the embryos of what might become an entirely new form of government whose lifeblood would be the kind of continuous, active participation in politics exhibited in the revolutions'.

The continuous revolution Jefferson wanted would have liberated each person to the highest degree, requiring their active participation. It would have been based on 'elementary republics' that were autonomous, regenerative and self-determining. It is similar to the kind of anarchism that Kropotkin and others imagined as 'an everchanging and fugitive equilibrium between a multitude of varied forces and influences'.

Postmodern society thwarts our innate desire to participate politically. Just voting in an election every few years, marching once in a while, or signing petitions on Avaaz or MoveOn doesn't count for much. We need new avenues for passionate participation – not just in elections every few years, but continuously. The desire for this is so effectively masked and covered up that most people don't even feel it as something they have forfeited.

Today's communications infrastructure could support a permanent revolution. In fact, I think this would be its logical endpoint. It seems possible – let's try a thought experiment – to design and launch a social networking infrastructure, via the Internet, that seamlessly supports political collaboration, direct democracy and resource sharing, based on transparent exchanges. Along with launching such a global platform, we would need to undertake a mass educational initiative through the media. We would have to disseminate the values and principles of a cooperative, trust-based society to people across the world.

As media critic Clay Shirky writes in *Here Comes Everybody,*

> Our social tools are not an improvement to modern society; they are a challenge to it. New technology makes new things

possible: but put another way, when new technology appears, previously impossible things start occurring. If enough of those impossible things are important and happen in a bundle, quickly, the change becomes a revolution.

We have already seen the power of our new social tools to raise awareness and coordinate social action in movements like the Arab Spring, Occupy, Black Lives Matter and WikiLeaks. This could be just the beginning. Over the next years, we have the potential to use the Internet to design, as a new global template, a participatory infrastructure for direct democracy that remains transparent and flexible, without hardening into a new institutional monstrosity. Many initiatives point in this direction.

Manufactured Mind

In *Multitude: War and Democracy in the Age of Empire*, Antonio Negri and Michael Hardt explore how a global revolution might become a universal phenomenon – and happen quickly. Negri, a political philosopher, was jailed by the Italian government in the 1980s, accused of supporting the Red Brigades, a leftist terrorist organization. In fact, it seems the government was just trying to silence him. Hardt is a professor of political science at Duke University. The two thinkers wrote a series of books together, balancing poetic flights of Continental theory with Anglo-Saxon pragmatism. The focus of their work is our potential for global revolution, based on their analysis of the forms of power and the productive forces inherent in post-industrial society. Negri and Hardt see new opportunities in the waves of social changes that have taken place in the last half-century and continue today.

During the Industrial Age, the focus was on the production of material goods. In a post-industrial world, the most important, or 'hegemonic', form of production is no longer physical objects. Today, above all in the developed world, the majority of work is in the realm of 'immaterial production'. This includes the making of ideas, memes, narratives, images, financial instruments and social technologies that shape how people form commercial or personal relationships. This is a significant change. Today, the biggest taxi company in the world, Uber, owns no cars. The biggest company for accommodation, Airbnb, owns no hotels. These companies – and others like them – seek monopoly control over the networks which define and mediate commercial relationships.

What immaterial production produces, most of all, is consciousness itself. Negri calls it, 'the production of subjectivity'. Our mass media and communications tools continuously produce, and reproduce, a certain level or frequency of consciousness with particular patterns of thought and action. For instance, people's consumer habits and values are subconsciously shaped by advertising. Corporations don't only respond to the desires of the masses; they use psychological techniques to create what Herbert Marcuse called 'false needs' – new desires for high-status or 'positional' goods. Mass consciousness – subjectivity – is manufactured, mass-produced, by the corporate media and advertising industry.

Edward Bernays, a nephew of Sigmund Freud and the founder of the modern discipline of public relations, put it plainly: 'The conscious and intelligent manipulation of the organized habits and opinions of the masses is an important element in democratic society. Those who manipulate this unseen mechanism of society constitute an invisible government which is the true ruling power of our country.' Bernays applied techniques of social psychology to reach into the subconscious of the public and change their behaviour. He famously organized 'freedom parades' in the 1920s, where glamorous young flappers would smoke cigarettes, inspiring other women to pick up the habit. These techniques have been refined in the decades since.

How people should relate to authority, what kinds of relationships they consider appropriate, what they should buy, and many other cues are given to them through advertisements, television shows and film. The primary function of media, as I understand it, is not to entertain or educate, but to coordinate behaviour on a mass scale, syncopating modern society around patterns of consumption, work and leisure. The positive side of this is that it suggests how a new form of subjectivity, a new level of consciousness, could be transmitted and imprinted quickly, if the mass media expressed a different intention.

Although the idea that 'subjectivity' is mass-produced may seem strange at first, I think it is crucial that we realize this. We tend to believe that our subjectivity – our consciousness and worldview – is a personal and private matter. Most people don't realize that the internal landscape of their thoughts and feelings has been constructed for them, produced by an extremely powerful and supple corporate-industrial entertainment system. This system has been brilliant at integrating rebellion and dissent, absorbing and nullifying it. I tend to think, in fact, that the battle for our future will be conducted through the media, which mass-manufactures and programmes human subjectivity. People have been programmed – but they can also be deprogrammed, and this can happen quickly.

The 1960s and its aftermath provide a useful case study. Back then, a political counterculture seemed to pose a threat to the dominant power structure. What Negri and Hardt call empire fought this menace in two different ways: the police and security services ferociously clamped down on the radical political aspects of the counterculture. Many leaders of the black liberation movement in the US – Malcolm X, Martin Luther King, Fred Hampton – were assassinated. White movement leaders were also put in prison, often on trumped-up drug charges. Nonviolent anti-war protestors at Kent State were shot and killed, sending a clear signal that dissent, past a certain point, would not be tolerated.

At the same time, the cultural ambience of rebellion was assimilated seamlessly into the machinery of immaterial production, feeding the consumerist system that the countercultural pioneers sought to resist and undermine. Rebellion – being 'cool' – was cut off from politics, ecological or social issues. It became merely a stance or a pose, used to sell products like cigarettes, alcohol and motorcycles.

Marx and Engels believed that factory workers – the proletariat – would be the class to launch global revolution and overcome oppression. This didn't happen as they predicted. Negri and Hardt seek to update this idea by defining a new revolutionary subject of history, which they call multitude. Since we are now in the Information Age, the multitude are 'immaterial workers who become a new kind of combatant, cosmopolitan *bricoleurs* of resistance and cooperation. They are the ones who can throw the surplus of their knowledges and skills into the construction of a common struggle against imperial power.' The software designer, the media maker, the hacker become foot soldiers in Negri and Hardt's revolution – neo-romantic, postmodern superheroes.

According to *Multitude*, revolutions follow a pattern of 'resistance, exodus, the emptying out of the enemy's power, and the multitude's construction of a new society'. In the past, this sequence took many years or even decades to unfold. But because our new social tools allow for instantaneous global communication and coordination, Negri and Hardt believe that 'insurrectional activity is no longer divided into such stages but develops simultaneously'. I find this a crucial insight – an amazing and also a hopeful prospect.

In the past, when news travelled slower than it does today, insurrections and revolutions were generally local affairs, confined to a single region or nation. Because humanity is now linked together through instantaneous networks of electronic communications, new social movements can spread rapidly, in a nonlinear way. They can become global phenomena, suddenly, without prelude or build-up. When it succeeds, a local initiative, a new idea, can be distributed everywhere, all at once, as we saw with the sudden global emergence of the Occupy movement or, on a technological level, the rapid spread of smart phones.

It is therefore possible to conceive of how a global 'revolution' – a new set of values, beliefs and behaviours, transforming our relationship to Earth – could become accessible, on a planetary scale. The ecological mega-crisis could be the lever that causes this sudden shift. Our immediate mission, then, is to be ready with working, peaceful, sustainable alternatives that can be scaled up when the time is right.

Part Five

Post-Capitalism: Property, Money and Power

11

Possession Trance

I've dealt with the big picture stuff, the overarching mythological frameworks that I believe to be the most helpful at this time of crisis. In what follows, I will explore the more material, everyday aspects of the current structures that we live in that no longer work for us, or that actively obstruct our progress: areas such as power, property and money. All of these areas represent social relationships, collective agreements, that become so ingrained in our approach to the world that we take them entirely for granted. We reject any alternative view of the world that doesn't seem possible, given the existing structures. We forget that these structures are, in the end, mental constructs. They can, in fact, change. If we are going to transition from our current predicament to a post-capitalist world, we will need to make new agreements.

It was 1985, a long-distant autumn day, when, as a sophomore at Wesleyan University in Middletown, Connecticut, I chewed a bunch of dried mushroom stems for the first time. During that first trip, I saw the entire concrete, steel and glass edifice of postmodern civilization as an artifice, a pompous fraud. We had imposed an abstract order over nature. By comparison, every tree, shrub and rock radiated patience, humility and good-humoured wisdom.

By briefly detaching my awareness from my ego, the mushrooms showed me that we live in a society based on layers of collective delusion. I saw how our system constantly tries to convince us of its importance and permanence – to intimidate us – while it suppresses those subjects that are most worthy of our interest, such as the nature of our own consciousness. The people around me seemed absent, hypnotized, watching baseball on television or reading reports on the stock market. I still recall going into a local deli and feeling embarrassed – ashamed – that the crumpled dollars I pulled from my wallet were what our culture valued highly. I felt that a joke had been played on humanity.

That semester I also read Jean-Jacques Rousseau's *Discourse on the Origins of Inequality* for the first time. Much like that first mushroom journey, that essay left an imprint, staying with me for my whole life. Like a fistful of psilocybin, Rousseau's thoughts peeled away at my understanding of the world, to reveal a wider viewpoint.

In his *Discourse*, Rousseau sought to understand 'the different accidents which may have improved the human understanding while depraving the species, and made man wicked while making him sociable'. He looked for 'the moment at which right took the place of violence and nature became subject to law, and to explain by what sequence of miracles the strong came to serve the weak, and the people to purchase imaginary repose at the expense of real felicity'.

Rousseau believed the origin of civilization was private property. 'The first man who, having enclosed a piece of ground, bethought himself of saying "This is mine", and found people simple enough to believe him, was the real founder of civil society.' Inequality didn't exist for man in what Rousseau called 'the state of nature' – in nomadic, aboriginal societies.

Rousseau believed this innovation led, eventually, to a state of collective suffering. In a society based on property rights, people find their positions insecure. They are forced to compete against each other – undermine and attack each other – to gain or protect their wealth. 'It has indeed cost us not a little trouble to make ourselves as wretched as we are,' he wrote. While those who hold wealth become vain and self-important, those without it often feel depressed and marginalized.

The Problem with Property

If we think about it, we can see that private property – a mental construct we protect by laws and police forces – has made our world an unfree world. A pigeon, a rat, a squirrel, has far more freedom of movement than a human being, who confronts fences and walls in most directions he might like to go. These fences and walls also live within us. We internalize them. It is possible that our world will always remain unjust and unfree until we end the system that protects private ownership, above all other rights. As unlikely as it is to imagine, this could be done humanely and benevolently. Eventually, we will supersede property rights through new cooperative arrangements.

Three of my favourite social thinkers – Karl Marx, Oscar Wilde and Buckminster Fuller – agree with Rousseau that private property is at the root of our society's sickness. For Marx, one problem was that property contorted the human personality, making us 'stupid and one-sided'. We confused the abstract 'sense of having' with a real sense. We got lost in this abstraction.

Marx wrote, 'In the place of all physical and mental senses there has therefore come the sheer estrangement of all these senses, *the sense of having*.' If humanity abolished private property and collectivized resources, Marx reasoned, people would be free to live in the present again. They would open their senses to the world around them.

Like Marx, Oscar Wilde saw that private property damaged human psychology by substituting a removed, abstract relationship to the world for immersion in the present: 'By confusing a man with what he possesses, it has led Individualism entirely astray. It has made gain not growth its aim. So that man thought that the important thing was to have, and did not know that the important thing is to be. The true perfection of man lies, not in what man has, but in what man is.'

All the world's mystical traditions tell us that we cannot truly own or possess anything – everything in the universe is energy undergoing processes of transformation. Chief Seattle said, 'How can you buy or sell the sky, the warmth of the land? The idea is strange to us. If we do not own the freshness of the air and the sparkle of the water, how can you buy them?' Ownership supports the low-frequency delusions of the ego that wants to control, possess, dominate the world. We turned *the sense of having* into something concrete, forgetting this is just an illusion of our minds.

Wilde similarly believed a new socialist arrangement was necessary.

> Socialism, Communism, or whatever one chooses to call it, by converting private property into public wealth, and substituting co-operation for competition, will restore society to its proper condition of a thoroughly healthy organism, and insure the material well-being of each member of the community. It will, in fact, give Life its proper basis and its proper environment.

Wilde did not see a contradiction between art and individuality – which he prized as the highest ideal – and a socialist or post-capitalist civilization. He thought socialism would allow the people's individuality to flourish for the first time. He noted that ownership of property 'has so many duties that its possession to any large extent is a bore. It involves endless claims upon one, endless attention to business, endless bother. If property had simply pleasures, we could stand it; but its duties make it unbearable. In the interest of the rich we must get rid of it.'

I think we need at least to consider the possibility that we can never have a truly regenerative society as long as the basis of it is private property and hoarded capital. I find obvious reasons this is the case. First of all, property (and the rents or interest collected from it) divides the world into two classes of people: Haves and Have Nots.

When somebody becomes wealthy, a Have, a huge amount of their intellect and energy gets channelled into protecting the wealth they have gained, rather than working for the comprehensive good of all. Perhaps they originally wanted to create things that helped and improved the human condition. With personal success, however, their focus inexorably shifts to protecting their own assets and their family's interests against everyone else.

Those without property, the Have Nots, feel little incentive to fight for the future of the Earth, because the world is already cut off from them. It is owned – lock, stock and barrel – by the wealthy. They don't feel the state of the Earth is their problem or responsibility. It is significant that indigenous people around the world have been courageously leading the battle against the extractive industries. Of course, this is partially because their homelands are directly threatened, but it is also because they come from cultures where private property either didn't exist or had limited value as a construct.

In today's 'Brave New 1984', a gigantic surveillance and security apparatus hangs over us like an invisible spider web. Its main purpose is to protect property rights, both physical and intellectual forms of property. 'When private property is abolished there will be no necessity for crime, no demand for it; it will cease to exist,' Wilde wrote. The enormous waste generated by the capitalist system is caused, at the root, by the individual's thirst to attain personal wealth – the only way to be secure in such a system.

Like Wilde, Fuller thought that private property would become a thing of the past once humanity liberated its creative powers through a design revolution. Already in the 1960s, he noted, 'Possession is becoming progressively burdensome and wasteful and therefore obsolete.'

Masses of people, particularly younger people, are starting to realize this now. We see a major cultural trend away from ownership towards a new sharing economy. Even the *New York Times* has noted, 'Sharing is to ownership what the iPod is to the 8-track, what solar power is to the coal mine.' This trend could be the start of a large-scale metamorphosis. Ideally, in the future, people will own little – or absolutely nothing – yet live abundantly, joyfully, able to access whatever they need or desire, when they need it. As virtual tools proliferate, property matters less to us than intangible assets, such as time and attention.

In *The Ecology of Freedom*, Murray Bookchin declared that we need to end the 'private ownership of the planet by elite strata' if we want to survive. As an alternative, we must establish 'a fully participatory society literally free of privilege and domination'. Bookchin expressed suspicion of partial 'solutions to the ecological crisis, like green consumerism, renewable energy, or carbon taxation'. He believed these reformist initiatives only concealed the deep-seated nature of the crisis, and 'thereby deflect public attention and theoretical insight from an adequate understanding of the depth and scope of the necessary change'. I think Bookchin makes a valid point – although one that will be difficult for many people to accept. The fundamental basis of capitalism – private ownership of physical and intellectual property – may be ecologically unsound.

What Do We Do?

I realize that the idea that we can voluntarily engineer a transition to a society where private property is either eliminated entirely or reduced to a minimum seems far-fetched. However, as Wilde noted, the progress of humanity is based on the progressive realization of utopias. Human nature is not fixed, but changes constantly. We first must realize – as Wilde and Marx did – that our civilization made a mistake in prioritizing *having* over *being*. We don't yet know what might happen to us once we correct that error.

Wilde proposed a transition to a system in which humanity was liberated from drudgery through automation and freed from the burden of property by socialism. He admitted he was offering an idealistic, utopian programme – but he did not think it was unattainable, even so.

> It is unpractical, and it goes against human nature. This is why it is worth carrying out, and that is why one proposes it. For what is a practical scheme? A practical scheme is either a scheme that is already in existence, or a scheme that could be carried out under existing conditions. But it is exactly the existing conditions that one objects to; and any scheme that could accept these conditions is wrong and foolish. The conditions will be done away with, and human nature will change.

Some radicals still believe that the only way we can have an authentic social transformation is through mass uprising and violence. They note that millions of people remain subject to violence, incarcerated in prisons for drug use, and so on. We live in a world dominated and controlled by military force. While this is true, I don't think violent revolt is possible in our current circumstances. The preponderance of military force, surveillance systems, killer drones, biological weapons and other insidious things makes an overthrow of developed world governments pretty much unthinkable. The consequences would be horrific. I also agree with the Gandhi-esque principle that violence can only beget more violence.

The alternative, then, is to engineer a peaceful transition of global civilization, superseding the current system of private property and hoarded capital by developing new infrastructures that convert property into cooperatively owned resources or trusts, over time. In order to accomplish this, we would need to establish a global network of early adaptors who have committed to making a transition into a system of open cooperativism and peer-to-peer production. If cooperation and symbiosis are evolutionary advances over competition and domination, then such a system should outperform the old model. Within a few decades or at most a few generations, it should be possible to engineer a global conversion – a planetary reboot of our social operating system.

Stewardship and Usufruct

When I try to envision how we might eventually abolish private property, I foresee a new model based on stewardship instead of ownership. Rather than bringing about an abrupt and disruptive change, people could transfer their property over time. There are already many examples of land trusts and worker-owned cooperatives that provide models for this. One possibility is to revive the medieval concept of usufruct. Usufruct means people have the right to continue to use a property or a tool productively, as long as they do not damage it, and particularly if they add value to it.

This is how people in many traditional societies still live today. For instance, in Ladakh, a Tibetan Buddhist enclave in India, many families farm the same plot of land for generations. They build their houses without title or legal claim. Another contemporary example is an urban community garden, where citizens cooperate to enhance the beauty of a plot of land or vacant lot, without anyone gaining economic advantage from their efforts.

I don't reject the possibility that we might transition to a regenerative society while perpetuating some forms of private wealth and ownership. Perhaps we can. No doubt we would require, at the least, a redistribution of wealth to create a much fairer and more equitable world. Wealth redistribution through taxation can happen during declared emergencies like wars – there's no reason we can't do it as we face global ecological meltdown.

People today assume private property is good and natural. We think it motivates free enterprise and drives innovation. In any event, we believe it is a fixed and irreversible aspect of our lives. Examples of collectivized property from Marxist countries like the Soviet Union, where the state owned the land and the factories, have no appeal (although there were some benefits to this system which have gone under-appreciated). But state ownership of land and factories is not what we should seek. Our goal should be to develop a programme which, over time, dissolves the concept of ownership entirely.

People would need to know their basic needs are fulfilled. Guaranteed a basic income, they would not have to prove their worthiness, or work to survive. Rooted in a shared sense of security and social trust, freed from the anxiety of market fluctuations, they would then participate in models based on stewardship and usufruct.

I think we need seriously to consider how we can make a peaceful transition to a propertyless society. An open-source, peer-to-peer network designed to facilitate cooperation, democratic decision-making and conservation could spread, much as Google and Facebook did over the last decade. Such a social infrastructure could take over many functions now managed by governments. When humanity becomes more comfortable with sharing rather than ownership as a model, we will convert private assets to commonly held resources. This might take decades or even generations – but we first have to recognize it as our goal.

A peer-to-peer network can make surplus or unused resources – a room, a piece of land, a second car – available to those who need them. As now happens on sites like Couchsurfing, eBay and Airbnb, people would have a rating based on past exchanges. Social trust then becomes a new essential currency, on all levels. People will be able to use collectively held resources, as long as they agree to abide by a set of principles, which would include caring for the land and buildings, and sharing with others. When multitudes of people find it to their personal advantage to pool their resources voluntarily in a cooperative network, the movement towards a post-ownership society will be under way.

12

The Money Problem

The force that transforms human nature is, ultimately, our desire to find meaning and order in the world. As an idealist, I believe no possibility – however far-fetched it sounds, at first – is truly out of reach. It is a question of what we choose to pursue together – how we define our purpose and what we consider meaningful. Most of us will agree that our current system – based on property, privilege, the brutal exploitation of people and nature – is not the best we can do. Apart from leading to ecological ruin, it doesn't make us truly happy. It induces anxiety, stress and fear, and it creates an insecure and unfree world.

The contrast is obvious if you visit a place where people still live in traditional ways, in intact communities. One finds a baseline level of happiness far above that of the middle class or the wealthy of the developed world. People don't have that disappointed, jaded, suspicious look in their eyes. They don't innately expect to be ripped off or shafted.

My question, again, is how do we transition to a regenerative society in the time available? There is no doubt that this requires a far more equitable sharing of the world's wealth and resources. There are two ways this can happen: either through social convulsions, or through the construction of a viable alternative supported by some subset of the elite and the privileged – the 1 per cent. We know we need to reduce excess consumption, redesign industry and shift back to organic agriculture. All of this is necessary – but it is utterly impossible within the current economic system. Why is that the case?

What's Wrong with Money?

People think of money as a natural phenomenon, similar to air or fire or water. Actually, money is an instrument that was designed by human beings to accomplish certain goals.

The modern form of a debt-based currency, issued by central banks, which are actually private institutions, and decoupled from any tangible resources, is a recent development that has accelerated the global dominance of finance capitalism. The inherent tendency of this system is to convert every natural resource into a profit source and constantly expand markets by privatizing aspects of the commons. Today, the small privileged financial class who control how money is issued literally control the world.

Since the 1970s, the financial sector has undergone a rapid, cancerous growth. We now live in a hyper-leveraged, deeply indebted 'financialized' society ruled by banks. In 2008, the global economy collapsed when we found that 'subprime mortgages', packaged into securities, were the basis of a massive Ponzi scheme. The beneficiaries of this scheme were the financial elite, and the losers were everybody else – the middle-class and working-class people who actually produce value for society.

When you think about it logically, it is obvious that those who profit excessively through the financial services industry are parasites. They don't create wealth. They extract it from the productive classes. The year after three million people lost their homes, Wall Street handed out $36 billion of bonuses. Through the alchemy of the financial system, the loss of assets of those three million people got transmuted into those bonuses. Virtually none of the bankers who created this fiasco were punished – quite the opposite. Today's monetary system is like a source code that has been thoroughly corrupted.

After the subprime meltdown, the governments and central banks worked together to prop up the existing system. They decided to protect the 'too big to fail' financial institutions. Rather than fixing the flaws or returning funds to the poor and the shafted, they rewarded the perpetrators. They created vast sums of money and gave them to the corrupt banks and securities firms, to ensure their continuity.

In the months after the 2008 collapse, the Federal Reserve bought $1.75 trillion in bonds, including US Treasury Bonds and mortgage-backed securities, and engaged in successive rounds of 'Quantitative Easing'. In September 2008, with the recovery still weak, the Fed started to buy $85 billion worth of bonds per month, and continued to do so for a number of years. They bought $600 billion worth of bonds in 2010 alone. The amount of US debt is currently $13 trillion, and still growing.

People will eventually realize our economic system failed – kicked the bucket – back in 2008. Since then, it has continued as a kind of virtual simulation of itself, a ghost, based on ever-growing debts that everyone knows will never be repaid. Around the world, global debt is increasing at 7 per cent per year, while global gross domestic product lags behind at 2 per cent. Debt forces unsustainable development. The system has only perpetuated itself by artificially inflating the monetary supply.

Masters of the Universe

Whoever controls the money system and the money supply controls the world. In January 2012, Kevin Roose, a reporter for the *New York Times*, managed to sneak into an annual dinner of a Wall Street secret society called Kappa Beta Phi, held at the St Regis Hotel. The 250-person party featured a 'Who's Who' of Wall Street plutocrats, including the CEOs of Citigroup and the Blackstone Group.

In a series of skits and comedy routines, the financial bigwigs mocked the poor as well as liberals, lampooning the system which rewards them. They changed the lyrics of 'I Believe' from *The Book of Mormon*, singing, 'I believe that God has a plan for all of us. I believe my plan involves a seven-figure bonus.' ABBA's 'Dancing Queen' became 'Bailout King'.

Roose was astonished. 'Here, after all, was a group that included many of the executives whose firms had collectively wrecked the global economy in 2008 and 2009. And they were laughing off the entire disaster in private, as if it were a long-forgotten lark.'

A major problem we confront in engineering the necessary transformation of our current political-economic system is that the people who currently run the show tend to be greedy and self-serving. Postmodern capitalism fosters winner-take-all competition and treats social and environmental costs as meaningless externalities. It self-selects its leadership from sociopathic character types. Given this system, those who seek to maximize self-interest in any circumstance, with no moral qualms or compunctions, naturally rise to the top.

I don't believe that the political and financial ruling elite, whose short-sighted greed and hypocrisy corralled us into this disaster, will be able to lead us out of it. Lawrence Summers was one of President Obama's key economic advisers and a former chief economist for the World Bank. Summers – himself worth an estimated $40 million – is on the record as stating, 'There are no limits . . . to the carrying capacity of the earth that are likely to bind at any time in the foreseeable future . . . The idea that we should put limits on growth because of some natural limit is a profound error.' Somehow or other, the financial elite who exercise such tremendous power and influence must be displaced. This can be done either by leaders like Bernie Sanders, who respond authentically to the problems they have unleashed, or through a 'leaderless revolution' where the people govern themselves via direct democracy, or some hybrid of the two.

John Fullerton, founder of the Capital Institute, resigned from JP Morgan in 2001, after a 20-year career. Believing the banking industry had lost any connection with the values and principles of earlier times, he went on a search to find answers to the underlying problems of the global financial system. He discovered that we were facing 'profound, interlocking crises', which included the reality that we are 'destroying the ability of the planet to support life as we know it'. The most startling discovery he made was that 'the modern scheme of economics and finance – what Wall Street "geniuses" (like me) practiced so well – formed the *root cause* of these systemic crises'.

Fullerton believes our greatest challenge 'is to address the root cause of our systemic crises – today's dominant (neoliberal) economic paradigm and the financial system that fuels it and rules it – by transitioning to a more effective form of capitalism that is regenerative and therefore sustainable over the long term'. He considers this to be our economy's 'Copernican moment', requiring the emergence of a new systemic and holistic worldview, embedded in an interlocking set of social and financial institutions.

Money Is a Design Problem

According to the Belgian financier Bernard Lietaer, one of the architects of the euro, there are a few important design features of our money, which he calls 'our most pervasive information system'. Money is issued by a country, or, in the case of the euro, a group of countries. It is issued by fiat – in other words, it is not linked to any tangible resource, whether gold or energy. It is created out of nothing. Because our money comes into existence as bank debt, it accrues interest over time.

When you get a loan from a bank, the bank doesn't create that money physically. It credits your account for the amount, which you can then use to buy a mortgage, or for some other purpose. While the bank issues you the initial amount of the loan, it does not create the extra amount you will need to return – in other words, the interest. You have to compete against everyone else in society to bring back that excess. Money is 'destroyed' – it disappears – when the loan is repaid.

The current financial system is designed to perpetuate artificial scarcity. In such a system, there will always be losers – in other words, bankruptcies. There will always be competition for money, which is artificially maintained as a scarce resource. Central banks control the global money supply by manipulating interest rates, among other means. Such a system is based on fear. It forces excessive, destructive growth.

'Conventional national currencies and monetary systems are programmed to produce competition and remain scarce,' Lietaer writes. Over time, interest has the effect of concentrating wealth in fewer and fewer hands. We have seen an extraordinary increase in wealth inequality over the last decades. It is estimated that 50 plutocrats currently control more wealth than that of half of the planet's 7.2 billion people. The poorest 80 per cent of the world's population control less than 1.4 per cent of global wealth.

Can we resolve the systemic problems – the ecological mega-crisis, the ever-increasing wealth inequality – unleashed by our current system by reforming finance capitalism, even drastically? Or do we need to transition to a different economic system, consisting of new instruments for exchanging value, which support social equality and ecological health?

Reformist Approaches

According to scientists, we are up against hard limits in how much more CO_2 we can produce before our planet becomes unliveable. We have released an estimated 1,900 billion tons of CO_2 into the atmosphere in the last two centuries. We have raised global temperatures more than a degree. We can only release another 500 billion tons of carbon dioxide, roughly, if we want to stay below the two degrees Celsius limit considered necessary to avoid runaway climate change. At current rates of CO_2 emissions, we will release that amount in the next 15 years. This gives us very little time. It underlines the urgency of our situation.

Unfortunately, we now know that even two degrees above pre-industrial levels is too much. It will produce catastrophic feedback effects. It may make large-scale methane eruption inevitable. Therefore, a massive, globally orchestrated restriction of CO_2 emissions must be combined with a comprehensive, global scaling up of renewable energy as well as all practical techniques to remove excess carbon from the atmosphere. This is what we must do – at least I can't see any alternative – if we decide we want to try to salvage our civilization and protect the world's children, including our own kids and their kids, along with the integrity of our biosphere. The change will have to happen exponentially, not incrementally.

At present, the main proposal for dealing with CO_2 while maintaining the current capitalist system is by taxing carbon pollution. Ways to do this include 'cap and trade' schemes that establish markets for the right to pollute and emit greenhouse gases, and ways to make companies pay for 'ecosystem services'; as well as systems of financial reward where money is given to companies and countries for not polluting or for leaving CO_2 sequestered in forests or underground.

'Cap and trade' seeks to regulate emissions by providing a profit incentive for companies to transition away from polluting. The market defines a certain number of 'allowances' for pollution which can be auctioned off to companies. These companies can then trade or sell off these allowances, if they are unable to reduce their emissions fast enough. The number of allowances can be reduced annually, limiting the total amount of CO_2 production, and forcing companies to innovate and switch to non-polluting sources, over time.

'Cap and trade is itself an innovation in how we operate as a society', Ramez Naam optimistically writes. 'It combines the best traits of the market – the rapid rate of innovation and the ability to find ever more efficient ways to do things – with the unique ability of government to set goals around things that the market is blind to, like damage to the environment. And it's worked.'

Naam points to the George Bush-led efforts to cap and trade sulphur dioxide emissions in the 1990s as a model. Between 1990 and 2000, sulphur dioxide emissions in the US declined by half, to under seven million tons. Unfortunately, sulphur emissions started rising globally again after 2000, largely due to China's intensive use of coal as an energy source.

That points to the deeper problem: as long as we maintain a global economic system that forces rapid growth, we will be unable to address the biospheric crisis at its root. We will keep shuffling deckchairs on the *Titanic*. Left-wing critics argue that creating new markets for CO_2 within the existing financial system will not help. The growth imperative underlying our system will simply lead to new forms of harm.

The Indian activist Vandana Shiva makes a compelling argument against carbon trading and similar markets. 'Creating a market in pollution is ethically perverse,' Shiva writes in *Soil Not Oil*. 'Some things should not be tradable – water and biodiversity are too valuable to be reduced to marketable commodities. Other things, like toxic waste and greenhouse gases, should not be generated. To turn them into tradable commodities ensures that they will continue to be produced.' On the other hand, if we can design a system that protects natural assets using market mechanisms, it would be far preferable to not doing so.

Carbon taxation is another strategy. 'The key to building a global economy that can sustain economic progress is the creation of an honest market, one that tells the ecological truth,' writes Worldwatch founder Lester Brown. 'To create an honest market, we need to restructure the tax system by reducing taxes on work and raising them on various environmentally destructive activities to incorporate indirect costs into the market price.'

Theoretically, if new taxes aggressively penalized CO_2 emissions, as well as other forms of pollution and environmental degradation, this would have the effect of transforming the capitalist system. It would force corporations radically to change their practices, embracing renewable sources of energy and regenerative processes on all levels. The likelihood of establishing such an aggressive tax policy, however, remains very remote, considering the power of corporations and their ability to evade or wriggle out of restrictions.

The underlying problem is that truly addressing the hidden costs and externalities involved in the current form of capitalist production will make the things we use every day far more expensive. For instance, a smart phone might cost $5,000 or more – which probably is closer to the actual value of its manufacture and materials. Prices have already been rising on many goods over the last decades. Without a transition to a system that resembles socialism in some ways – that applies technical efficiency rationally to satisfy people's basic needs – we will see extreme privation and misery, preceding a deeper doom-spiral.

Brown proposes a carbon tax of $240 per ton by 2020. He notes that this may seem steep, but it is still far less than petrol taxes in Europe. When he wrote the 2008 version of his book *Plan B*, Britain's petrol tax was £3 per gallon, equivalent to a carbon tax of £1,239 per ton. 'The high gasoline taxes in Europe have contributed to an oil-efficient economy and to far greater investment in high-quality public transportation over the decades, making it less vulnerable to supply disruptions.'

The market bases the valuation of the major energy corporations on the stored reserves of fossil fuel they plan to extract over the next decades, while they still spend $90 million per day searching for hydrocarbons. These reserves also play a major part in national planning. As much as $20 trillion of fossil fuel reserves must be recognized as stranded assets, because extracting them would lead to biospheric collapse. Those trillions of dollars of stranded assets are also structural underpinnings of the global economy. This is a knotty problem. It may be impossible to resolve within the current system.

It is possible, in the near term, that we will require a combination of state socialism to manage the energy and banking centres, anarchism to allow for myriad experiments in political and economic systems, and capitalism. In *Postcapitalism*, Paul Mason argues we must nationalize the central banks as well as the energy companies, in the short term. The state would take control of 'the energy distribution grid, plus all big carbon-based suppliers of energy'. He points out that the energy corporations 'are already toast, as the majority of their assets cannot be burned without destroying the planet'. Once made public institutions, central banks could focus on ecological goals: 'In addition to its classic functions – monetary policy and financial stability – a central bank should have a sustainability target: all decisions would be modelled against their climate, demographic and social impacts.'

The options are either that we build a global people's movement that forces these corporations to capitulate to the public will, or that we disband these destructive corporations, or that we find a way to compel them to change from within. They could, in theory, redirect their immense store of capital – as well as their capacity for technical innovation – to help engineer the global transition to renewable energy and conservation of threatened resources. One way to stop these companies from extracting those resources would be to compensate them financially for leaving them untouched. As painful as this idea is – like rewarding a tobacco company for not promoting smoking to teenagers – it is preferable to planetary meltdown.

No matter what tactic we choose, the only hope I can see is that we commit to an evolution of consciousness that must be intentionally engineered. We must somehow use the mass media and social media to provoke a mass awakening. The human populace must willingly accept serious limitations – on wealth, consumption and travel – over the next decades. We must voluntarily enrol ourselves in a worldwide effort to accelerate the systemic transition to a regenerative society based on renewable power, sharing, conservation of scarce resources, local farming and distributed manufacturing.

I believe that if the mass media is used as a megaphone – if a chorus of public artists and other public figures use their platforms in an organized way – the people of the world will agree that a period of shared sacrifice is preferable to the end of our species in a universal collapse of the Earth's life support systems. However I consider it, I can't see another option. The ecological mega-crisis is destined to unite humanity through either a universal collapse or a global awakening.

Systemic Change

Buckminster Fuller noted that 'under lethal emergencies vast new magnitudes of wealth come mysteriously into effective operation'. During the Second World War, for instance, the United States engineered a rapid shift of its industries towards military production within a few short months.

Now we need a mobilization, on a planetary scale, beyond what any human society has ever undertaken. We know the techniques and technologies that we need to deploy rapidly. We also know we must conserve our dwindling fossil fuel reserves and extract as little of the remaining hydrocarbon reserves as possible. We must intentionally redesign our political-economic system to bring about this transformation – and this is something that has never been attempted before.

Our best approach would be to pursue both solutions – the reformist and the radical – simultaneously. By all means, let's introduce a carbon tax as quickly as possible, if we can, as well as cap-and-trade agreements that may help limit carbon emissions in the short term and encourage investment in renewable energy. Let's also put a price tag on ecosystems services, charging industries for their consumption of natural resources. But at the same time, let's design and launch new instruments for sharing and creating value that will hopefully supersede the current system.

Bernard Lietaer draws an essential distinction between 'Yang' (masculine, aggressive) and 'Yin' (feminine, receptive) currencies. Our modern form of standardized national currency is entirely Yang. It is designed to be scarce. It forces incessant competition and hoarding.

Reviewing the history of monetary systems, Lietaer finds many examples of Yin currencies. These currencies are designed to increase social, rather than financial capital. They do this by building cooperation. They are issued in such a way as to discourage private accumulation or make it impossible. Currencies with a negative interest, or 'demurrage' charge, were widely used in Egypt and in medieval Europe. These societies had such an extraordinary excess of social wealth, despite their comparatively low level of technology, that they built enduring monuments like the Pyramids and cathedrals.

The simplest way to stop excess hoarding of a currency is to give it a negative interest rate, so it automatically declines in value over time. If you are using a currency that loses value the longer you hold on to it, you will want to get it back into circulation as quickly as you can. If there is nothing productive you can do with it, you will share it with other people and organizations who need it, building up goodwill instead of storing profit.

We have recent examples of negative-interest currencies used in Germany and Austria after the First World War, and in the United States during the Great Depression. Currencies such as the Wara in Germany, the Wörgl in Austria, and a number of 'stamp scrips' in the US depreciated in value. These alternatives rapidly reduced unemployment and supported the growth of local economies by keeping money flowing within the community. The reason we don't know about these experiments today is not because they failed but because they were surprisingly effective. The governing elites realized they threatened their central bank's control over the monetary supply and quickly made them illegal. President Roosevelt, for instance, prohibited these 'emergency currencies' in 1934, at the height of the Great Depression.

Lietaer proposes a negative-interest currency, the Terra, as a global standard for making trades. The value of the Terra would be linked to a 'basket' of commodities sold on the stock market, and therefore would not float in an abstract void, like today's currencies. The Terra would feature a 'demurrage' charge, losing value over time. The way that money currently accrues interest – eternally – has no relationship to nature. In nature, things degrade, break and rot over time. A negative-interest currency like the Terra could bring human activity more in alignment with natural processes.

A trading currency like the Terra could be combined with local currency initiatives, such as Time Banks and Local Exchange Trading Systems (LETS). These currencies would be designed to keep value circulating within communities, instead of flowing to distant rentiers or corporations. Instead of only using one type of currency – debt-based, issued by central banks – for everything, we would have an 'ecosystem' of currencies used for different purposes, intentionally designed as an interdependent whole that supports ecologically restorative activities.

We can develop many different instruments for exchanging value. Local and complementary currencies can be designed to keep value circulating within communities instead of flowing out to corporations. 'Local currencies work best for locally generated goods and services, or when a commodity's markup is derived from a locally added value, such as atmosphere or labor,' writes Doug Rushkoff in *Throwing Rocks at the Google Bus*. 'Complementary currency's purpose, more often than not, is either to kick-start a local economy or to make local transactions less burdened by the cost of currency and thus more competitive with non-local corporate, chain store, or big-box offerings.' Rushkoff, like many thinkers, believes we need to reprogramme 'the operating system of money . . . from the ground up to be biased less toward preserving passive wealth for the rich and more toward exchanging value among everyone else'.

One simple way to measure value is through hours of work exchanged. This is how Time Banks operate. On the time-banking platform TimeRepublik, for instance, people can offer skills to each other on an hour-per-hour basis. A carpenter might come to your house to fix your shelves. You pay them with hours you have accrued, and they then use those hours to get a babysitter. A Time Bank system can be a useful complement to other forms of currency. A time-dollar network makes great sense in areas where traditional employment is scarce. Cities in Italy and Spain are currently working with TimeRepublik to encourage skill sharing locally.

In a LETS, local businesses, service providers and manufacturers come together to back their own interest-free currency. 'Any group of traders can organize to allocate their own collective credit among themselves – according to their own criteria, and interest-free,' writes Tom Greco, in *The End of Money and the Future of Civilization*. Such systems can 'open the way to more harmonious and mutually beneficial trading relationships when done at a large enough scale that includes a sufficiently broad range of goods and services, spanning all levels of the supply chain from retail to wholesale, to manufacturing, to basic commodities'.

LETS are a means for local communities to exchange goods and services without debt or interest – without being controlled or influenced by multinational companies and predatory financial institutions. They can also support new initiatives that help build diverse, healthy, mutually supportive enterprises. Utilities that fulfil basic needs – like electricity or water – provide extremely stable foundations for community currencies, as everyone accepts the value they provide.

I am not going to pretend that I have The Answer to the money problem. However, the work of Lietaer, Greco, Fullerton and many others suggests that we can reprogramme our economic operating system to reduce wealth inequality, incentivize conservation and increase cooperation – just as our current system creates artificial scarcity and forces accumulation, waste and competition. The current money system actually deforms human nature, which is innately altruistic. It forces people to compete against each other in order to survive. Because human nature is inherently malleable, new forms of currency can reshape our behaviour towards altruism, conservation and communal cooperation – in fact, this would be closer to our original, premodern condition.

A new system must incentivize ethically grounded action based on long-term forethought over the pursuit of short-term, self-centred goals. We can accomplish this by changing the reward system – but we will also need to transform our society's values. Instead of the private accumulation of wealth, we must prioritize efficient sharing, mutual aid and the rational redistribution of resources. The share of global wealth controlled by the tiny class of the financial elite must be reduced significantly – but this can happen within a global movement towards a society that produces greater happiness and opportunity for everyone, including the 1 per cent.

To replace the single monolithic currency, we require a combination of diverse instruments for exchanging value. These would include community currencies, negative-interest currencies for global trading, Time Banks and so on. New currencies – ranging from local to global instruments – would support equitable development and cooperative social ventures. The need for constant economic growth would be reduced if people were given a universal subsidy, freely provided with the basic means to live a decent life.

Instead of moving towards a more hopeful future, we are currently seeing automation displace millions of jobs, and this problem will get far worse in the next decades. Our current economic system perpetuates outmoded forms of the struggle for existence, and forces excess waste, unnecessary development and ecological destruction. I don't see how reforms will be enough. What we need, instead, is to launch a new operating system.

What's After Money?

With the Internet, humanity now possesses a globally interactive medium for enhancing knowledge, building consensus, sharing value and supporting collective action, on every scale. We are continuously connected with each other, globally. When it comes to engineering social transformation, this means we don't have to undergo a slow, linear progression any more. We have the potential to supersede our outmoded systems and institutions rapidly. We can bring about changes in a handful of years that would have previously taken decades or centuries.

In the short term – there is no getting around it – we must undertake severe restrictions in CO_2 emissions. No market mechanism can help us here, as this move goes directly against the capitalist system and our profligate lifestyles. As draconian as this sounds, I think we need something like a global moratorium on meat eating, excess consumption and exotic vacationing until we bring about a technical and economic transition. Surely, if we expressed it to them properly, the vast majority of our human family would agree that a period of shared sacrifice is preferable to a total breakdown in the planet's life support systems. The potential also is that we make a shift into a post-capitalist mode of existence where people everywhere work far less and have more opportunity for self-development.

One way to do this is, I believe, would be through collective agreements or voluntary social contracts. We merge the breakthroughs we have seen with online crowd-funding like Kickstarter and movement-building platforms like Avaaz to ask people to commit to changing their lifestyle for the benefit of the whole. A social network could provide instant support groups for people who wanted to shift to vegetarian diets, form solar energy cooperatives or engage in building wilderness corridors to protect threatened species. What would happen, I wonder, if, through the Internet, 100 million US citizens made an agreement not to pay taxes until the US redirected funds from military weapons programmes to renewable energy? The government might be forced to change its priorities. Globally, through online referendums, the people can ratify a universal code of conduct, agreeing to follow something like the already existing Earth Charter, which seeks to define 'interdependent principles for a sustainable way of life as a common standard by which the conduct of all individuals, organizations, businesses, governments, and transnational institutions is to be guided and assessed'. In other words, humanity needs to agree on a universal code of ethical behaviour that will align our actions as a species with the limits of our biosphere.

As part of this process of building a truly participatory and democratic planetary culture, we must also design new instruments for sharing and storing value. We have a recent example in the partial success of Bitcoin. Bitcoin is not perfect, but it proves that virtual currencies can work without a central banking system. Entirely decentralized, managed by peer-to-peer technology, Bitcoins are virtually 'mined'. What this means is that each Bitcoin depends on the outcome of a complex mathematical operation, which takes a great deal of time and computer processing power to solve. Bitcoins are designed in such a way that only 21 million of them will ever exist. This alone doesn't limit their potential, however, as a Bitcoin can, in theory, be divided forever.

'Bitcoin gives us, for the first time, a way for one Internet user to transfer a unique piece of digital property to another Internet user, such that the transfer is guaranteed to be safe and secure, everyone knows that the transfer has taken place, and nobody can challenge the legitimacy of the transfer,' tech investor Marc Andreessen wrote in the *New York Times*. 'The consequences of this breakthrough are hard to overstate.'

I know this is a fairly abstract idea, but since Bitcoins have no tangible value, when you get a Bitcoin what you are actually receiving is a 'share' in the greater entity of Bitcoin. Bitcoin is something like a distributed, leaderless and autonomous organization or corporation. This opens up the possibility that we can use the blockchain – the under-lying architecture of Bitcoin – to build other kinds of companies and organizations. The blockchain functions as a transparent ledger where all exchanges get stored and can be permanently tracked. In theory, the blockchain could take away the opacity that currently obscures many aspects of our financial system. Compared to the blockchain, the actual Bitcoin currency may be of negligible importance. The blockchain could be the infrastructure for something like the resource-based economy envisioned by the Venus Project.

Vitalik Buterin, founder of Ethereum, calls these new enterprises, Distributed Autonomous Organizations (DAOs) or Distributed Autonomous Companies (DACs). DAOs and DACs can be based on self-executing contracts, defined by mathematical rules. It is possible to have 'an organization whose organizational bylaws are 100 per cent crystal clear, embedded in mathematical code', he writes. This could be a new way to operate a non-profit organization, a trust, a media company, or to issue any number of currencies. As I write this, the first major initiative of this type, called The DAO (for Distributed Autonomous Organization), has raised $150 million from small-scale investors, which will be used to develop more applications using the blockchain.

For instance, a DAO could be a worker-owned cooperative, or a network of permaculture projects, meditation centres or urban farming collectives. These kinds of distributed organizations might replace the current form of corporations, which are hierarchical, proprietary and profit-driven. As an example, Doug Rushkoff asks us to imagine 'a platform-independent Uber, owned by the drivers who use it. There's no server to maintain, no venture capital to pay back, no new verticals or horizontals in which to expand, no acquisition and no exit. There are just drivers whose labour and vehicles constitute ownership of the enterprise.' He points towards one experiment, La'Zooz, 'a blockchain-managed ridesharing app', where 'drivers are co-owners of a trans-portation collective organized through distributed protocols'. It is conceivable that every social function could be reconfigured in such a manner.

Rushkoff notes that the potential for such 'platform cooperatives' actually answers the original egalitarian dreams promised by the digital revolution:

> The basic behavior of downloading an app in order to work or rent property has already been anchored in users by Airbnb, Uber, TaskRabbit, Mechanical Turk, and countless others. Using a blockchain is just a small step further, compared to the original leap into digital labor and exchange. It is the disintermediation that all these supposedly disruptive platforms were promising in the first place.

I know it is hard to imagine reinventing the global financial system. But I don't think we have any choice: debt-based currency is inevitably destructive, forcing unsustainable growth. We need to inspire people to become active agents in bringing about this systemic change, providing them with the tools to facilitate it.

13

Power and Leadership

I must have been around three years old when my babysitter brought *Abbey Road* to our apartment on St Marks Place. She let me peel the plastic wrapper off the cardboard sleeve, overcoming the faint, crackly resistance of static cling. The photo on the cover showed the four Beatles crossing a London street. John wore a pristine white suit and sported a long beard. Paul went barefoot. They looked relaxed, slightly sheepish, somehow sublime. The image seemed to have a totemic significance. All of their album covers did.

To my child's mind, the Apple logo of the Beatles represented some cosmic force – liberated creativity, pure good – only just touching down on our world. The Beatles seemed to foreshadow a happy future on Earth. Their music has informed my politics – fuelled my utopian cravings – ever since.

The Beatles conveyed the message that humanity was going to triumph, somehow, in the end. I don't know how this filtered through, exactly, or, even today, what it means. Was it their particular mix of irony and innocence, formality and spontaneity that suggested this? Did their gentleness reveal a no-longer character-armoured or warlike masculinity – the victory of Orpheus and Dionysus over Pluto and Hades, of Eros over Thanatos? Was it because they embraced psychedelia and Indian mysticism? Was it because they harmonized with such irrepressible joy?

In just a handful of years, the Beatles evolved from the pop tradition of romantic love, expressed in songs such as 'I Want to Hold Your Hand' and 'She Loves You', to the all-encompassing compassion, the universal love, in late works like 'All You Need Is Love' and 'Let It Be'. In retrospect, one senses the impulse towards communion even in their earliest melodies. It felt like the Beatles were messengers – angels of history, bearing news from the future.

Listening to the Beatles, one felt that humanity was almost done with the horrors of the past. We were ready to leave behind our tortuous legacy of world wars, concentration camps, famines, depressions, gulags and forced marches. This didn't have to be a long, drawn-out process. It could happen in one sudden leap of collective will and imagination. It was imminent.

John and Yoko, inspired by LSD and mass adulation, must have believed they were riding this wave. Ahead of their time, they made a brilliant attempt to market and brand the concept of peace. They took out black-and-white billboards proclaiming, 'WAR IS OVER, IF YOU WANT IT'. They accompanied this by their performance-art bed-ins, exposing themselves to ridicule and scorn from the media, to make their humble point. They were right, of course. If everyone on Earth had joined John and Yoko and jumped into bed, war would have become impossible.

A generation later, Apple popped up as an icon once again. The Apple of Steve Jobs symbolized the union of silicon technology and human creativity. The alchemical apple of Eve's desire, borne along the centuries, touched down in Liverpool and Silicon Valley. We still follow the fable.

The music of the late 1960s seemed to point towards an imminent insurrection – an electrified upsurge of creative Shakti, destined to remake civilization. To succeed, to become the new baseline, such a revolution needs a steady foundation, a strong backbeat. The radical movements of the 1960s failed to provide that stability. In the end, they were easily dismantled by those craven Blue Meanies who work behind the scenes, pulling the levers of the shadow government and the military-industrial complex.

'We shall overcome', they used to sing during civil rights marches – a profound, moving, beautiful anthem.

But when shall we overcome?

What are we waiting for?

Wisdom Revolution

The level of transformation required now is inconceivable without a change of consciousness and a new planetary culture. But we may be on the cusp of a wisdom revolution – and it could happen quickly. As the futurist Peter Russell points out, revolutions in human culture unfold in exponentially shorter timeframes. The Agricultural Revolution started eight to ten thousand years ago, leading to the development of a surplus which was necessary for the growth of cities, and a complex, differentiated social system. The Industrial Revolution took around five hundred years, with its roots going back to the Middle Ages. The Information Revolution – the linking of the planetary community together through networks of data and communication – has happened within a half-century or so.

Russell thinks we are approaching what he calls the Wisdom Revolution. 'The growth of human information technologies is taking us rapidly toward a time when all human knowledge will be instantly available to anyone on the planet, in any medium.' Increasingly, he writes, we are connected to 'an emerging global mind'. This is leading to a qualitative shift, first, from information to knowledge and then from knowledge to wisdom.

If we agree that incremental reforms will not save us, then we can explore how we work together to accelerate the wisdom revolution, building the new planetary culture necessary to support it, based on values such as empathy, responsible forethought and resilience. Personally, I believe the media has a crucial role to play if we are going to make this transition. We need to reprogramme the values and ideals of the masses. Most don't even realize that much of what they believe to be true is just a programme that has indoctrinated them.

Revolt of the Masses

Antonio Negri noted that post-industrial civilization uses memes, narratives, media and networks to 'produce' mass subjectivity – to engineer a certain kind of consciousness. The detached, passive consciousness of the masses props up a centralized, industrial society based on consumerism, but has become a threat to our collective future. Now we need people to be educated, flexible, adaptive and active in remaking our world. We must quickly change our social nature as a species as we adapt to new conditions. In the same way that corporations created consumers continuously seeking to satisfy 'false needs', we can create a new model for our collective and individual patterns of behaviour, based on the authentic needs of the Earth.

Writing in the 1930s, José Ortega y Gasset proposed that civilization needed to be directed towards a collective mission – a goal that would carry the individual, as well as the masses, beyond their personal concerns. Without such a mission, society degenerates. 'Human life, by its very nature, has to be dedicated to something, an enterprise glorious or humble, a destiny illustrious or trivial,' he wrote in *Revolt of the Masses*. Ortega believed that most people needed to be given goals to believe in and strive towards.

A liberal Spanish philosopher who served as a civil deputy in the second Spanish Republic, Ortega thought civilization had lost its direction in modern times, causing a collapse of civic life. Since the Renaissance, Europe had established the ideals and values which the world followed. But in the twentieth century, Europe entered a crisis of nihilism, losing faith in its own principles, leaving a void which Fascism and totalitarian governments rushed in to fill.

He argued that some group – some subset of humanity – needed to lead, to establish a moral centre, a vision, for the mass of people to follow and rally around. 'To command is to give people something to do, to fit them into their destiny, to prevent their wandering aimlessly about in an empty, desolate existence.' As an elitist, he could be quite caustic in his views. 'The majority of men have no opinions, and these have to be pumped into them from outside, like lubricants into machinery.'

Ortega thought it was the role of the elite to establish a civilization's goals and shape its opinions. The alternative was chaos. 'Can we be surprised that the world today seems empty of purposes, anticipations, ideals?' Ortega asked. 'Nobody has concerned himself with supplying them.' Today, the closest approximation we have to long-range 'purposes, anticipations, ideals' is the cultural faith in the Singularity, where humans merge with machines or get replaced by sentient robots.

Although it has been 80 years since he wrote his idiosyncratic masterpiece, I still agree with many of Ortega's ideas. The mass of people are followers – this is neither good nor bad. It is a neutral fact. Most people simply want to be shown a path to a good and meaningful life. They seek values, ideals and beliefs to give them meaning, hope and inspiration. As the ecological crisis deepens, the value system of capitalism will inevitably give way to something else. We must be ready with an alternative. Those who have integrated the new paradigm, the urgency as well as the great opportunity of our time, must find the courage to lead, despite personal faults and flaws.

What I've been seeking to do in this book is to look at our current situation comprehensively, and offer systemic solutions. I am aware that, up to this point, many of these solutions may sound somewhat abstract – or so extreme as to be off-putting. One of my basic ideas is that we must learn from the ways tribal or traditional societies organized themselves for long-term resilience. We can use our virtual infrastructure and corporate techniques to scale some of these practices for a global civilization of over 7 billion people. This doesn't mean regressing to a tribal way of life, but advancing, based on the realization that we are collectively one human tribe.

When we look around the world, we find indigenous people, who are among the poorest and the most disenfranchised, on the front lines, fighting against the extractive industries, often at a terrible cost. To take just one example, there is the fight waged by the Ogoni people in the Niger Delta against Shell Oil. In 1993, 300,000 Ogoni staged a massive nonviolent protest against Shell's 'ecological wars'. They managed to stop oil production on Ogoniland. In retaliation, the government tortured and killed thousands, eventually executing the leaders of the uprising.

Many young people in the developed world – even children – feel the injustice and the weight of the ecological destruction we have unleashed. But they don't have the connection to the land or the basis in community, or ancient traditions, that would allow them to mobilize effectively. Our culture is also incredibly good at spreading all kinds of distractions and deceptions that keep people from acting effectively, or courageously.

I understand that, in our current situation, it seems unlikely, if not impossible, that we can make the level of change we require in the time we have without some kind of miracle. As horrible as it is to consider, it may be that a devastating crash of civilization and a massive population die-off is unavoidable and inevitable. In fact, it is easy to imagine a range of terrible outcomes, from our total extinction as a species through loss of biodiversity and nuclear war, to the survival of a tiny percentage of humanity in remote mountaintops and domed cities.

Still, we must admit that if the human community suddenly worked together as efficiently as the cells in an organism, without the obstacles caused by our economic and political system, the current population of the Earth could – in large part or altogether – survive. Resources could be shared and allocated efficiently as we innovated quickly, transitioning to no-waste, carbon-neutral, sustainable practices. Even if we lost 5 per cent of our global landmass to a hundred feet of sea-level rise, as now predicted, populations could be resettled on higher ground, with redesigned towns and urban centres featuring vertical farms and rooftop gardens, powered renewably.

We still don't know what is going to happen. The schizophrenia of our time is extreme – the tension keeps growing. Futurists like Jeremy Rifkin and Peter Diamandis argue we are on the verge of abundance for all through distributed manufacturing, renewable power and nano-technology. Scientists say we are on the cusp of driving ourselves to extinction. I see the validity in both viewpoints. But I also can't forget the mystical possibility – expressed by many prophecies and modern visionaries – that we are on the cusp of a phase-transition to a different 'world' or 'dimension'. Perhaps this sounds far-fetched, but I tend to believe that, once we change our focus as a species, we will be able to access the latent powers of the psyche to bring about rapid planetary transformation.

Two Forms of Power

We possess working models for non-hierarchical, non-commercial societies in the blueprint of many indigenous and traditional cultures. The design of tribal societies reflects the wisdom of tens of thousands of years of social innovation, and trial and error. We can rediscover these basic principles. We can look at how various tribal societies handled power dynamics, for instance, while maintaining egalitarian communities.

In *Society Against the State* (1974), the anthropologist Pierre Clastres contrasted the power relations within the Amazonian tribal cultures he studied with the power politics of modern civilization. Whereas power in modern societies depends on hierarchies, secrecy and centralized control, small-scale tribal cultures reveal an alternative in which power is collectively shared. As he lived with Amazonian tribes, Clastres found himself forced to solve the riddle of a 'powerless power'.

According to Clastres, in tribal societies the chief was unable to command anyone or give orders. 'In primitive societies, in societies without a State, power is not found on the side of the chief: it follows that his word cannot be the word of power, authority, or command.' The role of the chief is to mediate conflicts, tell the stories and myths of the past, and maintain the stability of tribal life. In many cases, the elder women of the tribe – the council of grandmothers – had the power to remove the chief, if he abused his position. The authority of the chief depended on his mastery of communication, the power of his speech – not on his capacity for violence.

Tribal societies, cultures without hierarchy, are the basic way that humans have organized themselves for tens of thousands of years. They are the most natural and enduring social form. This kind of social system can be contrasted with modern civilization – empire – based on domination, hierarchy and artificial scarcity, requiring constant expansion to exploit more resources. In the same way that we can redesign our economic system so that it supports ecologically viable behaviour, we can reinvent our political system to be based on cooperation and sharing, on principles of nonviolence.

In *The Unconquerable World* (2003), Jonathan Schell defines, like Clastres, two contrasting forms of power. One is based on mutual aid, and the other on violence:

> I suggest that the power based on support might be called cooperative power and that the power based on force might be called coercive power. Power is cooperative when it springs from action in concert of people who willingly agree with one another and is coercive when it springs from the threat or use of force. Both kinds of power are real. Both make things happen. Both are present, though in radically different proportions, in all political situations. Yet the two are antithetical. To the extent that the one exists, the other is ruled out. To the degree that a people is forced, it is not free.

Gandhi, similarly, distinguished between two kinds of authority: 'One is obtained by the fear of power, and the other by acts of love.'

Liquid Democracy

To realize the still latent potential of our digital communications networks, we would build decentralized, peer-to-peer systems designed to be perpetually evolving, supporting peer-to-peer production and social cooperation, making it easy and hyper-efficient to share skills and resources. Politically, we would establish something like a functional anarchy, based on nonviolent *satyagraha* principles, to supersede the current system of military and corporate control. New social technologies would train people to make effective decisions together, based on consensus methods as well as ongoing referendums.

Liquid Democracy is one platform for participatory decision-making where people can assign delegates to represent them in different areas. Most people don't have the time or knowledge to gain expertise on every issue. Using Liquid Democracy, they can pass their votes to the representatives who they feel best represent their interests, in different areas. Instead of a multi-year election cycle, voters can take back their vote, and assign it to a different representative, at any time. The goal is to give all participants equal rights in determining their political destiny.

Similarly, DemocracyOS, a web-based platform from Argentina, is designed to allow for participatory decision-making on the scale of municipalities and beyond. 'We are 21st-century citizens, doing our very, very best to interact with 19th century-designed institutions that are based on an information technology of the 15th century,' notes Pia Mancini, one of its founders. 'If Internet is the new printing press, then what is democracy for the Internet era?' she asks. 'What institutions do we want to build for the 21st-century society?' Another platform for democratic decision-making – on smaller scales, based on Occupy principles – is Loomio.org. Loomio is currently being used by Podemos, a grassroots movement in Spain.

Over the next decade, we must make a species-wide effort at self-limitation, conserving oil, restricting our use of resources, until we have made a systemic transition to a regenerative technical infrastructure and social system. I don't see how this can happen under the current regime of nation-state governments and multinational corporations. I also don't think a revolutionary overthrow of these inherited systems is conceivable. We therefore need to create new systems and supersede the old system from within – just as the imaginal cells within the dying caterpillar reprogramme the organism to make an astonishing metamorphosis.

We can't look to our current leadership to save us. We therefore need to participate in a broad-based movement of civil society. We need authentic leadership, and this kind of leadership could emerge from a consensus-based, open-source, peer-to-peer process, orchestrated transparently through the Internet. Just as we can devise an ecosystem of currency tools that support ecological restoration, so we can build a scaffold for direct democracy – we can, in fact, try true democracy for the first time.

The Occupy Manifesto of October 2011 states:

> As one people, united, we acknowledge the reality: that the future of the human race requires the cooperation of its members; that our system must protect our rights, and upon corruption of that system, it is up to the individuals to protect their own rights, and those of their neighbors; that a democratic government derives its just power from the people, but corporations do not seek consent to extract wealth from the people and the Earth; and that no true democracy is attainable when the process is determined by economic power.

We can use existing legal structures – such as the International Court of Justice, established by the United Nations – to slow down or stop the corporate juggernaut. The destruction of ecosystems could become a prosecutable crime, following the precedent of genocide, which was defined as a legal category after the Second World War. The British barrister Polly Higgins has developed the concept of 'ecocide' as a legal framework for protecting our remaining resources.

'Currently there is no law to prosecute those who are destroying the planet,' Higgins writes. 'Instead, climate campaigners do not have the support of the judiciary in preventing the corporate ecocide that is daily occurring under our very noses.' Higgins argues that ecocide could be recognized as the '5th Crime Against Peace', a category which currently includes Crimes of Aggression, War Crimes, Genocide, and Crimes against Humanity. This is a great idea but, like many great ideas, it seems extremely difficult to pull off, considering the entrenched forces that will fight against it.

Epilogue

Conclusion and Action Plan

Conclusion

What Do We Do Now?

I realize the task facing us is an enormous and daunting one. But initiations are meant to be difficult, to push us to the edge, where we will either change or die. As part of this planetary initiation, we must unite the many movements for justice and liberation that already exist. We can inspire people by pointing to a vision of a post-capitalist future where abundance is universally shared, where science and spirituality have merged, where everyone has the time and opportunity to learn, live and love.

The alternative – I get that it seems the most likely course of action – is a few more years of 'business as usual', then doom-spiral and catastrophe. We keep the party going, pretend we don't know the consequences, until we have ensured the collapse of global civilization, probably the crash of the biosphere and the extinction of most complex forms of life on Earth. I don't think that is what anyone wants.

We possess the innate ability to analyse, understand and overcome our conditioning. We can make the free-willing choice to transform our own inner nature. I believe the only way we can change humanity's fate is through our voluntary, free-willing choice as individuals to take on the ecological mega-crisis as our single-minded mission. When you think about it, there really isn't anything else to do but this right now. My personal experience is that once you make that choice, the heaviness of the situation lifts away. You find yourself joyfully infused with purpose, and united with something greater than yourself.

When I have shared aspects of this vision with people over the last decade, the most common question is, 'What can I do?'

Somewhat ironically, I have found this a difficult question to answer. One reason for this is that, as a natural anti-authoritarian, I don't want to prescribe behaviours or actions. Another reason is that my eccentric tendency has been to think in terms of collective consciousness and social systems – to focus on the macro level, more than the individual level. I believe we need a systemic overview of what is happening and what is at stake. Without this, I don't think people can make good decisions about what to do in the time just ahead.

But the main problem is that the scale of the planetary crisis is so enormous that individual actions can seem kind of meaningless – until we figure out how to weave them into a unified global movement. Remember Al Gore's *Inconvenient Truth*? He presented mountains of data on the climate emergency, but then proposed, at the end, almost ridiculously trivial 'solutions', like switching to energy-saving lightbulbs (which I did).

Of course, you can, and should, take all sorts of individual actions. Here are some of them:

- Become a vegetarian or a vegan, or reduce your consumption of meat to a minimum.
- Cut down on air travel. Stop taking unnecessary business trips and vacations. Focus on creating local utopias rather than travelling long distances for exotic experiences.
- Give up your car, or share a vehicle with other people. New digital platforms are making this easier. For instance, Bla Bla Car, a European company, has recently launched a new ride-sharing platform, which connects 'people who need to travel with drivers who have empty seats'. This is a beautiful and simple solution. It could quickly become a global standard.
- Reuse, recycle, conserve, compost.
- Buy less stuff, particularly new stuff.
- Support the transition to renewable energy sources such as solar and wind.

  When it comes to energy, there are many innovative companies moving into this space, all across the world. One example near me is Brooklyn Microgrid, which is developing 'a decentralized and sustainable energy management solution that combines the transparency and security offered by blockchain-based "smart contracts" and currencies, in an emerging peer-to-peer economy'. Members and businesses can directly trade energy with each other, buying excess solar power generated locally, reducing their dependence on utility companies. Assuming this system works successfully in Brooklyn, the model could be replicated in many neighbourhoods.

Solar entrepreneur Tom Dinwoodie has launched an app, MyDomino, an 'energy concierge' that helps individuals and businesses make the transition from fossil fuels to renewables. The service analyses their current energy needs and matches them with products and vendors that can save them money while reducing their burden on the planet. This is one of many new products and services aimed to support the energy transition.

- In the digital domain, support the movement away from closed, proprietary platforms that extract value to a small financial elite towards platforms that are open-source, peer-to-peer, cooperatively run and democratic. Tech entrepreneurs are building open-source replacements for mainstream platforms in many areas. Lacking the resources of the corporate platforms, many of them struggle to scale effectively. Two examples of social networks that could become alternatives to Facebook are Diaspora and Minds.com. On Minds.com, all communication is protected from data mining, and content creators are guaranteed to reach all of those who choose to follow their content.

- Food: grow some of your own food, if possible. Sprouting is relatively easy to do at home. Windowfarm is an online platform that helps crowd-source creative solutions for urbanites who want to experiment with food growing. You can also participate in community supported agriculture programmes that support local farms.

- Join a cooperative or start one. As business ventures, cooperatives are democratically controlled, collectively owned, voluntary associations of people. They are based on common economic, social and cultural needs and shared values. Some friends of mine in the tech world started a cooperative, Enspiral, which now has over 200 members and a larger network of contributors around the world. Individual members voluntarily donate some of their income to support the organization, which is based on the mission of 'more people working on stuff that *matters*'. Their model is inspiring, and can be transferred to other fields and types of work.

- Create your own media about what inspires you: With our smartphones alone, each of us is now a broadcaster able to spread ideas, stories and so on. In the best-case scenario I can envision, at least a portion of the wealthy elite in the developed world will model the path to self-sufficiency, sacrificing excess, choosing to address the planetary emergency as an initiatory path. Through media, they can explain to the global multitudes – the rest of the world – what they are doing, and why.
- Join an already existing, purpose-driven, social change movement. Some examples of ongoing global movements are Transition Town, the Zeitgeist Movement, the Global Eco-Village Network and the World Social Forum. There are also non-profits like Rainforest Action Network and Greenpeace. I admit I am terrible at joining things, but many of these organizations do great work.
- Join a community, or start one with your friends. I currently know many groups buying land or buildings together. Some of these communities are in Costa Rica, Nicaragua and elsewhere, Some are scattered around the United States. Some of these communities have business plans seeking to produce exotic superfoods or work with local farmers. Some of them are 'off the grid'. Depending on your resources and the work that you do, it may be possible to join and support such a community without living there full time.

   While many of my friends developing communities are relatively affluent, communities can also be started by those with modest means who have perseverance. People can also activate and organize their local communities. For instance, the members of Avalon Village in Detroit, started by low-income residents in an area marked by urban blight, are seeking to transform their neighbourhood by creating an academic support centre for local kids, taking over local water and power services, and building an organic community garden and local cafe.

   'Detroit has always been at the forefront of social change: the cradle of the labor movement, home of the automobile, and now we're redefining community development in a 21st century economy,' write the founders of Avalon Village. 'Urban farmers,

start-up technologists, futurists, and visionaries of every kind
are descending on Detroit to envision new ways of living and
working in a post-industrial economy.'
- Help disenfranchised communities. The science-fiction writer
  William Gibson quipped, 'The future already exists – it's just
  not very evenly distributed.' This seems to be the case to an
  ever more extreme, even schizophrenic degree. A growing
  community of people in the developed world have integrated
  ecological ethics. They seek to realize new business models and
  practices that support progressive goals. They are exploring
  freedom and spiritual development in their daily lives. At the
  same time, billions across the planet struggle to survive.

  Walter Benjamin wrote, 'For those without hope, hope was
  given to us.' There are now 60 million refugees worldwide.
  That number may skyrocket in the next decade as climate
  change intensifies. How we choose to understand and embody
  Benjamin's idea is, I think, part of our spiritual mission and
  evolutionary journey, individually and collectively.
- Protest or fight against corporate- and government-sanctioned
  activities that further degrade the planet, impair human health,
  degrade collective intelligence or hurt vulnerable communities.
  Sometimes, direct action is the only way to focus attention on
  the failures of governments and the malfeasance of corporations.
  However, we must realize that these kinds of actions only make
  sense as part of a larger strategy seeking to move us towards
  post-capitalism.
- Reckon with yourself honestly. If your work is contributing to
  the problems we face – exacerbating consumerism, purveying
  more distraction, extracting wealth from the poor – then change
  careers. Use your skills and resources to do something that helps
  address the situation in some way.

Unify

I agree with Murray Bookchin that 'green consumerism' or 'going
organic' is not going to lead to our salvation. While personal sacrifices
can be important, the kind of commitment we make must be deeper.

We must realize and accept that, while we are individuals with our own desires, we are also catalytic agents, expressions of a living biosphere. We can only enact our responsibility to care for and protect the greater community of life if we work collaboratively.

Our indigenous ancestors understood this innately, as native people around the world still do today. We can learn from them, absorbing their values as well as some of their practices, where applicable. The humbling realization that our civilization has failed to protect the most important thing – the Earth itself – could be the basis for a new alliance between post-industrial civilization and those native communities which have preserved the old ways.

We need more than 'social entrepreneurship', 'conscious capitalism', organic sections in supermarkets, and 'impact investing' – although all of these are important as part of the transition facing us. Ultimately, we need a structural transformation of our political and economic system, and this requires a unified, global movement of civil society. Considering we are racing against an ecological emergency that could bring about humanity's extinction, we need to be able to move quickly, without obstruction from outmoded institutions and broken ideologies.

As I have suggested, this will require profound shifts in how we exchange value. The money we currently use – issued by central banks which are private institutions – is corrupted source code. We therefore need new forms of currency that support a redistribution of wealth. We also require truly participatory decision-making structures, where people can practise direct democracy in real time. Individually, we can participate in creating, applying and disseminating these alternative structures.

Personally, I think we will need to engineer, eventually, a peaceful transition from ownership and private property to stewardship, trusts and other cooperative models. Particularly I would like to see a liberation of intellectual property rights, so that all of our human family can access our shared resources of knowledge and creativity. I realize this is not going to happen tomorrow. The only way to bring this about is through a change of the collective consciousness. Such a change can be designed, or in a sense, engineered.

We have to accept – I realize it sounds a bit creepy – that people's worldview, their 'subjectivity', is manufactured by the media. The great mass of people have already been programmed to be consumers and detached spectators. They have been deluded, indoctrinated, to act against their own best interests, instead of being trained to think for themselves. The same tools of media and advertising that have been used so successfully to dominate and control the human mind can be repurposed, transformed into instruments for liberation.

A change of global consciousness will be accomplished, quickly, when we can enrol the mass media, social media, social networks and other social tools in accelerating this transition. People can be de-programmed from their consumer trance, their cynicism. They can be given a new set of values, ideals and habits. I think that many if not most (if not, eventually, everybody) would be happy to embrace a new vision that infuses life with meaning and purpose.

If you agree with this thesis, then it is up to you to think about your own life accordingly. Where do you fit into the changes that need to take place? Whether you are an engineer, a lawyer, a pop star, a landscape architect, a chef, a banker, a pot farmer – or whatever – only you can decide how your skills and talents should be applied. Each of us has a role that is appropriate for us.

Social Networks

When I think about the systemic crisis we confront, I see that the potential – perhaps the only hope – for a solution is to extend the logic inherent in our new social tools. We tend to forget that Facebook, Google, Amazon and so on have only been around for a decade. The Facebook community is 1.6 billion people, while 1.2 billion use Google regularly. This makes them also the largest media companies in the world. Unfortunately, as publicly traded companies, they are locked into the financial structure of global capitalism, fuelled by advertising and the need for incessant growth.

Facebook is a private company that happened to invent something like a public utility – the twenty-first-century equivalent of the post office. In the spring of 2015, I helped organize a two-day summit at Facebook on climate change. In their new headquarters in Palo Alto – a vast open hangar, designed by Frank Gehry, with a green roof – we convened executives from Facebook, Oculus, WhatsApp and Instagram, along with representatives of NGOs including Greenpeace, Rainforest Action Network, 350.org and Climate Reality Project.

I helped put this meeting together because I think Facebook could be an incredibly powerful instrument for helping humanity learn about and respond to the ecological emergency. But to do this, unfortunately, they would have to break with the avowed 'neutrality' of their platform. They would have to take sides – siding with environmentalists and against corporations. This would hurt their profits. The results of our meeting were disappointing, but perhaps there will be another opportunity in the future.

Imagine if Facebook – reaching a billion people per day – decided to broadcast the urgency of the ecological crisis. They could put a panel on the top of every page, speaking directly to their user base. The panel would say something like: 'Hey People! We are in an ecological emergency! We are all in this together! Here is what we can do.' People could be enrolled in an exciting real-time game.

Imagine if people were able to vote in Facebook groups. These groups would suddenly be able to function like mini-nations. As an example, I started the Evolver Social Movement page, which currently has 2 million followers who share more or less the same values. If we were able to launch a campaign to boycott a company like Monsanto (for instance), asking everyone to vote on whether or not to join up, probably a huge proportion of our followers would get on board. Currently, we have no way of reaching out to all of them. In this and many other ways, Facebook currently obstructs the movement towards a truly democratic and participatory society that the underlying technology innately supports.

All the latest information on climate change, species extinction, ocean acidification and the other planetary boundaries could be presented and updated in real time. Facebook could build an infrastructure for people to start local community groups, including tools for voting together online. It could use its geolocating capabilities to help people share tools and resources, start local gardens, car pool – anything that would support conservation of fossil fuel use, reduction of CO_2 emissions and ecological restoration. If Facebook won't do this, hopefully another platform will emerge to captivate public imagination – but we only have so much time.

Although Facebook's mission is to make the world more open and connected, the company is limited by its responsibility to its investors, and the vision of its founders. This is yet another example of our current predicament: we have the tools and technologies to bring about a rapid, even sudden evolution of human society in all of the ways I have previously discussed. But our political-economic 'operating system' is obstructing our ability to move as swiftly as we must.

We need a virtual infrastructure to disseminate a shared understanding and coordinate mass collective actions. Ideally, this infrastructure will be open-source and peer to peer. We need to scale it rapidly, much like Facebook or Google grew exponentially. Alternatively, Facebook or Google could be decommercialized – made into public trusts – and transformed into this infrastructure.

Individually, people are highly susceptible to peer pressure; collectively, the multitude has a powerful herd instinct. If we are going to disseminate a successful alternative to self-destructive over-consumption, we need to leverage what we know of human psychology. We must create a tipping point phenomenon in the opposite direction, away from unconscious consumerism, where making personal sacrifices to help 'save the planet' will become trendy, cool – the next thing everybody has to do, like the Ice Bucket Challenge, if they don't want to lose the respect of their peers.

Many organizations make skilful use of the Internet for activism around social and ecological causes. These include Avaaz, Change.org, and MoveOn. But we must go far beyond engagements that end with signing petitions or making monetary contributions. We must find a way to engage people, ever deeper, in an ongoing process of transformation. Through a switch in social and economic priorities, we must make building a regenerative and resilient society our dedicated focus. We also must make it fun, seductive and inspiring.

I like the model of launching decentralized, volunteer organizations where local chapters can be started simultaneously in many different cities, towns and regions. MoveOn has organized nationwide phone banks in this way. Transition Town provides a model for autonomous local groups focused on preparing populations for peak resources and climate change. The 12-step programme of Alcoholics Anonymous is an amazing example of a successful decentralized organization which propagates itself through a set of rules that anyone can adopt. Burning Man follows a similar pattern, providing core principles that organizers follow to create Burning Man Regional organizations and festivals locally. The Zeitgeist Social Movement has launched local chapters globally, where people meet to explore approaches to system change.

As mentioned above, I helped start a similar organization, the Evolver Network, which, at its peak, had as many as fifty local groups around the world – mainly in the US, but also in Europe, Latin America and South Africa. We created monthly themes which the different local organizers could explore as they chose, ranging from psychedelic shamanism to permaculture to economic alternatives. Two Evolver communities launched local currencies from their meetings, starting the B Note in Baltimore as well as a Time Bank in Long Beach, California. The Evolver Network tended to attract the already psychedelically informed cutting-edge – the success of the movement made me think it would be possible to do something along similar principles, aimed at a much larger mass audience.

The blockchain offers us the potential to create organizations defined by 'smart contracts', where all exchanges are recorded and can be tracked. This could allow us to build the infrastructure for a global direct democracy, in which everyone on Earth has the right to contribute to ongoing decisions about our collective future. Using blockchain, it is theoretically easy to build new platforms – social networks – where masses of people can make collective decisions together, or sign social agreements, like personal pledges to become vegetarian or restrict unnecessary air travel. These pledges can be backed up with money held in escrow or other forms of capital.

Realizing the urgency, we must look at all current institutional structures not as obstacles or enemies, but potentially as ready-made social infrastructures that can help transition human society towards resilience. To take one example, we can consider the Catholic Church. In his recent encyclical on the environment, *Care for Our Common Home*, Pope Francis calls for an 'ecological conversion' and shared sacrifices – particularly sacrifices on the part of the wealthy, developed nations – to create a sustainable world.

Ecological Conversion

The Pope's ecological manifesto gathers together many strands of Christian thought, proposing a new direction for Catholicism. 'Once we start to think about the kind of world we are leaving to future generations,' Pope Francis writes, 'we look at things differently; we realize that the world is a gift which we have freely received and must share with others.' If the 'common good' includes the health of future generations, then Catholics have a responsibility to make the planet liveable for those to come. This is a new addition to Catholic doctrine.

> The pace of consumption, waste and environmental change has so stretched the planet's capacity that our contemporary lifestyle, unsustainable as it is, can only precipitate catastrophes, such as those which even now periodically occur in different areas of the world. The effects of the present imbalance can only be reduced by our decisive action, here and now.

This reframing of Catholic belief provides an opening to make use of the global network of Catholic institutions for ecological restoration. Churches, monasteries and Catholic schools could be used to retrain the 1.2 billion faithful in ecological principles and permaculture practices. Local gardening and other skills can be taught after the weekly sermon. We can realize a new redemptive vision that encompasses care for the Earth – our common home – in tangible form, in cooperation with Catholicism and the other major world religions. All the world's religions anticipate a peaceful, harmonic reunification of humanity.

We Are the Super-organism

By now, if you have stayed with me to this point – I know it is hard to read books in this era of shattered attention spans – you will understand my argument. The human species, still a work in progress, faces a stark choice: we can continue our current trajectory and probably drive ourselves to extinction, or we can leverage the ecological mega-crisis as an opportunity to make a mutational leap, a metamorphosis, into a new condition of being. By undergoing this initiation, we learn consciously to direct our own evolution, and transform our relationship with the Earth. We master our projection of technologies, beliefs, narratives, memes, ideologies.

Our mission, if we choose to accept it, is to bring about the next threshold of human liberation – socially, politically, economically, spiritually. Where the bourgeois revolutions of the eighteenth century allowed people to trade, consume and explore personal freedom, the next level of evolution-as-revolution will free humanity from vacant consumerism and hyper-individualism. As we realize our inter-dependence, we will establish a global system based on mutual aid, where everyone is guaranteed basic security. As part of this process we will realize authentic individualism. People will be free to be – no longer surfing waves of anxiety, guilt, status envy, fear; no longer driven to compete against each other for survival.

We know we possess the technical capability to transform our civilization rapidly. No physical force prevents us from radically reducing our dependence on fossil fuels within a decade or two, and then eliminating their use, as we transition to clean technologies like solar, wind and ecologically sound biofuels. Similarly, the agricultural system can be transformed, and much of the world reforested. Only capitalism – and human greed – stand in the way.

As the ground crumbles beneath us, we have the opportunity to create something unforeseen and new – a meta-programme to reinvent human society, combining aspects of a social movement, an advertising campaign, an open-source religion, a conceptual art project, a carnival, a nonviolent uprising. We can use the corporate, commercial and communications infrastructure to propagate cooperation, empathy, flexibility and local autonomy. Every successful resistance movement and counterculture throughout history developed tactics that we can learn and apply. What we need is something like a creative synthesis of extreme corporate efficiency, participatory democracy, socialism and mystical anarchism.

Festival Earth

What needs to be communicated is that, if humanity comes together now, we can thrive into the far-distant future. In order to do so, we need to make some immediate changes in how we live. We must also evolve and change some of our beliefs and values. People need a vision of the future that is so inspiring they find the will and desire to sacrifice to attain it.

I think we should reject the idea that robots and artificial intelligence are meant to replace us in a monstrously dehumanized world. We should also reject high-tech solutions that could have terrible unforeseen consequences, worsening the mistakes of the past. At the same time, we can make use of technical innovation in fields like biomimicry, renewable energy and ecological farming to make the world comprehensively successful for all. We should seek to master our projections of technology for humane and benevolent purposes. As Oscar Wilde realized, back in the 1890s:

> At present machinery competes against man. Under proper conditions machinery will serve man. There is no doubt at all that this is the future of machinery, and just as trees grow while the country gentleman is asleep, so while Humanity will be amusing itself, or enjoying cultivated leisure – which, and not labour, is the aim of man – or making beautiful things, or reading beautiful things or simply contemplating the world with admiration and delight, machinery will be doing all the necessary and unpleasant work.

I think this remains a valid goal for us – and is now an attainable one.

I believe also that a deeper liberation of Eros will be an essential element in recreating our global civilization on regenerative principles. I think we will see a movement to build local communities that are multi-generational and autonomous. Those who desire it can deprogramme themselves from the belief that monogamy is the only way for people to have fulfilling relationships and secure partnerships. We can develop new relationship models and new ideals of love. I realize this transition is already taking place – particularly among millennials – and for some of them I am stating the obvious. Sometimes the obvious needs to be stated.

In a liberated society where we apply our conscious focus to love and sexuality, we will realize many new forms of love. New relationship models will only work, for most people, as part of a systemic redesign that integrates cooperative childcare. Beyond the nuclear family, we can develop new forms of community, integrating care for children and elders. As we reduce the time needed for labour, people will have more time to explore fulfilling relationships of all sorts.

This transformation will also require a new spiritual initiative that will supersede outmoded religious structures. As Albert Camus pointed out, humans live either in the world of rebellion or in the world of the sacred. We appear to be undergoing a polarity switch from one to the other. Overcoming nihilism, we can identity the seeds of truth in the world's religious and mystical traditions. We can integrate mysticism with recent scientific discoveries that reveal consciousness to be the fundamental basis of the material universe. We can see science and mysticism as two complementary pathways towards knowledge and self-realization. We will then be able to live again in an undivided world, worthy of our devotion and care.

The Outer Reaches of Inner Space

I foresee two missions humanity can undertake together to satisfy our innate yearning for new frontiers and new worlds to conquer. These adventures will shift humanity's focus away from individual egotism, competition and warfare, as we seek communion with something far greater than ourselves. One direction is 'down and in', exploring the vast fields of the psyche, revealed by psychedelics, meditation and other esoteric practices. The other is 'up and out', investigating the inconceivably vast regions of the surrounding universe, settling in other worlds – as science fiction from *Star Trek* to *Star Wars* has prepped us for.

Dean Radin, a scientist who researches Psi effects, believes that we are at a point in our investigation of psychic phenomena similar to the period just after serious study of electricity took off in the eighteenth century. It took scientists several decades to learn how to channel, transmit and store electricity – to turn it into a reliable current. Once we mastered electricity, we transformed the geophysical environment of the Earth in just two centuries. Presumably, we could transform the world once again, if we discovered a new form of energy, with different properties. This energy could be Psi, which scientists like Radin are just beginning to explore and understand.

We seem to tell the same story, over and over. In films like *The Matrix, Star Wars, Harry Potter, The X-Men* and *Avatar*, the heroes must be initiated, trained at a kind of school, to master their psychic powers. These stories could be more than fantasy; they may foreshadow what's ahead of us as we transition to a psycho-technic civilization. We will use our technical powers to explore and enhance our cognitive and visionary capacities. For instance, we will learn to harness subtle energies like *Chi* and *kundalini*. We will apply technologies, ranging from virtual reality systems to biofeedback devices, to upgrade our neurological operating system. We will train our young people to develop clairvoyance, ESP, telekinesis; to lucid dream and astrally project.

We will legitimize the study and use of psychedelic chemicals and visionary plants, bringing prohibition to an end. This process is already under way, and I believe it is crucial. In April 2016, cutting-edge research on LSD was presented to the Royal Society, the most respected institution for scientific discovery since the seventeenth century, where Isaac Newton was president. Brain scans of subjects under the influence of LSD reveal usually dormant areas of the brain lighting up like a Christmas tree. Subjects 'experienced images through information drawn from many parts of their brains, and not just the visual cortex at the back of the head that normally processes visual information', noted the *Guardian*. 'Under the drug, regions once segregated spoke to one another.' According to researchers from Imperial College, London, the evidence revealed 'the LSD induced experience of "ego-dissolution" results from increased communication and integration across brain systems (networks)'. A great deal of evidence supports the value of psychedelics for creative problem solving and for healing of depression, post-traumatic stress disorder and other syndromes.

I think it is quite natural that the investigation of the psychocosmos – infinite worlds within worlds – will become a central focus in the future. As I discussed in my last book, there is evidence that indigenous peoples like the Hopi in Arizona were able to change weather patterns through 'psycho-technical' rituals and initiations. Much of their spiritual culture was focused on bringing the rain needed to grow their crops to their dry desert environment. Perhaps we will someday understand scientifically how the electromagnetic environment of our brains can influence the delicate ionosphere, and other regions of the surrounding cosmos. Once again, I consider it possible that humanity has unconsciously created the ecological mega-crisis to force ourselves to access the latent powers of the psyche. Psi abilities were known and recognized by indigenous cultures around the world.

The philosopher Alan Watts once noted that, just as an apple tree naturally 'apples' – producing apples in extravagant supply – the Earth 'peoples', constantly producing more and more of us. The apples from an apple tree are meant to reach other orchards, where seeds will take root and produce new trees. Probably, as humanity reaches maturity as a species, we are meant to leave the Earth, bringing the biosphere with us, producing new orchards, gardens of organic life, on currently barren worlds.

Private entrepreneurs like Elon Musk and Richard Branson have launched new initiatives in space travel. These plutocrats have revived the great hopes of the space programme that went unfulfilled after we landed on the moon in 1969. The exploration and colonization of space could become a new collective dream – a mission for humanity, unleashing innovation and creativity. What awaits us is the collective dream of an infinite frontier. Before we can launch ourselves into the cosmos, however, we must first pass this final exam the universe has set for us.

We can use the imminent threat of ecological collapse to awaken ourselves, making a quantum jump beyond our current state of being so that we can establish a peaceful, planetary home for our human family, protecting the community of life – here, on Spaceship Earth.

We have the option to embark on a utopian adventure that will satisfy our deepest yearnings for communion, self-actualization, creative innovation. We can let the ecological crisis overwhelm us, or we can use it as our 'cosmic trigger', impelling us to reach a new state of being.

'I slept – and dreamed that life was joy. I woke – and saw that life was but service,' wrote the Indian sage Rabindranath Tagore. 'I served – and understood that service was joy.' Beyond denial, cynicism, despair and grief, we have the option to embrace our role as agents of planetary regeneration, helping to redeem and restore our world – to find joy in surrendering limited forms of self-interest for planetary communion.

Undergoing metamorphosis means letting go of everything we thought we knew. When we shed the skin of the past, we create the potential for rebirth into a new condition of being, beyond anything we might imagine or conceive. Until it happens, we can never know if an alternative exists that we can realize. Once we free the butterfly from the chrysalis, there is no going back.

Further Reading

Ecology

Books that helped me understand the current ecological situation included *The God Species* (National Geographic, 2011) by Mark Lynas; *Eaarth* (Henry Holt, 2010) by Bill McKibben; *Infinite Resource* (University Press of New England, 2013) by Ramez Naam; *The Sixth Extinction* (Holt, 2014) by Elizabeth Kolbert; *Whole Earth Discipline* (Viking, 2009) by Stewart Brand; *The Ecology of Freedom* (AK, 2005) by Murray Bookchin; *Hot* (Houghton Mifflin, 2011) by Mark Hertsgaard; *A Paradise Built in Hell* (Penguin, 2009) by Rebecca Solnit; and *This Changes Everything* (Simon & Schuster, 2014) by Naomi Klein.

Evolution

I found the idea that our social evolution is meshed within a larger evolutionary process supported by many works, including *Microcosmos* (University of California, 1997) by Lynn Margulis and Dorion Sagan; *Spontaneous Evolution* (Hay House, 2009) by Bruce Lipton and Steve Bhaerman; *The Hidden Connections* (Doubleday, 2002) by Fritjof Capra; and *Nonzero* (Pantheon, 2000) by Robert Wright; as well as the works of José Argüelles, Barbara Marx Hubbard and Buckminster Fuller, particularly *Utopia or Oblivion* and *Operation Spaceship Earth*. Fuller's ideas on design as an instrument of evolution were extended by William McDonough and Michael Braungart in *Cradle to Cradle* (North Point, 2002).

Society

Books I recommend on the changes we need to make to our social, political and economic systems include *On Revolution* (Penguin, 1963) by Hannah Arendt, *The Great Turning* (Berrett-Koehler, 2006) by David Korten; *Multitude* (Penguin, 2004) by Antonio Negri and Michael Hardt; and *The Democracy Project* (Spiegel & Grau, 2013) by David Graeber.

Post-capitalism

A number of recent books suggest we have the capacity to make a rapid transition to a post-capitalist and post-work society. These include *The*

Zero-Marginal Cost Society (St Martins, 2014) by Jeremy Rifkin; *Post-Capitalism* (Penguin, 2015) by Paul Mason; and *Inventing the Future* (Verso, 2015) by Nick Srnicek and Alex Williams. I was also inspired by anarchist works like *The Conquest of Bread* (AK, 2008) by Pyotr Kropotkin, and the Situationist classic, Raoul Vaneigem's *The Revolution of Everyday Life* (PM, 2012).

Finance

Books on how we transform the money system include *The Future of Money* (Random House, 2001) by Bernard Lietaer; *The End of Money and the Future of Civilization* (Chelsea Green, 2009) by Thomas H. Greco; and *Alternatives to Economic Globalization* (Berrett-Koehler, 2004), edited by Jerry Mander.

Media

Books that shaped my perspective on media include *Mediated* (Bloomsbury, 2005) by Thomas de Zengotita; *Here Comes Everybody* (Penguin, 2008) by Clay Shirky; and *The Revolt of the Masses* (1930) by José Ortega y Gasset.

Love and Sexuality

Books that influenced my views include *Eros and Civilization* (Vintage, 1961) by Herbert Marcuse; *Sex at Dawn* (HarperCollins, 2010) by Cacilda Jethá and Christopher Ryan; *Eros Unredeemed* (Verlag Meiga, 2010); and *Terra Nova* (Verlag Meiga, 2015) by Dieter Duhm.

Spirituality and the Psyche

I found the idea that we are moving toward a 'psycho-technical' civilization in Jose Argüelles's *The Transformative Vision* (Shambhala, 1975). This idea is developed in recent works, such as Dean Radin's *Supernormal* (Deepak Chopra, 2013) and Tom Roberts's *The Psychedelic Future of the Mind* (Park Street, 2014). The notion that we will develop our psychic, supersensible or 'supra-mental' faculties is central to the work of thinkers like Gerald Heard, Pierre Teilhard de Chardin, Sri Aurobindo, Rudolf Steiner and Carl Jung. Other influential books were Albert Camus's *The Rebel* (Vintage, 1991), Frithjof Schuon's *The Transcendent Unity of Religions* (Quest, 1984), and Georg Feuerstein's *Tantra* (Shambhala, 1998).

Index